DEVELOPMENTAL SYSTEMS THEORY

This book is dedicated to those very special aspects of our contexts who have played and continue to play a key role in our own developmental processes:

Jacqueline, Justin, Blair, and Jarrett Lerner
Carol, Cameron, Douglas, Martin, and Russell Ford

DEVELOPMENTAL SYSTEMS THEORY

An Integrative Approach

DONALD H. FORD
RICHARD M. LERNER

SAGE Publications
International Educational and Professional Publisher
Newbury Park   London   New Delhi

For information address:

SAGE Publications, Inc.
2455 Teller Road
Newbury Park, California 91320

SAGE Publications Ltd.
6 Bonhill Street
London EC2A 4PU
United Kingdom

SAGE Publications India Pvt. Ltd.
M-32 Market
Greater Kailash I
New Delhi 110 048 India

Printed in the United States of America

Library of Congress Cataloging-in-Publication Data

Ford, Donald H.
    Developmental systems theory: an integrative approach/ Donald H.
Ford, Richard M. Lerner.
      p. cm.
    Includes bibliographical references and index.
    ISBN 0-8039-4661-9
    1. Developmental psychology. 2. Systems theory. I. Lerner,
Richard M. II. Title.
BF713.5.F67 1992
155'.01'1—dc20   92-12462

92 93 94 95 10 9 8 7 6 5 4 3 2 1

Sage Production Editor: Diane S. Foster

Contents

Preface

OUR PERSONAL PATHWAYS of intellectual development illustrate the principle of equifinality. Starting from different initial professional contexts and commitments, we have arrived at similar ideas concerning the nature of human development. The purpose of this book is to create a synthesis of our ideas. The book combines a way of representing the content of development and developmental outcomes with principles for understanding developmental processes and dynamics. It will be called Developmental Systems Theory or DST.

ORIGINS OF DEVELOPMENTAL SYSTEMS THEORY

Like individuals, conceptual frameworks have developmental pathways. Here we will summarize how our conceptual developmental pathways have progressively converged, resulting in the creation of DST. In turn, throughout the book, we will convey how the work of many other scholars has contributed to the developmental pathway of DST.

Richard M. Lerner's work on this book was supported in part by NICHD Grant HD23229.

Donald H. Ford began his career in the early 1950s at the Pennsylvania State University as a professional psychologist, teacher, and scholar focused on the phenomena of counseling and psychotherapy. For more than a decade he taught psychology and helped develop and served as Director of the University's comprehensive program of psychological services, which covered all of the University's 20 campuses.

In his professional work with clients, training of doctoral students in clinical and counseling psychology, supervision of a large staff of professional psychologists, and research, he struggled to understand how individuals operate as coherent entities in their life context, how they change, and how positive or desired change could be facilitated. He was impressed with the necessity of understanding individuals' development and functioning within their life contexts and formulated counseling programs that emphasized a developmental rather than pathological perspective and family influences on individual development. His search for a comprehensive theory lead to a comparative study of theories of personality development and psychotherapy with a colleague, Hugh Urban, titled, "Systems of Psychology" (Ford & Urban, 1963).

He continued to struggle toward finding or developing such an integrative theory between 1967-1977, while serving as an academic dean and creating a new multidisciplinary, multiprofessional College of Human Development at Penn State. He resigned that role to devote all his teaching and scholarly energies to this theoretical quest. The ensuing decade of effort resulted in two books describing and testing the conceptualizations that resulted: *Humans as Self-Constructing Living Systems* (Ford, 1987) and *Humans as Self-Constructing Living Systems: Putting the Framework to Work* (Ford & Ford, 1987).

Richard M. Lerner began his career in the late 1960s. At Eastern Michigan University his teaching and research were focused primarily in the domain of developmental psychology. His program of empirical research focused on issues in child and adolescent personality and social development. His search for more general theoretical formulations about development that could integrate the fruits of specific empirical studies resulted in a book, *Concepts and Theories of Human Development* (Lerner, 1976, 1986). In it he identified key issues in developmental theory and then compared the views of several theories of development on those basic issues. Each approach, he argued, had certain strengths and limitations.

In 1976 he joined the College of Human Development at the Pennsylvania State University, where several colleagues were attempting to formulate a view of development that encompassed the entire life span. There he continued his efforts to formulate a view about the nature of development in an attempt to produce a more comprehensive and integrative perspective. The resulting series of theoretical and empirical papers emphasized the dynamic interaction of nature and nurture variables as they influence development; the importance of understanding individual development as a function of person-context interactions and fit; and the role of individuals in shaping their own development (e.g., Lerner, 1984, 1986; Lerner & Kauffman, 1985).

During a year at the Center for Advanced Study in the Behavioral Sciences in Palo Alto, California, he examined the limits on the plasticity of human development across the life span. Evidence supporting his conclusion that considerable plasticity exists throughout life was reported in his book, *On the Nature of Human Plasticity* (Lerner, 1984).

He also created and served as the founding Director of the Center for the Study of Child and Adolescent Development at the Pennsylvania State University from 1984 to 1989. By stimulating collaborative efforts among scholars from many disciplines and professions, the Center was designed to encourage relevant research and the evolution of more comprehensive and more adequate conceptual frameworks for understanding and for enhancing development.

The flow of his two decades of work has resulted in a developmental metamodel termed "developmental contextualism." Most recently, in 1991, he moved to Michigan State University, where, as Director of the Institute for Children, Youth, and Families, he seeks to use the developmental contextual perspective and developmental systems theory to devise a multidisciplinary and multiprofessional approach to integrating science and service for developing people and their contexts.

Therefore, although the authors' developmental pathways have been different, they have converged on similar ideas about the nature of human development. Developmental contextualism provides a metamodel of guiding assumptions about human development but does not try to formulate specific proposals about the actual content or the processes of human development. It is precisely the latter that the LSF seeks to do, building on assumptions similar to those of developmental contextualism. A synthesis of the two should produce a more comprehensive representation of development than any that presently exists.

PLAN OF THE BOOK

To this end, the book is organized as follows. In Chapter 1 the influence of metatheoretical assumptions on research and professional work in human development is considered. We will illustrate these influences by several historically important metatheoretical perspectives concerning development and relate them to the developmental contextualism metamodel. In Chapter 2 we will define what we mean by development and distinguish among the concepts of stability, variability, change, and development. Developmental Systems Theory (DST) is constructed by merging developmental contextualism and the living systems framework. Therefore the presentation of DST begins with Chapter 3, where the developmental contextualism metamodel is presented. It provides the overarching framework for DST. In Chapter 4 we will present the operational model of the content and organization of the person as a structural-functional, contextually embedded unit, an open system, and describe the basic functional dynamics. Developmental outcomes can be represented as changes in the content and organization of these components in relationship to different kinds of contexts.

As a basis for considering the "how?" of development, in Chapter 5 the basic processes regulating change and development will be presented and illustrated. Such principles must underlie all efforts to influence the development of individuals. One way to evaluate a conceptual framework is to ask "What will it do for me?" Therefore in Chapter 6 we will illustrate the implications of DST for the kinds of research questions that might be investigated, for research design and types of data analytic models, for professional applications, and for the formulation of social policy.

We believe the present book will be useful to three kinds of audiences. One comprises researchers seeking to put the understanding of human development on firmer scientific grounds. Any individual study must necessarily focus only on some aspects of development in some specific contexts. Only by being able to integrate the results from many investigations into a larger framework can the pieces of knowledge that result from particular studies culminate into a fuller understanding of human development.

The second audience consists of professionals who design intervention programs and methods to facilitate desired developmental pathways and to interrupt or redirect undesirable ones. Such professionals necessarily must work with persons in their natural life contexts; they cannot focus just on their minds, hearts, or hands. To be effective they need a framework that facilitates understanding of the person as an integrated unit engaged in his or her daily contexts; and, second, of how changes might be facilitated.

The third audience is made up of students. To serve them we have tried to keep technical jargon to a minimum and to clearly define basic concepts. In addition, we have used many and diverse research and everyday examples. Preliminary versions of most of the chapters have been used in graduate seminars and in upper-level undergraduate classes involving juniors and seniors. Student evaluations have been quite useful in shaping our writing. One useful way to employ the book as a text is to familiarize students with DST and then help them use it as a tool to analyze and compare other proposals about development such as those by Erikson, Piaget, and Vygotsky.

We are grateful to Martin E. Ford, John R. Nesselroade, and Laurie Mulvey for their critical review and commentary on earlier versions of these chapters. In addition we are grateful to all our colleagues in Human Development and Family Studies at Penn State and in Family and Child Ecology, Psychology, and Pediatrics and Human Development at Michigan State for providing stimulating and warm collegial environments that provide a fertile context for scholarly creativity. We also want to thank Teri Charmbury for her invaluable help in producing this manuscript. Her skill, efficiency, and good humor in working with us was admired and valued.

CHAPTER ONE

The Past as Prologue to the Present

ALL THINKING AND ACTING, in science as well as in society and in personal behavior, start with prior assumptions. Understanding the basic nature of human development is probably not ultimately answerable based solely upon "facts" (e.g., Murphy, 1949), but, rather, rests upon some initial philosophical assumptions about the nature of humans (Lerner, 1982; Royce, 1961). Being clear about and periodically reexamining one's guiding assumptions is important because different assumptions will lead one in different directions. Science is not value free (McMullen, 1983). The model of human nature we use to guide us influences the selection of phenomena considered relevant and how we interpret our observations as well as the way we construe ourselves and the world. Through their selective influence on our behavior, guiding assumptions may become self-fulfilling prophecies, that is, we may select our observations and interpretations to fit what we already believe, and, over time, turn ourselves into what we assume ourselves to be.

Sets of guiding assumptions are sometimes called world views, metamodels, or metatheories in science. For clarity we will use the term metamodel. Because a metamodel about human development represents a set of starting assumptions that guide the choice of variables considered important and the kinds of explanations considered

1

plausible, it follows that different metamodels will lead to somewhat different theoretical and empirical emphases. This is not just an interesting intellectual issue. Such differences may have important practical implications as well.

Consider, for example, the following developmental patterns. A boy and girl are fraternal twins. At the age of 2 years the boy is taller, heavier, and stronger than the girl. He has better motor skills than she has; however, she has a larger vocabulary and considerably greater language competency than he. How might these differences in developmental patterns be explained? Should the parents be concerned about either of them? Should they do something to try to change the pattern? If so, what? Later in this chapter we will use these children to illustrate how different metamodels guide one toward different explanations and different patterns of action.

Because of their fundamental theoretical and practical importance, we have chosen to begin this book with a brief examination of the kinds of metamodels that have been historically influential, and how growing recognition of their limitations has led to the construction of alternate metamodels designed to encompass what we currently know and believe about development. The past is prologue to the present.

Several significantly different metamodels have guided the study of human development in the past. This book summarizes and builds upon a particular one called developmental contextualism and a model of individual development and functioning based upon a similar framework of assumptions called the Living Systems Framework (LSF). Developmental contextualism specifies and justifies the guiding assumptions of a metamodel about development that is in accord with current knowledge, but does not attempt to derive from that metamodel and current knowledge a specific theory of the nature of individual humans and how they function and change. On the other hand, the LSF focuses on the creation of a representation of the nature of humans and their development rather than on metamodel construction. Because the assumptions that guided the creation of the LSF are similar to the developmental contextualism metamodel, a synthesis of the two is possible. We believe that the synthesis of the developmental contextualism metamodel with the LSF represents a more comprehensive framework for understanding human development than presently exists. We have labeled this synthesis Developmental Systems Theory (DST). In addition, we believe that the other metamodels and their related theories of development are not as useful as DST for the derivation of intervention programs and policies designed to enhance human development. Though we outline our position about such applications in the final chapter of this volume, we plan to discuss such applications in more detail in a later book. The purpose of the present chapter is to provide an historical and conceptual review of the metatheoretical context for the presentation of Developmental Systems Theory; we do this by comparing and contrasting alternative metamodels of development and by briefly reviewing changes in metamodel perspectives over the last two decades. This is only one aspect of the history of efforts to understand human development (e.g., see Chapters 1 and 2 in Mussen, 1983, Volume 1, for a broad historical summary). First, two historically dominant metamodels will be identified. Then efforts to construct alternate metamodels during the past 20 years will be considered. (These efforts resulted in metamodels termed contextualism and developmental contextualism.) Finally, some implications of three different metamodels will be compared. DST builds upon the ideas and evidence generated by many distinguished theorists and scientists during the past 100 years. The past is prologue to the present.

Changes in Philosophy and Theory in Human Development

"Theory" in human development has evolved quite dramatically over the past 20 years. At least two interrelated changes have occurred. First, and due primarily to the contributions of Hayne W. Reese and Willis F. Overton (e.g., Reese & Overton, 1970; Overton & Reese, 1973), developmentalists were reminded of the embeddedness of their theoretical and derivative methodological endeavors in superordinate philosophies of science. Second, developmentalists explored the potential of several of these different philosophies for use in integrating existing ideas and data for generating new ideas and data, especially with regard to the plasticity and multidirectionality of relations between developing people and the changing contexts of their lives.

HISTORICALLY INFLUENTIAL METAMODELS: ORGANICISM AND MECHANISM

Reese and Overton (1970) explained that two metamodels—termed organicism and mechanism—had been associated with the major theoretical formulations extant within the study of human development in Western cultures. Organicism is illustrated by cognitive developmental theory (e.g., Piaget, 1950, 1970). Mechanism is illustrated by behavior analytic theory (e.g., Bijou & Baer, 1961).

Metamodels prescribe certain views (for instance, "development involves qualitative change," as in organismic stage theory) and proscribe others (for instance, "development in a later stage cannot be reduced completely to phenomena involved in a prior stage," as also held in organismic stage theory; see Lerner, 1986, for elaboration). Through such prescriptions and proscriptions, the same metamodel is manifest in "families" of theories (Reese & Overton, 1970), such as the set of mechanistically oriented social learning theories generated from the 1940s through the early 1970s (e.g., Bandura, 1965; Bandura & Walters, 1959; Davis, 1944; Dollard & Miller, 1950; Gewirtz & Stingle, 1968; Homans, 1961; McCandless, 1970; Sears, 1957).

The Organismic Metamodel

Theories associated with the organismic model are holistic, emphasizing the organism as the unit of analysis, with parts to be understood as components of an integrated whole. They stress movement toward a final end state and emphasize the predetermined bases, usually hereditary or maturational, of developmental change (e.g., Gesell, 1946; Hamburger, 1957). Such changes are typically of an epigenetic, and, hence, qualitatively discontinuous, stage-like nature, resulting in emergent properties. Examples are the theories of Freud (1949) and of Erikson (1959). In such theories the structural developments through which a person progresses are "predetermined" by heredity or maturational variables. Developmental change is presumed not to be able to be influenced in regard to sequential emergence or structural character by experience per se (Gottlieb, 1983). The contextual variables of experience and environment play only a secondary role in development in that they can only speed up or slow down (or even arrest) these intrinsically determined developmental changes (Emmerich, 1968; Lerner, 1976).

The Mechanistic Metamodel

Theories associated with the mechanistic model are elementaristic, emphasizing basic components as the unit of analysis, with the organisms to be understood as an assemblage of basic parts. They stress the quantitative addition of structural units, emphasize continuity in the laws of their combinations that rule out emergent properties, and, typically, (in psychology) stress the primacy of organism-extrinsic (e.g., environmental) determinants of behavior. Examples are the psychological theories of Kendler (1986), Bijou (1976), and earlier of Bijou and Baer (1961). Each is a theory that stresses environmentally based, behavior-theoretical (S-R) processes, with little attention given to intrinsic biological and psychological processes. For instance, to Bijou and Baer (1961), personality is equivalent to behavior, and behavior is seen to be exclusively a function of patterns of stimulation. For example, they specify that: $B = f(S)$, where $S = S_1$ (the current stimulus situation) S_2 (the history of stimulus situations; p. 8).

There are other, more macrolevel instances, of mechanistically oriented theories. Examples include sociogenic formulations that emphasize the sociocultural determination of personhood in general and of any specific feature of the person in particular (e.g., see Dannefer, 1984; Meyer, 1988). Indeed, in the latter theories individual constancy and change are both epiphenomenal in that all features of ontogeny are held to be derived solely from superordinate social institutions. For instance, Meyer (1988) contends that the person's belief that he or she has a "self" and that both the person's *and* the scientific community's conception of the self as developing through different periods or stages are products of society's embeddedness in age-graded social institutions. For political and economic reasons, these institutions create the categories of self and the age changes therein and inculcate ideologies to foster their adoption (Meyer, 1988).

THE CREATION OF NEW METAMODELS: DIALECTICS AND CONTEXTUALISM

The renewed recognition of the role of metamodels in influencing the shape of theory and research was associated with the exploration of the usefulness of other metamodels for the elaboration of new theoretical formulations, for the integration of existing data, and for the generation of new data about development (Baltes, 1979). Motivated by the Reese and Overton (1970) and Overton and Reese (1973) papers, there was considerable intellectual excitement in the 1970s and early 1980s about the scientific potential of models derived from these "alternative" metamodels (Lerner, Hultsch, & Dixon, 1983) and, as well, there were numerous instances of these "new" models. Sameroff's

(1975) "transactional" conception, Looft's (1973) "relational" notion, and Lerner's (1978, 1979) model of "dynamic interactionism" were all examples of such formulations. The perspective provided by the work of Klaus Riegel, however, was particularly influential.

Klaus F. Riegel's Dialectic Metamodel

Arguably the most important early examples of these "new" models, that is, the dialectical view of human development, were formulated by Klaus F. Riegel (1975, 1976a, 1976b). In many ways Riegel was both the intellectual leader of and catalyst for the exploration in the 1970s of the use of alternative models for the study of human development. This was the case, first, because he was a prolific and passionate writer, illustrated by his book, *Psychology Mon Amour: A Countertext* (1978), and, second, because he was editor of the journal *Human Development*, a prime outlet for theoretical scholarship in the field of human development.

Of the many important contributions of Riegel's scholarship, two are particularly pertinent to the present discussion. First, his dialectical model emphasized that the primary goal of a developmental analysis was the study of change, not stasis. Second, his model stressed that any level of organization—from inner-biological, through individual-psychological and physical-environmental to the sociocultural—influences and is influenced by all other levels. Thus Riegel (1975, 1976a, 1976b) "developmentalized" and "contextualized" the study of the person by embedding the individuals within an integrated and changing matrix of influences derived from multiple levels of organization.

Riegel's model, however, which was both a product and a producer of the 1970s' intellectual *zeitgeist* in human development, was only one example of the growing interest during this period in the importance for human behavior and development of the interaction of the changing physical and social context with individuals' characteristics. Riegel's ideas, as well as those of Sameroff (1975), Looft (1973), Lerner (1978, 1979), and others (e.g., Baltes, 1979; Bronfenbrenner, 1977, 1979; Elder, 1974, 1975), were similar in their emphasis on change and context—and, to this extent, may be interpreted as being part of a common "family" of theories. As scholarship about this family of theories advanced, however, it became increasingly clear that important distinctions existed among family members (e.g., compare Lerner, 1978, with Lerner, Skinner, & Sorell, 1980, with Lerner et al., 1983, with Lerner & Kauffman, 1985). For example, scholars raised two interrelated issues about Riegel's ideas.

First, Riegel (1976a) saw his dialectical views as both a model and a metamodel; that is, dialectics was, for Riegel (1975, 1976a, 1978), both a world view *and* a theory of developmental change derived from that world view. Indeed, Riegel (1976b) explicitly argued that dialectics constituted a metamodel of development distinct from organicism. For example, he argued that the (dialectical) model of cognitive development he derived from his (dialectical) metamodel led to a formulation quite different from the one of Piaget (1950, 1970). As an illustration, Riegel contrasted Piaget's proposal that formal operations was the final stage of cognitive development with the alternate view that the dialectic resulted in a fifth, open-ended stage of cognitive development.

Thus, in merging his model of cognitive development with his metamodel, Riegel did not attend to the similarity between, or the association of, his emphases on change and context with the metamodel of "contextualism." This latter metamodel not only stresses the very features of the human condition emphasized by Riegel—change and context—but, as well, was attracting considerable attention in the literature at the very time of Riegel's own writings (e.g., see Lerner et al., 1983, for a review). Nevertheless, the present writers have found no reference by Riegel to Pepper (1942), much less a discussion by Riegel of the embeddedness of his ideas in the contextual world view described by Pepper (1942).

Second, Riegel's (1975, 1976a, 1976b) ideas, while similar to those of other theorists in the "family" in regard to the common stress on context and change, were also distinct from many of these other formulations in respect to the *format* of change specified in his dialectical model. Indeed, in relying on the dialectic as a model for change, Riegel inadvertently undercut his effort to create a new metamodel that was significantly different from the organismic one. As will be argued, the nature of dialectical change is, in fact, entirely compatible with the view of change found in organicism—and thus, although Riegel (1976b) may have been correct in stressing that postformal operational thought is possible (e.g., see Alexander & Langer, 1990), his reliance on the dialectic to go beyond Piaget (1950, 1970) was ill conceived.

Indeed, there are at least two reasons why the dialectical model of Riegel (1975, 1976a, 1976b) has not remained a conception of prime focus among developmental scholars. First, dialectics, as presented by Riegel, is but one of several somewhat similar metamodel approaches concerned with change and context. Second, dialectics is a flawed conception in that it rests on a limited view of change—one quite difficult to use to integrate the wealth of empirical data that exists about the multidirectionality and plasticity of human development (e.g., see Baltes, 1987; Brim & Kagan, 1980; Lerner, 1984).

The next section of this chapter will examine the shortcomings of the dialectical view of developmental change. In so doing, we will explain why theorists should not rely on such a perspective if there is an interest in modeling the variability of the developmental pathways associated with development across life. We will argue that such representations may be made better through use of Developmental Systems Theory.

Limitations of Dialectical and Organismic Metamodels

The search for alternative metamodels that occurred in developmental theory over the last two decades resulted in a focus not on dialectics, but, rather, on the contextual metamodel (Lerner, 1986; Lerner et al., 1983; Pepper, 1942). Indeed, it can be argued that the growing interest in contextualism metamodels (e.g., see Bandura 1978, 1986; Jenkins, 1974; Mischel, 1977; Rosnow & Georgoudi, 1986; Sarbin, 1977) resulted in the recession of the mechanistic and (to a much lesser extent) the organismic metamodels to the "back burner" of intellectual concern and empirical activity among developmentalists (Lerner, 1990). In their place, activity associated with the contextual metamodel moved to the "cutting edge" of the scientific study of human development. A key basis for the shift of interest from other metamodels toward contextualism was the view of human developmental change contextualism involves. It is important, then, to examine the conception of change found in organicism and, as well, dialectics so that it can be contrasted with the assumptions of contextualism about change.

As explained by Pepper (1942), Overton and Reese (1981), Lerner (1986) and Lerner and Kauffman (1985), organicism and contextualism are closely related. Both metamodels are nonreductionistic, involve the consideration of variables or events at multiple, qualitatively distinct levels of organization, and are change oriented; however, it is in this last similarity—change—that the two metamodels diverge as well. The process of change is seen quite differently in the two perspectives.

Within organicism, change is teleological (Lerner, 1986; Nagel, 1957). The final cause producing the goal-directedness of such change means that despite the "strands" (Pepper, 1942) of change that may exist over the course of life, development will eventually channel into a single direction. Despite individual differences in change that may exist at some earlier time in life, organicism proposes that development will have a common (i.e., interindividually invariant) end point—be it the attainment of formal operational thought, the emergence of the ego crisis of integrity versus despair, or the development of postconventional moral reasoning. People may differ only in how fast or in how far they develop toward this universal end point. In other words, because of the telos of change, development follows a predetermined path. Change, when seen from the perspective of the entire span of life, is thus unidirectional; and, accordingly, interindividual differences are not emphasized in organismic conceptions of life span change.

By what process does the telos of development, that is, the final cause of change, pull the antecedent events of life toward this common, final point? From Plato to Piaget, the answer has been the dialectic (Pepper, 1942; Piaget, 1970; Riegel, 1975, 1976a, 1976b). As explained by Dixon, Lerner, and Hultsch (1991), the dialectic describes a teleological process of change: Thesis and antithesis (e.g., the "strands" of change, as in Pepper's 1942 account) lead to synthesis. In other words, in the dialectic, as in the predetermined formulation of the direction of developmental change found in organicism, there is a universal, necessary, and single direction to change. It is through dialectical change that the telos of development is revealed.

In their essence, then, a predetermined organismic view of change is isomorphic with a dialectical one: Both conceptions stress that change of a single pattern or a common developmental pathway (Wohlwill, 1973) characterizes human life. Plasticity of change (Lerner, 1984; Willis, 1990); multidirectionality of life span development (Baltes, 1987); and increases across age in interindividual differences in intraindividual change (Schaie, 1979) cannot be dealt with adequately from a predetermined organismic or dialectic view of change (Dixon et al., 1991). Given the substantial empirical documentation that developmental change evidences a diversity of patterns (e.g., Baltes, 1987; Brim & Kagan, 1980; Elder, 1974; Featherman, 1983; Gollin, 1981; Hetherington, Lerner, & Perlmutter, 1988; Lerner, 1984, 1986; Riley, 1979; Sorensen, Weinert, & Sherrod, 1986), it is not surprising that many human developmentalists have turned from organismic/dialectic models to a world view that may seem to hold more promise for leading to formulations that can integrate data about the plasticity and multidirectionality of and individual differences in developmental changes across the life span. These interests, then, were key factors in the burgeoning of attention to contextualism over the last 20 years (Lerner et al., 1983).

Contextual Metamodels and Change

Pepper (1942) argues that within contextualism change is dispersive. His metaphor for this metamodel is the historical event—the totality of phenomena, from all levels of organization, as they exist at a given instance in time. Although all phenomena within an instant of history are interconnected (and here the parallel with the holism of organicism is apparent), the dispersiveness of contextualism arises because the multilevel structure of one historical event bears no *necessary* connection to the structure of a prior or succeeding event. Thus, although change is continuous within contextualism—that is, time/history continues incessantly—there is no necessary integration to the change from one time to another.

PROBLEMS WITH "PURE" CONTEXTUALISM

Thus if contextualism were to be adopted as the metamodel for developmental theory, it would be able to deal with plasticity, multidirectionality, and individual differences—but only in the most radical of ways. The extreme dispersiveness of the contextual world view would mean that plasticity was infinite, that any direction of developmental change was possible, and that there were no necessary commonalities of human development. In that extreme, contextualism becomes similar to a mechanistic metamodel and development can be explained as a form of cultural determinism. In fact, Morris (1988) argues that contextualism is the metamodel for operant behaviorism. Clearly these possibilities are counterfactual and, just as clearly, contextualism in its "pure" state—that is, as Pepper (1942) described it—cannot serve as an adequate metamodel for the study of human development (Lerner & Kauffman, 1985).

Simply, plasticity is relative, not absolute; the nature of and levels of organization that combine to structure an historical event both _constrain_ as well as _permit_ particular instances of change. Such patterns of constraining and facilitating conditions promote or preclude certain patterns or directions of change. Finally, these same biological through social contextual variables act to both make people _different from all others_ in some respects; _different from some others_ in some respects; and _similar to all others_ in some respects (Lerner, 1988; Lerner & Tubman, 1989).

DEVELOPMENTAL CONTEXTUALISM

Accordingly, if contextualism were to serve as a metamodel for developmental theory alternative to predetermined organicism/dialectics, it could not do so in its "pure" form. For this reason a conceptual framework that has attracted increasing interest among human developmentalists is a modified view. It is associated not only with contextualism but also with the systems (Brent, 1978, 1984; von Bertalanffy, 1933) and probabilistic epigenetic views (Gottlieb, 1983) of organismic structure and function. This metamodel has been termed _developmental contextualism_ (Lerner, 1986, 1989; Lerner & Kauffman, 1985) and is described fully in Chapter 3. As we will stress throughout this volume, both the developmental contextual and LSF formulations (e.g., Baltes, 1987; Featherman & Lerner, 1985; Ford, 1987; Ford & Ford, 1987; Lerner, 1986; Lerner & Kauffman, 1985) stress the reciprocal, or dynamic, influence of biological and psychological (or organism) processes and environmental (or contextual) conditions. In these conceptions, the reciprocal relation between the interrelated features of the person and his or her context are held to not merely "interact" in the linear sense used in analysis of variance. Instead, person and context transact (Ford, 1987; Sameroff, 1975) or "dynamically interact" (Lerner, 1978). By virtue of their reciprocal relation, each of the features is transformed by the other.

In a "conventional" notion of interaction, particular combinations of organism variables and context variables influence behavior in ways different than either organism or context variables alone; but neither organism nor context are transformed by their "interaction"; both remain qualitatively the same after their interaction is completed (Riegel, 1976a). In dynamic interactions, however, organism and context variables each alter the quality of the other by virtue of their interaction. The organism becomes something different than it was, or would have been, because of its interaction with a particular context.

Moreover, the possibility that both organismic and mechanistic types of development may occur in some aspects of humans at some phases of development can be encompassed in the multilevel framework proposed in Developmental Systems Theory.

It is of historical interest to note that Russian developmental theorists independently evolved a similar view in the first quarter of the twentieth century. In his review of previously untranslated Russian work by Bogdanov, Bosov, and Leontiev, Valsinger (1988) emphasizes their similarity to modern interactionist, contextual, and system's models. The better known work of Vygotsky (1962) emphasizes social contextual influences on development.

In essence, then, a major stream of developmental theory has evolved to stress this systems or probabilistic epigenetic view of the interaction of context and organism and, as such, to include an emphasis on developmental changes as involving relatively plastic, multidirectional trajectories shaped by the fusion of dynamically interacting levels of organization. The synthesis into DST of the developmental contextual metamodel and the LSF representation of the actual content and organization of human characteristics and how they develop stands in contrast to formulations representing predetermined organismic and mechanistic metamodels. In the final section of this chapter we will describe and illustrate some of the differences.

Mechanistic, Organismic, and Developmental Contextualism Metamodels Compared

To illustrate their differences, the mechanistic, organismic, and developmental contextualism metamodels will be compared on four different characteristics: Variables and units of analysis emphasized; the form of change processes proposed; and their implications for the basic issue of continuity-discontinuity in development. Of course, there are other characteristics on which they might be compared, but our purpose here is not to be exhaustive in the comparison; rather, we simply want to illustrate the assertion that the nature of the guiding metamodel does lead to different approaches to trying to understand development.

Table 1.1 illustrates the kinds of variables, units of analysis, and form of change processes emphasized by each of the three metamodels. It also identifies some of the scholars whose approach manifests each type of metamodel. We will not present a detailed discussion of these metamodel

TABLE 1.1 A Comparison of Variables, Units of Analysis and the Basic Form of Change Processes Emphasized in Mechanistic, Organismic, and Developmental Contextualism Metamodels

Type of Metamodel	Illustrative Variables	Illustrative Units of Analysis	Basic Form of Change Processes
Mechanistic (e.g., Bijou, 1976; Bijou & Baer, 1961; Kendler, 1986,)	Extrinsic Environmental Variables (e.g., reinforcers; socialization practices)	S-R Connections (e.g., conditioned responses)	Conditioning/Socialization (e.g., operant behavior modification; social modeling)
Organismic (e.g., Freud, 1949; Erikson, 1959; Gesell, 1946, Hamburger, 1957, Piaget, 1950)	Basic Biological and Behavioral Variables (e.g., genes; reflexes)	Universal Organism Patterns (e.g., physical growth; cognitive stages)	Predetermined Epigenesis (e.g., heredity; maturation)
Developmental Contextualism (e.g., Baltes, 1987; Featherman & Lerner, 1985; Gottlieb, 1991; Lerner, 1989; Lerner & Kaufman, 1985; Lewontin & Levins, 1978; Schneirla, 1957; Tobach, 1981)	Organizations of Environmental, Biological, and Behavioral Variables (e.g., parent-child interaction patterns; gene-context relations, and patterns of temperament)	Bidirectional/Multilevel Organism-Context Intergractions (e.g., goodness of fit; attachment); changing relations between one person and his or her changing context.	Probabilistic Epigenesis (e.g., organism-context dynamic interactions or "fusions"; bidirectional parent child influences)

13

differences because that is available elsewhere (e.g., Dixon et al., 1991; Lerner, 1986, 1989; Overton & Reese, 1973; Reese & Overton, 1970). We will try, however, to demonstrate the practical implications of such differences when trying to understand, explain, and perhaps attempt to influence the developmental patterns of individuals in real-life contexts. To do that, let us return to the twins whose developmental patterns at 2 years of age were described at the beginning of this chapter. We will speculate about how the differences in their development might be explained from the perspective of each of the three metamodels being compared.

A MECHANISTIC METAMODEL EXPLANATION

Within this model one would look for environmental variables and socialization/conditioning processes to explain the patterns. For example, imagine that this boy and girl live in a culture that places a much higher value on male than female children. One manifestation of this value position is that male children are fed first, and after they are full the female children are fed with what is left. As a result, the female children often get far less nourishment and frequently end the meal still hungry. Naturally, the well-nourished child (the boy) will grow faster and larger than will the undernourished child (the girl); therefore their size differences at the age of two can be explained as the consequence of different patterns of nutrition. If the nutrition patterns were reversed, the girl could be caused to grow as large as most men and the boy's growth can be limited to the size of most adult women.

Differences in socialization practices may also differ for male and female children as a function of different expectations of boys and girls. Suppose that infant boys are given much attention by both parents and older siblings. They work at helping the boy grasp and manipulate objects as well as to learn to stand and walk as soon as possible. In contrast, suppose infant girls are given less attention. Interactions with them are more in the form of discussion and verbal instructions than in actions and physical demonstrations. So the boy's greater motor skills and the girl's greater verbal skills can be explained by differential patterns of environmental contingencies and reinforcers. These developmental patterns could be reversed simply by switching the patterns of contingencies and reinforcers each child experienced, that is, the girl could become the most motorically competent and the boy the most verbally competent.

AN ORGANISMIC METAMODEL EXPLANATION

Within this model one would look for person characteristics and genetic/maturational processes to explain the developmental differences. For example, suppose that in this group of people adult women are significantly smaller than men on the average, and this is characteristic across all the socioeconomic classes within their culture, that is, whether the women are well or poorly nourished. It may appear, therefore, that there are some gender-linked genetic differences that regulate maturational processes that control physical growth so that at maturity males will be larger than females. Because these are maturationally controlled processes, changes in nutrition or exercise patterns will have little effect on eventual adult size.

Imagine also that male children are regarded as "innately" more physically active and aggressive than female children. Boys, then, would be more exploratory and risk taking than girls. They would like to build things and knock them down and to have physical interactions with adults (e.g., wrestling). In contrast, suppose that female children are regarded as "innately" more interpersonally oriented. They would be more social and enjoy personal interactions with adults. So the boy's greater motor skills and the girl's greater verbal skills are by-products of the exercise of their different inborn predispositions. Any attempt to shape boys or girls into the opposite pattern will be relatively unsuccessful because it requires overcoming their natural developmental predispositions.

A DEVELOPMENTAL CONTEXTUALISM METAMODEL EXPLANATION

Within this model one would look for organized patterns of person-context variables operating to influence one another and leading to different developmental pathways depending on the nature of the variables and their dynamic interaction. For example, imagine that there is considerable diversity in the sizes of men and women in this culture: Both women and men come in large, medium, and small sizes. It is true, however, that on the average men are bigger than women; therefore it is clear that there must be some gender-linked genetic influence on physical growth; however, it is evident that when that predisposition interacts with different patterns of nutrition and exercise, both males and females can grow into relatively small or large adults. Their physical growth is a product of the dynamic interaction of environmental and genetic variables. It follows that the eventual adult size of a child can be influenced by environmental variables, but only within the boundaries permitted by their genetic "predispositions."

Infants differ in their initial biochemical, biological, and behavioral "tuning" as a result of the interaction of their genetic heritage with their embryonic and fetal environment before birth. As a result of such initial differences, infants function differently and, as a result, elicit different reactions from their contexts. For example, an energetic, active baby who smiles a lot will elicit more positive interactions from adults because he or she is "fun" to interact with. In contrast, a quiet, passive, unresponsive baby will elicit less and less variable interaction with adults, whereas an irritable, cranky, loud, crying child is likely to elicit more rejection and hostile reactions from adults.

In turn, adults' reactions, behaviors based on their own personalities, values, and socialization experiences, will further cultivate or inhibit different patterns of baby behavior. As a result, boys and girls both display a diversity of patterns of development of their initial characteristics with the people and things in their daily contexts. There may be some gender-linked genetic predispositions toward one pattern or another, but the extent to which a particular pattern develops will be a function of the person-context dynamic interactions. It follows that adults can exert some influence on the patterns of development of their children, but how they do so will depend on the nature of the initial pattern. Moreover, the extent of plasticity the child may display will be a function of the nature of the boundaries inherent in their own history. For some kinds of development those boundaries may be quite broad (e.g., the development of social skills) and for other quite narrow (e.g., eye color).

There are several basic issues over which developmentalists have argued for a century (e.g., Lerner, 1986). One of these is the extent to which development is continuous or discontinuous. As one final illustration of how different metamodels lead to different theoretical and empirical efforts, we will consider the continuity-discontinuity issue in relationship to these three metamodels.

DISTINGUISHING BETWEEN CONSISTENCY AND CHANGE
IN INTRAINDIVIDUAL AND INTERINDIVIDUAL DIFFERENCES

Before considering metamodel differences with regard to discontinuity in development, some definitional issues must be clarified. When we talk about developmental change, we are talking about differences in the same person from one time to another, that is, *intraindividual* change. On that basis we can talk about consistency and change in individuals, but there is another kind of difference that developmentalists study—differences between individuals or *interindividual differences* (often shortened to individual differences). Interindividual differences may display stability or they may change. Confusion about the meaning of these two kinds of differences and their relationship to one another has led to complications in the study of development.

The complication arises because alterations *within* the person (intraindividual changes) have been confused with differences *between* people (interindividual differences) in the extent to which they show within-person alteration over time, that is, development. In other words, there has often been a failure to discriminate between intraindividual developmental change (which involves continuity-discontinuity) and the stability-instability of interindividual differences in within-person change.

In traditional psychometric theory stability refers to the maintenance across time of interindividual differences, while instability refers to the alteration over time in these between-people differences; however, the constancy or change of intraindividual differences can be seen as distinct from the stability-instability of interindividual differences. Stability can occur when there is either constancy or change in respect to a target person's characteristics if there is no alteration in the distribution of individual differences around the person. Similarly, instability can occur where there is either constancy or change in respect to a target person's characteristics, if there is an alteration in the distribution of individual differences around the person. It is crucial that these distinctions be kept in mind in order to avoid making mistaken inferences about the absence or presence of intraindividual change (i.e., development) on the basis of information about stability (Baltes & Nesselroade, 1973; Baltes, Cornelius, & Nesselroade, 1977).

Table 1.2 illustrates that point. Note that the group means and the rank order of individuals remain identical across three occasions of

TABLE 1.2 A Hypothetical Example of How Patterns of Interindividual Differences for Five People Show Stability Across Three Occasions of Measurement Even Though the Patterns of Intraindividual Change Across the Three Occasions Are Quite Different

		Occasion				
		I		II		III
Person		Score	Rank	Score	Rank	Score	Rank
A		14	1	13	1	12	1
B		10	2	11	2	10	2
C		7	3	5	3	8	3
D		3	4	4	4	7	4
E		1	5	1	5	1	5
	Total	35		35		35	
	Mean	7		7		7	

measurement, that is, there is high stability of individual differences. Note, however, that each person's scores show different patterns of differences across the three occasions. For example, Person A decreases, Person D increases, Person E remains the same, and Persons B and C vary. Thus considerable intraindividual change may exist in regard to most if not all of the people in a group (Rogosa, Brandt, & Zimowski, 1982), even though interindividual differences remain quite stable. In short, in the large and complex data sets typically analyzed by psychologists and sociologists, the conceptual distinctions between continuity-discontinuity of intraindividual change and stability-instability of interindividual differences must be kept in mind because the differences between these constructs may not be readily discernible just by an inspection of some aggregate scores such as means and correlations.

As implied previously, of course, there is a key "protection" against interpreting a given data set as indicative of one versus another form of continuity versus discontinuity (and/or stability versus instability). This "buffer" is the a priori metatheoretical presuppositions (Kagan, 1980, 1983) and theoretical assumptions (Lerner, 1986) that proscribe and prescribe particular formats, or instances, of continuity or discontinuity.

Next we will provide a representation of the range of possible instances of continuity and discontinuity in intraindividual change patterns. We will then discuss which instances are prototypically included or excluded in theories associated with organismic, mechanistic, and developmental contextual metamodels of development.

POSSIBLE INSTANCES OF CONTINUITY AND DISCONTINUITY

Change per se, and developmental change in particular, can occur with variables at any level of analysis (Werner & Kaplan, 1963). In the study of human development, the individual level of analysis is the most typical focus of interest, but other levels of analysis have been considered (see Featherman & Lerner, 1985).

The categorization of intraindividual changes is a multidimensional issue (e.g., Baltes & Nesselroade, 1973; Lerner, 1986; Wohlwill, 1991). Change—or constancy for that matter—has both descriptive and explanatory components: When one is *describing* change, one is depicting or representing an attribute or process as it is altered over time. When one is *explaining* change, one is specifying the necessary and sufficient conditions that account for the attribute or process being depicted in the manner involved in one's descriptions. Continuity or discontinuity may be associated with either description or explanation.

One may depict a phenomenon over time in the same manner (descriptive continuity) or in a different manner (descriptive discontinuity); and one may specify over time the same causes for a particular phenomenon (explanatory continuity) or different causes at different times for a given phenomenon (explanatory discontinuity). In addition, one may distinguish between descriptions and explanations that change quantitatively versus those that change qualitatively. Of course constancy can exist in regard to quantitative and qualitative domains as well.

For example, a feature of personality (e.g., a component of temperament, such as mood) may remain descriptively the same over time. It may be depicted isomorphically at two different temporal points (e.g., positive mood may be represented by the percentage of facial expressions per unit time, which are scored as indicative of smiling). Such cases therefore may be instances of descriptive, qualitative continuity; however, *more* of this qualitatively invariant phenomenon may exist at Time 2 (e.g., there may be more smiles per unit time), and thus descriptive quantitative discontinuity may be coupled with descriptive qualitative continuity.

Moreover, both descriptive quantitative discontinuity and descriptive qualitative continuity may be explained by the same ideas. For example, smiling may be assumed to be released across life by biogenetically based physiological mechanisms. Alternatively, descriptive continuity or descriptive discontinuity may be explained by different ideas. For example, smiling may be assumed to be biogenetically released in early infancy and mediated by cognitively and socially textured processes across subsequent developmental periods. Indeed, if different explanations are, in fact, invoked they may involve statements that constitute either quantitatively or qualitatively altered processes.

In short, assessments of intraindividual developmental change in human behavior and of the processes that promote or constrain it are complicated because intraindividual development involves change simultaneously along three dimensions: descriptive continuity-discontinuity; explanatory continuity-discontinuity; and a quantitative-qualitative dimension. This complexity is illustrated diagramatically in Figure 1.1.

METAMODEL POSITIONS ABOUT DEVELOPMENTAL CONTINUITY AND DISCONTINUITY

The different metamodels of human development act to include or to exclude particular forms of continuity or discontinuity. For example, no true form of qualitative discontinuity in behavior can occur in mechanistic-behavioral formulations. Thus philosophical/theoretical proscriptions create empirical impossibilities.

Theories embedded within a given metamodel of development are not all alike. For example, while the organismic theories of Gesell (1946) and of Erikson (1959) emphasize an ontogenetic, maturational "ground plan" as constituting the key process explaining developmental change, Hall's (1904) organismic theory explains ontogenetic changes by positing a biogenetic recapitulation in ontogeny of phylogenetic changes (cf. Haeckel, 1868). In turn, the mechanistic, behavior analysis theory of Bijou (1976) emphasizes proximal stimuli as the material and efficient causes shaping behavior, but makes no proposals regarding how distal sociocultural institutional influences are translated into such stimulation. In contrast, the mechanistic-sociogenic views of Dannefer (1984) and Meyer (1988) discuss the distal, age-graded channeling of behavior by societal institutions, but do not discuss the links between these entities and proximal stimulation.

Despite such differences, however, theories within a metamodel "family" (Reese & Overton, 1970) are more similar to each other than

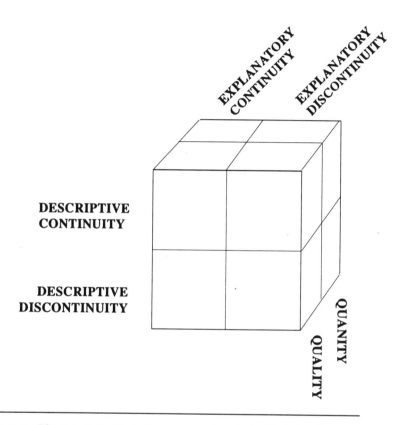

Figure 1.1. The Intraindividual Change Box. Intraindividual development involves change along three dimensions: (a) descriptive continuity-discontinuity; (b) explanatory continuity-discontinuity; and (c) a quantitative-qualitative dimension.

are theories associated with different metamodels (cf. Pepper, 1942). As a consequence it is possible to describe, at least for the general case, the prototypic views regarding continuity and discontinuity associated with theories from the organismic, mechanistic, and developmental contextual metamodel families (remembering of course that some individual differences may nevertheless exist among "family members"). Table 1.3 summarizes these prototypic views.

TABLE 1.3 Prototypic Views of Theories Associated With the Organismic, Mechanistic, and Developmental Contextual Metamodels of Development

Model of development	Representative theories associated with model	Descriptive continuity[a]	Descriptive discontinuity[a]	Explanatory continuity[a]	Explanatory discontinuity[a]
Organismic	Gesell (1946); Freud (1940, 1949); Erikson (1959)	Yes/yes	Yes/yes	No/yes	No/yes
Mechanistic	Bijou & Baer (1961); Bijou (1976); Dannefer (1984)	Yes/yes	Yes/no	Yes/no	Yes/no
Developmental contextual	Gottlieb (1983, 1987); Lerner & Lerner (1987); Baltes (1987); Featherman & Lerner (1985)	Yes/yes	Yes/yes	Yes/yes	Yes/yes

SOURCE: Lerner and Tubman (1989)

NOTE: a. Quantitative/Qualitative.

As can be seen from Table 1.3, theories associated with any metamodel can accommodate the presence, at a descriptive level, of both quantitative and qualitative continuity. This acceptance, however, is nothing more than admitting that things may stay the same across at least some portions of life. That is, there may be ontogenetic stasis. Quantitatively, this may mean that identical scores for a construct are present across time or that rates of growth remain constant (e.g., throughout the middle childhood years). Qualitatively, stasis can occur when there is no numerical or structural change in the components of the behavioral repertoire or of personality (e.g., traits).

Differences among the metamodels exist, however, for the remaining instances of continuity and discontinuity. Both organismic-based and developmental contextual-based theories recognize that, descriptively, both quantitative and qualitative discontinuities can occur in development; but descriptive quantitative discontinuities are largely irrelevant to organismic theorists, whose interest focuses almost exclusively on qualitative structural variation across ontogeny (e.g., Erikson, 1959; Piaget, 1950). In mechanistic theories of development, however, no true descriptive qualitative discontinuity can exist; no novelty can exist in development (von Bertalanffy, 1933). Given the mechanist's commitment to reduce all developmental phenomena to a common set of constituent elements (e.g., S-R connections), merely lightly scratching the surface of any claim of newness or novelty in development will readily reveal that the operationalization of such terms is made via recourse to the quantitative combinations (additions) of identically constituted elements; see, for example, the Bijou and Baer (1961) treatment of personality in childhood.

In regard to explanatory continuity and discontinuity, all models are distinct. In respect to continuity, organismic theories do not typically explain development by reference to quantitatively invariant laws. Instead qualitative invariance is stressed (for instance, to explain within-stage consistency or across-stage décalages, e.g., Levinson, 1978; Neugarten & Guttman, 1968; Piaget, 1950). The reverse of these emphases is found in mechanistic theories. That is, quantitative invariance is emphasized. Within developmental contextualism, development may be explained by either quantitative or qualitative continuity. For example, in regard to quantitative invariance, Haan and Day (1974) account for the maintenance of adults' style of engagement with their context by reference to a quantitative invariance over time in their scores for activity level. Schaie and Gewirtz (1982) account for the maintenance of adult personality structure by noting that adults select contexts in which to interact that provide a goodness of fit with their already-established personality structure and, as such, do not provide demands for qualitative change in personality.

Finally, while organismic theories do not discuss quantitative discontinuity as an explanation for development, in mechanistic theories qualitative discontinuity in the explanations of development are not possible. Within developmental contextualism both qualitatively and quantitatively discontinuous explanations may be used. For example, while Elder (1974) and Schaie (1984) both draw on the link between individuals and features of the historical epoch within which they live to explain individual differences in personality developments, they do so by positing different types of influences. Elder (1974) argued that individual differences in achievement, health, and in degrees of commitments to family values were influenced by whether a person experienced a qualitatively distinct historical event (the Great Depression) in his or her childhood or adolescence. Thus one age group's experience of an individual-context relation that was qualitatively discontinuous from that of a succeeding cohort was used by Elder (1974) to account for individual (in this case, cohort) differences in features of personality development.

Schaie (1984) posited that such cohort differences in development are explained by quantitative differences across historical eras in the accumulation of life events (such as epidemics, wars, unemployment, inflation, and technological innovations). To Schaie (1984) it is not the nature of the events per se that explain interindividual differences in development. Instead these differences occur because of historical quantitative discontinuities in the cumulative number of events that comprise the context of a given cohort.

In sum, theories associated with the organismic, mechanistic, and developmental contextual metamodels differ in the instances of continuity-discontinuity they see possible, demonstrating that continuity-discontinuity is not solely an empirical concern but is also a metatheoretical issue. In other words, the issue of continuity-discontinuity in human development is an empirical question, but only within the constraints of the variables considered relevant by the researcher's theory or metamodel; adopting alternative metamodels may introduce new variables that show a different empirical pattern. Moreover, this theoretical embeddedness of continuity-discontinuity leads us to note one key feature of our discussion of the categorizations made in Table 1.3: No instance of continuity or discontinuity is necessarily excluded within the developmental contextualism approach to human development.

Acceptance of all possibilities may seem like uncritical eclecticism, but we believe that such an appraisal is not correct. Theories associated with developmental contextualism do *not* maintain that all instances of continuity-discontinuity occur within and across developmental periods. Instead, the point is that several instances *may* happen. The empirical implication of this view is that the Developmental Systems Theory presented in this book seeks to identify the organismic and contextual conditions within which any particular instance of continuity-discontinuity occurs (Baltes, 1987; Ford, 1987; Lerner, 1984).

This search for the organismic and contextual conditions of continuity-discontinuity has a long tradition in developmental psychology, especially as it has been practiced by researchers who have conducted major longitudinal studies of multiple cohorts of people (e.g., Block, 1971; Eichorn, Clausen, Haan, Honzik, & Mussen, 1981; Elder, 1974; Nesselroade & Baltes, 1974; Schaie, 1979, 1984; Thomas & Chess, 1977). In fact, it is the attempts to make sense out of the plethora of combinations of continuity-discontinuity—of multiple directions in the course of human lives—that was a major impetus to the creation of the developmental contextual metamodel (Dixon & Lerner, 1988; Lerner et al., 1983), of the life span view of human development associated with this model (Baltes, Reese, & Lipsitt, 1980; Brim & Kagan, 1980; Lerner, 1986), and of theoretical formulations that are akin to developmental contextualism, such as the LSF (e.g., Baltes, 1987; Featherman, 1983; Ford, 1987; Lerner & Lerner, 1989).

In short, in the search for the organismic and contextual conditions of continuity-discontinuity, developmentalists whose work is developmental contextual in character would tend to agree with one implication of the orthogenetic principle of Heinz Werner (1957). The human life course is a synthesis of processes that, at one and the same time, make us both: (a) similar to ourselves, at other points in time, and to others as well through nomothetic processes affording continuity at both descriptive and explanatory levels (these are global and hierarchically integrated processes to Werner, 1957) and (b) different from ourselves, at other points in time, and from others as well through idiographic processes affording discontinuity at both descriptive and explanatory levels (these are differentiating processes to Werner, 1957).

In other words the search by scholars, following a developmental contextual metamodel, for the conditions of continuity and discontinuity may be translated into a search for nomothetic and idiographic change processes that, at one and the same time, make us similar and make us different. This search is admittedly a quite complex one, certainly more difficult than one involving the a priori theoretical exclusion of particular instances of continuity-discontinuity. That is, developmental contextualism and the LSF represent synthetic approaches to development (Ford, 1987; Lerner & Kauffman, 1985). As implied in Table 1.3, these perspectives integrate features of the active organism and of the active context. As such, the Developmental Systems Theory presented in this book must take an open stance in regard to the instances of continuity-discontinuity that are possible.

Next Steps

This chapter has sought to illustrate how different metamodels concerning human change and development influence the selection of variables, methods, and interpretations of empirical evidence, and practical actions regarding human development. It has also sought to show how the developmental contextualism metamodel on which this book is based emerged as a part of a more general historical stream of effort to understand human development. Before beginning the presentation of our synthesis of developmental contextualism and the LSF into Developmental Systems Theory, we must first be explicit about what we mean by the concepts of change and development. That is the objective of Chapter 2.

CHAPTER TWO

The Concepts of Stability, Variability, Change, and Development

HERACLITUS, THE GREEK PHILOSOPHER, provided the world with a famous insight about the ubiquity of change: You cannot walk into the same river twice. From a least this point in the history of Western thought, scholars have recognized that incessant change is the way of the world. Whether the changes are cyclical, as in the phases of the moon or the beating of the waves upon the shores of the beach; whether they are inexorable and progressive, as in the adaptational changes purported to characterize evolution; or whether they are chaotic, cataclysmic, and unique as in the onset of a worldwide epidemic, such as AIDS, there is no escaping the conclusion that change is a pervasive natural phenomenon characterizing all living and nonliving things.

The pervasiveness of change makes it a core focus of the interests of scholars from numerous disciplines. Geological changes, historical changes, economic changes, and the changes that characterize the human organism from conception to death have become prime topics engaging both intradisciplinary and interdisciplinary work. Simply, one must study change in order to deal with the basic phenomena of many natural and social scientific disciplines.

Many scholars claim, however, that they are studying a special type of change called development. Scholars differ in their use of the concept of development, and, therefore, in the extent of the diverse array of change phenomena that they encompass. In fact, many definitions of development do not have such integrative utility. Attempts to reduce complex sociological or psychological phenomena into common stimulus-response connections (e.g., Homans, 1974; Skinner, 1957) provide a case in point.

Other definitions, such as those associated with organismic or holistic metamodels, have potentially broader scope than mechanistic ones (Kaplan, 1983), but have not been systematically or successfully used to generate an integrative approach to change phenomena. Moreover, such organismic approaches continue to encounter problems because there seems inherent in them the concept that there are fixed goals toward which human development is directed (Dixon et al., 1991; Nagel, 1957; Pepper, 1942).

We believe, however, that a definition of development that provides the broad integrative power lacking in mechanistic and extant organismic conceptions is possible. The definition constructed in this chapter provides a basis for dealing with the problems of other metamodels discussed in Chapter 1 that include insufficient representation of the multidimensional, multilevel nature of development; lack of specificity concerning developmental processes and outcomes; inadequate recognition of the role of the environment in development; and a developmental teleology contradicted by current knowledge.

Any theory of development should start by clearly specifying its domain, that is, what it means by the concept of development. Therefore we will examine key components of our definition of development and indicate where they converge or diverge from other definitions of development. Because development is considered a type of change, it is first necessary to define change as a basis for identifying developmental change.

Differences, Variability, and Change

How can one know when something has changed? The inference of change rests upon the fundamental human capability to perceive that two or more things or events are dissimilar or different in some way.

IDENTIFYING DIFFERENCES

Nature is organized into things, relationships, processes, and events that can be perceived as dissimilar from one another because each has some distinguishing characteristic(s). Learning to recognize how things are different, often called discrimination learning, is a cornerstone for all learning. We cannot readily learn to behave differently toward different parts of our world unless we discriminate one part from another.

Qualitative and Quantitative Differences

Recognizing a difference requires a comparison process to decide if phenomena are dissimilar and, if so, how. Phenomena may differ in form (e.g., round or square; linear or circular motions); in quality (e.g., rough or smooth; red or green); or in amount (e.g., tall or short; heavy or light; fast or slow). Differences in form and quality are usually referred to as differences in kind or *qualitative differences*. Differences in amount are usually referred to as *quantitative differences*. For example, Scooter and Winston can be compared and certain qualitative and quantitative differences perceived because Scooter is a small beagle and Winston is a large sheepdog. Mathematical operations can be performed on quantitative differences but not on qualitative ones, although qualitative differences can often be indexed in a quantitative form (e.g., frequency counts).

Four Types of Differences

Several different kinds of comparisons are possible, defined by spatial/contextual and temporal conditions; each kind of comparison provides information about different types of differences. These are summarized in Table 2.1. *Occasion* and *state* differences are of special importance in understanding development. Occasion differences combine temporal and contextual differences. It is possible to compare the same phenomena with itself in similar contexts at different times (e.g., to compare a child's piano practicing on two different days); however, because contexts will vary from one time to another, it is impossible to ensure that the contexts are identical at two different times (e.g., exactly the same lighting, the same temperature, the same background noise). Therefore occasions usually differ both temporally and contextually. One cannot walk into the same river twice.

TABLE 2.1 A summary of four kinds of differences that may result from comparing levels of phenomena under different spatial/contextual and temporal conditions

Type of Difference	Type of Comparison
Concurrent	Differences resulting from a comparison of different phenomena at the same time and in the same context (e.g., compare different students' grades on a mathematics test in the same class).
Contextual	Differences resulting from a comparison of different phenomena at the same time but in different contexts (e.g., compare the grades of students sitting in the back rows of class with those sitting in the front rows).
Occasion	Differences resulting from a comparison of phenomena in similar or different contexts at different times (e.g., compare students' performance in their morning classes with their performance in their afternoon classes).
State	Differences resulting from a comparison of one set of phenomena with itself on two or more occasions (e.g., compare each students' mathematical performance at the beginning of the year with his or her mathematical performance in the middle and end of the year).

All four of these kinds of comparisons may reveal differences, but do they all provide a basis for detecting change? No! *Only state differences revealed by comparing some phenomena with itself on different occasions represent change.* But are all such between-occasion state differences to be considered change? No! Understanding why not requires consideration of the concepts of variability and duration.

VARIABILITY AND DURATION

The concept of *variability* means that something may take on different values. If it can, it is called a variable; if not, it is a constant. The concept of variability is used in two different ways in the study of humans.

1. *Interindividual* (or *individual*) *differences* result from comparing the states of different persons on the same variables.
2. *Intraindividual differences* result from comparing the states of individuals with themselves on the same variables on different occasions.

An inference that a person has changed or developed must be based on intraindividual differences or variability; but there are two different kinds of intraindividual differences: steady state variability and change. These can be illustrated with the summary in Figure 2.1 of one person's body temperature variability (i.e., intraindividual differences) across five days.

Steady State Variability

If one only measured this person's body temperature at 8:00 a.m. on Monday and Tuesday, no difference would be observed, but if temperature is measured at 8:00 a.m. and 6:00 p.m. on Monday and compared, an interindividual difference could be noted. Would this mean that that body temperature had changed? If one measures repeatedly from 8:00 a.m. Monday to 8:00 a.m. Thursday, it becomes apparent that each morning the person's temperature starts a little below the population norm of 98.6 degrees and increases to the norm or slightly above it as the day proceeds. This kind of stable or consistent pattern in which the value of some attribute varies in a regular way, but within limits, is called steady state variability. The periodic differences between 8:00 a.m. Monday and 8:00 a.m. Thursday do not represent significant changes but, rather, only normal fluctuations in body temperature.

This kind of dynamic stability, called homeostasis by Cannon (1939), is a "natural" (i.e., prototypic or ubiquitous) property of human biological functioning and of other aspects of humans as well. For example, people's habits of eating and sleeping often show such repetitive patterns. People vary in the way they think, feel, and act from occasion to occasion, even when trying to do the same things in the same contexts. This kind of apparent biological and psychological/behavioral consistency of humans is a dynamic stability, a steady state, not an equilibrium and is best understood as performance variability rather than change because the state pattern remains stable even though there may be moment to moment differences.

Recognizing that differences representing steady state variability have a meaning distinct from differences that represent change has practical importance. For example, suppose your physician measures your blood pressure once, compares it with a population norm (i.e., focuses on interindividual differences), diagnoses you as having high blood pressure, and puts you on a drug to lower your blood pressure. That single measure may have been the high point of your personal steady state fluctuations (intraindividual differences) and administering drugs may not be warranted (and may even entail dangers). Finkelstein's (1980) research on hormonal variation and change in adolescents illustrates the importance of this distinction. Individuals' serum levels of sex hormones varied so much during 24-hour periods that one measure could have been used to indicate that the adolescent was at the beginning of pubertal maturation, while another measure could have indicated the same person to be at the end of this period. Only by observing and comparing a person's states on multiple occasions is it possible to identify their normal steady state pattern for any attribute, illustrated in Figure 2.1.

CHANGE AND DURATION

By what criteria do we interpret the differences in body temperature measures on Monday to Thursday in Figure 2.1 as steady state variability rather than change? It is because the differences display a stable pattern of bounded variability, are of limited duration, and are reversible. In contrast, examine the consistent differences of nearly two degrees between the set of measures obtained on Monday to Thursday and those obtained Thursday and Friday. Because the higher level temperature persists (i.e., a 2-day duration), it is considered a change to a new steady state level. Therefore, distinctions between the concepts of variability on the one hand and of change on the other are *duration-dependent* (Featherman & Lerner, 1985).

Temporary and Enduring Changes

Changes may differ in their duration. Some changes are typically time limited, are eventually reversed, and the previous steady state restored, i.e., they are *temporary changes*. For example, the elevated body temperature on Thursday and Friday in Figure 2.1 will return to the normal steady state when the infectious process it signals is eliminated. Other changes are not time limited, i.e., they are *enduring changes*. They persist over extended periods of time, are not likely to be reversed, and, in fact, may be irreversible. For example, diabetes represents an enduring change that cannot be reversed but can be compensated for. Similarly, learning to communicate in English is an enduring change.

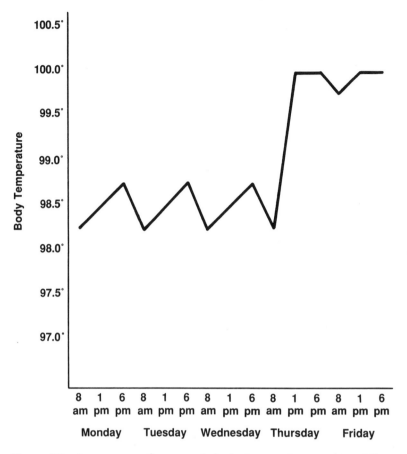

Figure 2.1. A summary of a person's body temperature measured three times a day at the same time for 5 consecutive days.

In fact when enduring changes are reversed, we are typically very surprised. For example, a man who had been in a coma for eight years (certainly an enduring change) suddenly began to behave normally after being administered a tranquilizing drug so that dental work could be performed. Similarly, if an adult discontinued normal speech and only babbled like a baby, that change would be considered a sign of pathology.

SUMMARY

Differences can be observed by comparing one thing, attribute, or event with others or with itself on the same or different occasions in the same or different contexts. Only comparisons of something with itself on different occasions (called intraindividual differences) provide a basis for an inference of change. Some intraindividual differences represent a stable pattern of variation between boundaries across occasions called steady state variability or performance variability. Some differences endure across a significant period of time. These are called change. Some changes are typically time limited and reversible while others persist and are often not reversible. These are called temporary and enduring changes, respectively. Understanding the dynamics of living and the distinctions between steady state variability, temporary change, and enduring change requires the comparison of intraindividual states on the same variables on multiple occasions.

The implications for professional practice of the distinctions between steady state variability, temporary change, and enduring change have been illustrated above. Their implications for designing research to study change processes and outcomes in humans are also significant and have been discussed elsewhere (Nesselroade & Ford, 1985, 1987). Nesselroade (1987) has also considered their implications for the trait-state distinction in the study of personality, issues of sampling and generalizability (Nesselroade, 1988), and individual differences approaches to the study of adult development (Nesselroade, 1990b).

Most of the illustrations used to this point to illustrate different types of change have been of biological processes because they are easy to understand; this is the case because we all experience these processes. Yet the same principles apply to other human characteristics as well.

For example, consider a young man who has sprained his ankle severely. He has to walk with crutches for several days until his ankle heals. The change in his walking behavior is a temporary change. A woman is beaten, threatened with death, and raped in an elevator on her way to work on the 12th floor of an office building. Thereafter anytime she enters an elevator or faces the possibility of entering an elevator she has an anxiety attack, and that state has persisted for a year. It is an enduring change, but it may be reversible with proper therapy. A young Hispanic woman from a poor family goes to college and becomes a successful, well-to-do pediatrician. That is an enduring change manifested in most aspects of her life.

ENVIRONMENTAL VARIABILITY AND CHANGE

The distinctions between and relationships among differences, variability, and change with regard to individuals' functioning also apply to the environments or contexts within which people live. Attributes of the environments in which people lead their lives also vary and change across time. Moreover, people create variability and change in their environments by their actions upon them and by moving from one context to another (Lerner, 1982). In addition, other people, who also vary and change, are key parts of each person's environments (Lerner & Lerner, 1987). Therefore in order to obtain needed and desired consequences, people must vary and change their patterns of living in synchrony with their varying and changing environments. Heraclitus's metaphor can be elaborated to say that not only can one not walk into the same river twice, but, also, because the river varies and changes, one must walk a little differently each time. Each moment of life is somehow different from every other moment. The profound implications of that fact for human development will be considered in later chapters.

ELABORATIVE AND DECREMENTAL CHANGE

It is both theoretically and practically useful to distinguish changes that elaborate from those that reduce a person's capabilities (cf. Baltes, 1987). An *elaborative change increases* the size, diversity, or complexity of organization of a person or of his or her characteristics, capabilities, and relationships with their environments. In the examples above, the changes in the young Hispanic woman's life are elaborative. That is, through her advanced education she elaborated her knowledge, skill, environment, and opportunities.

A *decremental change reduces* the size, diversity, or complexity of organization of a person or of his or her characteristics, capabilities, and relationships with his or her environments. The woman with the elevator phobia and the man with the sprained ankle represent decremental changes. That is, the elevator phobia restricted the woman from doing things she used to be able to do, and the man's sprained ankle prevented him from participating in his favorite activities of hiking, dancing, and playing basketball. Terms such as impairment and regression refer to decremental changes, while terms such as growth and learning typically refer to elaborative changes.

In general, elaborative changes are evaluated as "good" and decremental changes as "bad," but not always. For example, the growth of a malignant tumor is an increase in size of some aspect of a person (an elaborative change), but it is evaluated as "bad" because it disrupts and threatens the existence of the larger system of which it is a part, that is, the person. Similarly, overcoming an addiction to alcohol or drugs eliminates a pattern of behavior from a person's repertoire (a decremental change); however, it is evaluated as "good" because removing the addiction facilitates new potentials for future development (e.g., a successful career) and constrains other possibilities (e.g., potential for death from an overdose). Note that all such evaluations are relative to some frame of reference. For example, the recovered addict might evaluate that decremental change as good while his or her drug dealer might evaluate it as bad.

Some scholars (e.g., Baltes, 1987), have proposed that "developmental" outcomes at any phase of a person's life be viewed as a combination of "gains" and "losses." While we believe our proposals seek to convey the same general meaning intended by that formulation, we have avoided it. We think the concepts of "gain" and "loss" imply value judgments in contrast to the concepts of "elaborative" and "decremental" change, which we believe are more denotatively descriptive and less value laden. The terms *gain* and *loss* are also sometimes used to refer not to elaborative or decremental changes in current characteristics, but, rather, to changes in future possibilities. Each change, whether in a person or his or her contexts, changes the constraining and facilitating conditions under which he or she functions and therefore alters (often in unknown and unpredictable ways) future possibilities for elaborative or decremental changes.

The fact that an elaborate change often involves new constraints on behavior patterns does not mean that there is a "loss" in the sense of a decremental change in current characteristics, although elaborative and decremental changes are sometimes coupled; in life one often gives up one possibility to get something else.

For example, becoming married is an elaborative change that is coupled with decremental changes (e.g., giving up other close, affectionate relationships with members of the opposite sex and giving up living by oneself). It also changes one's potential futures, for example, it increases the probability of becoming a parent and decreases the probability of amorous involvements with others. It is of both theoretical and practical importance to carefully distinguish between actual changes and alterations of potential futures, as well as to keep separate the tasks of identifying different kinds of changes from their evaluation as desirable or undesirable.

CHANGE OUTCOMES AND CHANGE PROCESSES

Distinctions between qualitative and quantitative changes, kinds and durations of change, and elaborative or decremental characteristics of change all refer to aspects of the results or outcomes of change, that is, they refer to the what and when of change. If one wants to understand the conditions that lead to change or to try to promote or prevent change, however, then it is necessary to also understand the processes of change, that is, the how of change.

A focus on change processes leads to questions such as, "Are different kinds of outcomes—for example, biological versus cognitive—generated by different processes or by the same processes?" "Are the same kinds of outcomes generated by the same or different processes at different phases of life?" or "Are change processes that generate decremental changes different from those that generate elaborative changes?" Most theories of development have emphasized change outcomes. With these distinctions between the concepts of differences, variability, change, and change outcomes and processes we can now consider the concept of development.

Components of a Definition of Development

Why is a concept of development needed? Why isn't change enough? First, developmentalists claim that while all development involves change, not all changes represent development, and that a specific type or subset of changes has a specific array of change characteristics that require a special label: development.

Second, some scholars such as Bernard Kaplan (1983) and Heinz Werner (1957) champion a rationale for a focus on development that may be labeled the "developmental attitude." Here, as argued by Kaplan (1983), a developmental attitude (or "orientation") provides a framework with which to impose order on the flux and seeming chaos of the changes that ubiquitously characterize the world. A concept of development enables one to sort or partition changes that are unsystematic, disorganized, and lack progression from those that are systematic, organized, and progressive. A developmental orientation is a means of partitioning the world into meaningful and ordered changes versus random, unsystematic, destructive, or nonmeaningful changes. Thus the concept of development refers both to a type of change and to an orientation or strategy for studying and understanding change. Indeed, if those distinctions were not adopted, there would be little reason for a concept of development as opposed to the simpler concept of change. In fact, one source of confusion is that some people use the two terms as synonyms. Both science and clear communication require precision in concept definition and use. Therefore we will next attempt to specify key attributes that we believe help distinguish developmental change from other changes.

Although developmental scholars broadly agree that developmental changes differ from other changes, there is less agreement about the attributes that define the concept of development. In our view there are at least four attributes that characterize developmental change. Each successive component to be discussed next engages increasing debate within and across scholarly disciplines.

SYSTEMATIC CHANGE

Perhaps the most general definitional consensus that exists in the several relevant disciplinary literatures is that developmental changes, in contrast to other changes, are systematic in character. Although recent work in the natural sciences, specifically in physics (Gleick, 1987), has focused on the way order may emerge from chaos (e.g., Prigogine & Stengers, 1984), most scholars remain convinced that changes must be of a systematic nature in order to qualify as a developmental change. In fact many of the kinds of changes described by Prigogine and Stengers (1984) illustrate transformational systemic change.

Systematic change means that developmental changes must be coherent: they must be nonrandom and linked together in a meaningful spatial-temporal framework. They must occur in a way that maintains self-consistent, interdependent relationships with other parts of the entity or organization (i.e., "system"). A person is an entity composed of a complex organization of biological structures and interacting functional capabilities. Change cannot and does not occur in all components of a person simultaneously; however, because a person must maintain structural and functional unity to survive and be effective, any change in any component must be fit into the larger system or that unity will be destroyed. Therefore developmental change is systematic in the sense that it must occur within the constraints and possibilities of the current states of the rest of the system, including system-context relationships, or the rest of the system must go through some modification to accommodate the change that is occurring.

SUCCESSIVE VERSUS PROGRESSIVE CHANGE

Successive Change

When put into a temporal—that is to say, developmental—framework, systematic and organized changes have a successive character to them. This means that the range of changes seen at a later time are circumscribed, delimited, or facilitated by the nature of the changes seen at a former time. Each new state emerges from, but is not solely the result of, previous states. In other words, within an organized system the probability of a particular change at Time 2 is a function of the system states existing at Time 1. Thus there is not complete flexibility or plasticity within an organized system because at any moment the existing states of the system provide facilitating and constraining conditions that define the possibilities for, and the probabilities of, different kinds of potential changes. Each change in system states alters those conditions and therefore alters the next set of possible and probable changes.

Thus this successive character to systemic organized change means that the nature of developmental changes are at best relatively plastic, and not absolutely plastic (Lerner, 1984). In turn, relative plasticity means that change is a probabilistic phenomenon. One can, at best, say that, within certain limits of confidence, a particular set of changes in a system is likely to occur given the nature of earlier states, current states, and current contexts. On the other hand, however, the relative plasticity that exists because of the successive nature of change means that there is some possibility (albeit perhaps a small and potentially difficult one to implement) that a low probability change may occur or may be promoted by an interventionist seeking to influence change in a given system.

Progressive Change

The successive character of change is elaborated by some developmentalists into the concept of progressive change, by which they mean that the direction of successive change proceeds in terms of a particular universal end point or goal (Pepper, 1942). In contrast, there is no inherent teleology in the definition of development to which we subscribe (Lerner, 1986). Relative plasticity and probabilistic change means that developmental change is multidirectional in nature (Lerner, 1984; Ford, 1987). Indeed, because multiple end points of development are possible, there is no single, normative change trajectory—no one universal developmental format for change—that necessarily must apply to every component structure and function of each person over time as he or she is enmeshed in the complex flow of intraperson and person-context transactions that comprise human life. On the other hand, the propositions that multiple and changeable developmental pathways are possible for each person does not mean that "anything goes." The developmental possibilities for each person are both constrained and facilitated by: (a) their personal characteristics (e.g., genetic endowment); (b) their contexts (e.g., their family circumstances); and (c) their current states (e.g., their health and skills).

From our point of view, the concept of progressive change represents a value judgment that requires comparing actual changes to an idealized template for change. *Progress* involves an evaluative judgment that a pattern of change is in the direction of a correct, more valued, better, best, or more refined state of being or functioning. For example, one view holds that development is change toward "perfection" (e.g., Kaplan, 1983). Changes that move to the valued end state represent the "goal" of the developmental progression, and changes that do not match this idealized view are seen as other than progressive. They are seen at the extreme as inferior, degenerate, or unhealthy. This "developmental perfection" view is implicit in some popular concepts in personality, counseling, and clinical psychology, (e.g., "self-realization" or "self-actualization").

The belief in progressive change, while certainly not diminishing the presence of plasticity in development, gives such variability—both within and between individuals—a substantively different interpretation than definitions that emphasize only the successive character of change. Those who believe in progress must recognize the empirical reality of plasticity, but when such variability moves the organism off the idealized developmental trajectory, such plasticity is seen as, at best, error variance and as, at worst, degeneracy. That is, deviations from the ideal developmental trajectory may be seen as evidence of abnormal or undesirable growth and development; however, if every person's developmental pathway inherently has the potential for multi-directionality and, therefore, individual differences are the *rule* in life, then asserting that there is only one good or appropriate course for life to take can lead to serious and misleading consequences. A "perfection" conception limits on an a priori basis investigation into the empirical possibility that there may be several pathways through life that may subserve each person's healthy or positive functioning, and that these pathways may differ between persons or for the same person as they progress through life. Indeed the teleological notion of progress toward some ideal outcome diverts attention away from the investigation of the individual and contextual conditions that, first, promote individual differences in development and, second, foster or diminish the probability of different kinds of developmental pathways. In addition a "perfection" conception of development can lead to social injustice (e.g., persecution of those who do not match the idealized template) and/or personal distress and difficulty (e.g., self-evaluations as being unworthy, bad, or incompetent because one is different from the idealized template for development). This is another illustration of the many practical consequences of one's guiding assumptions.

The Role of Value Judgments in Development

This is not to say that developmental pathways are not influenced by value judgments or by personal and social goals, for they clearly are. Each society and each family tries to promote or facilitate the development of some kinds of patterns and to constrain others. For example, one group may promote striving for personal success and pleasure while another may promote sacrificing personal aggrandizement in the interest of the group. In fact, agreement about a guiding set of fundamental values is essential for effective social group living.

When such valued outcomes are socially defined, then it is possible to evaluate developmental pathways in terms of their progression toward the valued outcomes. What is important is to recognize that these values influence individuals' development as a part of their environment, they are manufactured by humans, and they may differ from society to society. They must be understood as culturally relative value judgments or religious beliefs about desirable developmental pathways rather than as inborn developmental goals toward which all humans must necessarily develop.

Similarly individuals may construct ideas about their preferred developmental outcomes (i.e., personal goals), and then organize their behavior to pursue a developmental pathway they think will lead to those outcomes. Individuals will differ in the outcomes they value and therefore the developmental pathways they will follow. For example, one person may seek to produce a heavily muscled, trim, fat-free body and may pursue a regimen of weight lifting and diet to produce this outcome. Another may seek to lead a righteous and moral life and may pursue a program of religious study and meditation to those ends.

Emphasizing successive rather than progressive change not only is in accord with evidence about the relative plasticity and multidirectionality of change, but also recognizes that there is a diversity of developmental pathways that may be associated with good functioning. Thus cultural differences may represent alternate pathways to a good life. The distinction between successive and progressive change leads to a third factor that is linked to the distinction between successive and progressive change.

ADAPTIVE VERSUS APTIVE CHANGE

The influence of Charles Darwin (1859, 1872) and the theory of evolution upon the study of development in many disciplines cannot be overestimated. For example, one finds reference in such diverse fields as biology, geology, history, psychology, sociology, and human development to the belief that through the natural selection process there is a refinement and improvement in the functional and morphological characteristics of organisms. While Darwin's theory was constructed to account for phylogenetic or species development, it has also been applied by analogy to try to understand ontogenetic or individual development.

Adaptive Change

Simply stated, in traditional Darwinian thinking evolution involves adaptation. That is, changes in organisms are shaped by natural selection to enhance the fitness of each species to survive and reproduce within the demands of the environment. It follows that all characteristics of each species must have evolved as a consequence of eons of rigorous, selective pressures within the natural world, a world "red in tooth and claw."

In this view development results from adaptive change, and adaptation represents progress. What exists now has to be better, more ideal, or more advantageous than that which existed at a prior time. By virtue of its present existence, that which currently exists has shown itself to be able to "win" the battle of natural selection, to compete, and to outdistance—in terms of survival and reproduction— prior patterns and, therefore, to survive and flourish as it currently does. Thus, in evolutionary theory, the notions of progress and of adaptation and fitness are linked.

Aptive Change

A growing body of knowledge suggests, however, that only some current species' characteristics are the direct adaptive product of natural selection. Darwin himself, in *The Origin of the Species* (1859), recognized that there were currently functional characteristics that did not originally evolve to serve that function as a direct consequence of natural selection. Such characteristics have been labeled *aptive* (Gould & Vrba, 1982)—that is, they may be fit, they may enhance current survival and reproduction—but they may not necessarily be *ad*aptive— that is, originally shaped by natural selection for the functions they now serve.

Darwin gave the example of the unfused skull sutures in the human head as a possible instance of an aptive evolutionary change. Certainly, unfused skull sutures allow the human infant, having a large cranium, to fit through the 10-centimeter opening in the mother's cervix. Clearly this seems adaptive; the unfused sutures "allow" the infant to be born with a brain larger than would be the case *if* infants' skulls had no unfused sutures. In turn, their large brain is an advantage for humans' survival in a complex physical and social world; if humans did not have such a large brain (which requires a large cranium to house it) human culture could not have evolved to its current level of complexity. Therefore humans' evolution of unfused skull sutures served an adaptive purpose, that is, permitting large-brained human babies to survive the rigors of the birth process without brain damage.

This scenario, however, is a "Just So Story," akin to those told by Rudyard Kipling. Snakes and birds are born from eggs. Yet, they too have unfused skull sutures. Clearly their unfused skull sutures cannot have an adaptive evolutionary history akin to that purported to exist for humans. Darwin (1859) recognized the problem that the unfused skull sutures of reptiles and birds posed for maintaining the ubiquity of the influence of adaptation in evolutionary change processes; however, people using the adaptation assumption have typically avoided the problem raised by such evidence, while others have not.

For example, Gould and Vrba (1982) have argued that there may be characteristics that exist because they are neutral to natural selection pressures *or* because they are correlated with characteristics that are selected. Thus these latter characteristics are merely carried along in evolution and may, like the unfused skull sutures of humans, be co-opted for later functional utility. Gould and Vrba call such characteristics *ex*aptations; Nesselroade (in preparation) calls them selection effects.

Ford's (1987) LSF provides an explanation for why and how such aptive changes could occur. Each person, as a living system, must maintain structural-functional unity to survive and reproduce successfully. If adaptive change occurs in one part of the system, the rest of the system may undergo modifications to accommodate the change. For example, imagine a baby born with three arms. For the third arm to be integrated into the rest of the body there would have to be many skeletal, neural, circulatory, and other system modifications. The third arm might evolve as an adaptive change (e.g., you could play a piano and scratch an itch at the same time) while the accommodating changes would be aptive ones.

The adaptive versus the aptive (or exaptation) "alternatives" lead to somewhat different explanatory strategies about development. The adaptationist explains existing human characteristics historically in terms of speculations about their probable utility when they first evolved. The aptive approach argues that once any characteristic appears, various uses for it may be found as life and contexts change. Therefore the current utility of a characteristic is not necessarily limited to the conditions under which it appeared or evolved. In other words, development is a function of both current and historical conditions. This emphasis on the importance of current conditions for development leads to a fourth characteristic of development.

DEVELOPMENT OCCURS IN THE HERE AND NOW

The adaptive and aptive change distinction illustrates a general and very basic problem regarding understanding the way past events and experiences relate to current development and functioning. Physics makes it clear that forces that occurred a year ago cannot influence the motion of objects today. Only current forces can influence current motion. Analogously, how could events that occurred a year ago influence a person's behavior today? The answer is they cannot! In human behavior, just as in physics and chemistry, what existed last year cannot *directly* influence what happens now, just as what may exist next year cannot *directly* influence what happens now. Past and future events cannot directly influence the present; only present events can directly influence present events. Yet it is apparent that human behavior is a function of past events and potential future ones. How is that possible? The only way the past and the future can have any influence on present development and functioning is through surrogates that represent them in current circumstances.

Schneirla (1957) labeled the effects of past experiences on current circumstances "trace effects." The past is gone, but the traces it left can influence present development and functioning. For example, it is not the parental treatment received when a child that directly causes an adult's current dysfunctional behavior; rather, patterns of cognition, emotion, and action developed because of that treatment (i.e., the past's traces), and that are manifest in current behavior cause dysfunction. Similarly, the future has not yet arrived, but possible futures can be imagined and this influences the present. For example, it is not the potential future treatment by a probable spouse that influences the development of a person's present relationship with his or her fiancee; instead, the person's current thoughts about such future possibilities (i.e., present surrogates for the future), and the interaction of such thoughts with observations about his or her fiancee's current behavior, affects the relationship.

The utility of studying a person's past experience is that it provides one basis for inferring the "trace effects" that may operate as influential surrogates of the past to influence the present. Similarly, studying a person's hopes, expectations, and goals for the future provides information about currently influential surrogates for possible futures. Thus "traces" of the past, present events, and surrogates representing possible futures can exist simultaneously in the here and now, making it possible for humans to deal with the flow of life and the world and to rise above the moment.

A person's current characteristics are important, but development is context dependent; therefore development must be understood to result from interactions between current characteristics of the person with his or her current environment. Development is the product of the flow of person-context transactions, and this is true from fetal life onward (e.g., Smotherman & Robinson, 1990). It is important to recognize that present environments also contain surrogates of the past (e.g., in books) and of the future (e.g., social/organizational goals). It follows that human development can only be understood through examination of the differences among temporally sequential sets of contextually embedded current human states.

Humans' capability for merging past, present, and potential future circumstances means that they do not react blindly to current circumstances without the benefit of past experience or future possibilities. Human cognitive and learning capabilities and cultural constructions free people from complete stimulus control by bringing current representations of past, present, and future conditions into interaction in organizing present functioning and development.

In summary the four characteristics of developmental change that have been discussed make it clear that development involves relative plasticity and multidirectionality—both at the ontogenetic and phylogenetic levels. Developmentalists do a disservice to the plasticity that does exist by preordaining that only those changes judged adaptive and progressive qualify as developmental change.

A Provisional Definition of Development

A definition is a way of trying to convey the precise meaning of a concept and of distinguishing it from other concepts. One task of science is to build categories (e.g., concepts) that as accurately as possible represent the phenomena of interest. Because nature is very diverse, the choice of which of its aspects one will focus upon and construct concepts to represent is somewhat arbitrary because many choices are possible. Such choices are not capricious, however, because they must demonstrate their utility in the search for deeper understanding of our world and ourselves and as tools for dealing with the practical affairs of life. Our proposed definition of development is designed to serve those purposes.

In this chapter we have argued that variability and change are properties of our world and ourselves that are of basic importance, and that there are different kinds of change. We have argued, further, that one subtype of change called developmental change is of particular interest to us. We have proposed a set of defining attributes for that type of change. We have tried to be as precise and explicit as possible. We will now synthesize all those ideas into a formal definition of that type of change called development and briefly examine the implications of that definition.

Though we do not expect everyone to agree with our definition, we urge those who disagree to formulate their own definitions with equal explicitness and justification so that points of disagreement can be clearly identified and examined theoretically and empirically. In the remainder of this book we will seek to make more evident the meaning, significance, and utility of the definition we propose and to embed it in a larger theoretical framework.

Our formal definition seeks to capture a view of human development as a continuous and sometimes unpredictable voyage throughout life, sailing from seas that have become familiar into oceans as yet uncharted toward destinations to be imagined, defined, and redefined as the voyage proceeds, with occasional, often unpredictable, transformations of one's vessel and sailing skills and the oceans upon which one sails resulting from unforeseen circumstances.

Humans are multilevel, contextually embedded organizations of different kinds of structures and functions. It is important to recognize in any definition that change and development can occur in any level and between levels in any kind of characteristic. Therefore, before proceeding to propose a definition of development, it will be useful to summarize the different kinds of change defined earlier and their relationships within and between levels of organization. Figure 2.2 represents a person as a complex, multilevel organization of biological structures and biological, psychological, and behavioral functional patterns. Changes may occur within or between levels.

Figure 2.2 refers to actual patterns of variability and change that occur in a person. In defining and discussing development, it is important to distinguish between actual changes in the system and

Level of Analysis

Type of Change

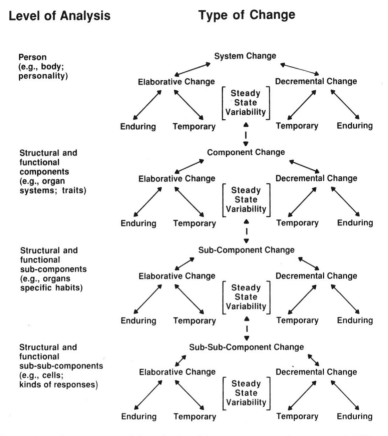

Figure 2.2. A summary of the relationships among steady state variability and different types of change at different levels of analysis for understanding a person.

the changes in potential futures for a person that result from developmental changes in the constraining and facilitating conditions manifest in current states. Any change makes some future possibilities more likely and others less likely. For example, an aspiring young painter who becomes blind may no longer be able to pursue the developmental pathway of a painter, but may shift to a different form of artistic expression such as becoming a sculptor or musician.

The multilevel representation in Figure 2.2 should not obscure the basic principle that humans must function as structural-functional units. This means that a change in any aspect of a person at any level must somehow be accommodated by the rest of the system to maintain unitary functioning. That accommodation may occur in various ways. For example, an elaborative change at one level (e.g., the growth of a malignant tumor in the brain) may produce decremental changes at other levels (e.g., loss of some cognitive or behavioral capabilities). Or a decremental change at one level (e.g., the death of a few neurons in the brain) may be accommodated locally and not affect other levels. Or a change at one level (e.g., loss of sight) may require changes in many other aspects (e.g., life-style changes) to accommodate the disruption. Thus the entire system does not necessarily have to change to accommodate every component change, but accommodating changes will occur insofar as necessary to maintain structural-functional unity.

If development is not a synonym for change, then to which kinds of changes summarized in Figure 2.2 does the concept of developmental refer? A person's characteristics and possibilities at any point in his or her life result from a combination of elaborative changes ("gains") and decremental changes ("losses"). If, however, the concept of development were applied to that combination, then development would have no distinctive meaning; development would be a synonym for change. Therefore our definition of development is limited to *relatively enduring elaborative change*. This idea is the common thread running through most other definitions of development and is illustrated by Werner's (1948, 1957) orthogenetic principle. The criterion of enduring elaborative change is combined with the other defining attributes of the concept of development discussed earlier to construct the following definition.

DEVELOPMENT DEFINED

Individual human development involves incremental and transformational processes that, through a flow of interactions among current characteristics of the person and his or her current contexts, produces a succession of relatively enduring changes that elaborate or increase the diversity of the person's structural and functional characteristics and the patterns of their environmental interactions while maintaining coherent organization and structural-functional unity of the person as a whole.

Several characteristics of this definition should be noted. First, it encompasses the four attributes previously discussed: systematic change, successive change, aptive as well as adaptive change, and change that occurs through the interactions of current conditions. Second, it represents development as open-ended; it has a direction but not preordained goals. The direction involves the elaboration and diversification of a person's characteristics; but many developmental pathways are possible leading toward different kinds of outcomes, that is, we define development as multidimensional and multidirectional. Our definition, however, remains neutral as to which kinds of development are to be valued over others.

IMPLICATIONS OF THE DEFINITION

Our view that development is open-ended has several very important implications. First, development is a never-ending possibility as long as a person lives; however, the kinds of development that are possible will be successively selectively constrained and facilitated by current states and contexts of the person. That is, developmental possibilities encompass the life span.

Second, because persons and contexts may change in unexpected ways, so too may individuals' developmental pathways take unexpected courses as a result. This does not mean that there are an unlimited number of potential developmental pathways for each person. The number of possible pathways may differ in the different levels of analysis summarized in Figure 2.2. For example, humans can never grow wings and fly like a bird, but they can invent machines that enable them to fly.

Third, viewing development as open-ended and a product of current conditions means that a person's future is not prisoner of his or her past. Future developmental pathways can be constructed that deviate from previous pathways. There may be discontinuity in life, discontinuity that emerges from the continuity of a person's ongoing relations with his or her contexts.

Fourth, development, defined as elaborative change, functions to create new possibilities for people. It is axiomatic in evolutionary theory that species with a greater diversity of capabilities are more adaptively successful than others. Analogously, individuals with a more diverse set of capabilities have more options for dealing effectively with changing environments and a more diverse base for future development than those with less variability in their behavioral capabilities. The more diverse one's capabilities, the more performance variability is possible;

the more performance variability that occurs, the more diverse are the related contingencies and consequences experienced; the more diverse one's experience, the greater the number of options likely to come one's way for future developmental possibilities.

Fifth, any developmental pathway will open up possibilities that did not exist before. Of course, foregoing alternate developmental pathways may foreclose other unknown possibilities. Development always involves both gains and losses in future possibilities (Baltes, 1987). For example, what possibilities might have emerged or disappeared for you had you chosen a different occupation, lived in a different location, or married a different person?

Sixth, because one's future is probabilistic and somewhat unpredictable, it is not possible to know which of one's capabilities may be most valuable in the future. A competence unimportant in one's current developmental pathway may become very valuable as future possibilities unfold. By analogy to phylogenesis, aptive changes may become adaptively valuable. Therefore multidimensional development prepares people for the probable diversity and unexpected twists and turns of their future lives (Bandura, 1986).

Seventh, the definition specifies that developmental change cannot be understood solely in terms of person or context characteristics. For example, genes do not drive development independent of environmental influences, and social and behavioral development are not simply reactions to environmental forces. Our definition requires a theory of human development in which person and environment factors interact dynamically to produce developmental change in which changes in relations between these factors reveal the basic process of development (Lerner, 1992). Indeed this conception of development can be applied to any level of organization, such as those represented in Figures 1.2 and 2.2.

Finally, the definition identifies two basic processes, incremental and transformational change processes, that can produce both continuities and discontinuities in development. They will be defined, illustrated, and justified in Chapter 5.

Other Concepts About Change

It may be useful to end this chapter by comparing our definition of development with some other popular concepts about elaborative and decremental change.

CONCEPTS EMPHASIZING ELABORATIVE CHANGE

Growth traditionally has referred to a permanent increase in the total mass of the body or one of its physical parts via tissue elaboration resulting from food exchanges with the environment interacting with biological processes (cf. Schneirla, 1957). Used in this way, growth is a subcategory of development; however, the concept of growth has sometimes been expanded to refer to all other aspects of a person as well, for example, cognitive growth or growth in competence. This broader usage makes the concept of growth a synonym for development.

Maturation traditionally has referred to the progressive differentiation and elaboration of biological structures and functional capabilities toward the prototypical adult steady state for that species (e.g., humans) that results from the interaction of genetic processes and environmental conditions (cf. Schneirla, 1957). Used in this way, maturation is a subcategory of development. Its usage is also sometimes expanded to include the acquisition of preferred patterns of belief and behavior of a particular culture, for example, social-emotional maturation. Such expanded usage approaches the status of another synonym for development. Conceptual precision would be served if the concepts of growth and maturation were restricted to their original biologically based meanings, and other terms were used for other types of developmental change.

Learning is the process through which knowledge and skills are acquired, elaborated, or modified as a result of study, training, or experience. *Socialization* is a learning process through which people acquire the beliefs, values, and social behaviors characteristic of their culture or subculture, largely through social modeling and instruction. Thus both of these concepts represent subcategories of development.

CONCEPTS REPRESENTING DECREMENTAL CHANGES

Injury refers to any damage to body structures resulting from an environmental assault. It results in temporary or permanent decremental change in some level or levels of Figure 2.2. The concepts of *illness, disease,* and *physical disability* refer to decrements in capabilities and functioning resulting from some material/energy disruption such as genetic anomalies (e.g., Downs syndrome), invasion by other organisms (e.g., flu), materials ingested (e.g., cirrhosis of the liver), and organ or cellular dysfunctions (e.g., diabetes).

Regression refers to a return to a pattern of functioning typical of and appropriate to an earlier stage of life (e.g., schizophrenic infantile behaviors), resulting in a reduction of current capabilities. *Aging* is a concept that has, until recent years, emphasized successive decremental changes in biological structures and functions resulting from the cumulative effects of irreversible physiochemical changes and accompanying decrements in cognitive and motoric capabilities. This definition of aging as decremental change tended to promote the view that people become increasingly incompetent and dependent as they age, resulting in social customs and policies of significant disadvantage to the elderly. More recently the concept of aging has been broadened to encompass elaborative changes as well, promoting understanding of the acquisition of desirable qualities as a function of age as with a fine wine (e.g., wisdom) (Baltes, 1987; Kleigel et al., 1990). One product of this definitional elaboration is the life span development orientation (Baltes & Willis, 1977).

These examples of other change concepts illustrate the theoretical and practical utility scholars and professionals have found in distinguishing between developmental (enduring elaborative) changes and decremental changes.

Next Steps

We have now defined the domain called development. The rest of the chapters in this book are designed: (a) to construct Developmental Systems Theory (DST) so that it captures our definition and deals with the what, when, why, and how of development of humans; and (b) to examine the utility of and implications of that more comprehensive theory.

Chapter 3 will summarize the basic assumptions, the metamodel, on which DST is based. It links the guiding assumptions of the LSF to the conceptual structure of developmental contextualism. Following that, a model of individual development and functioning that is based on and applies those guiding assumptions will be presented in Chapters 4 and 5. Chapter 6 will briefly consider implications for research, intervention, and social policy.

CHAPTER THREE

Developmental Contextualism: Biology and Context as the Liberators of Human Potential

[Our] conception of human development . . . differs from most Western contemporary thought on the subject. The view . . . is that humans have a capacity for change across the entire life span. It questions the traditional idea that the experiences of the early years, which have a demonstrated contemporaneous effect, necessarily constrain the characteristics of adolescence and adulthood . . . [T]here are important growth changes across the life span from birth to death, many individuals retain a great capacity for change, and the consequences of the events of early childhood are continually transformed by later experiences, making the course of human development more open than many have believed.
(Brim & Kagan, 1980, p.1)

IN THIS CHAPTER THE BASIC STARTING ASSUMPTIONS, or metamodel, for Developmental Systems Theory (DST) will be summarized and justified. The primary source of the metamodel for DST is called developmental contextualism. Developmental contextualism rests on two key ideas.

Multivariate, Multilevel Organization

First, there are variables from multiple, qualitatively distinct levels of analysis or levels of organization involved in human life and development (e.g., biology, psychology, society, and history). Scientists adhering to virtually *any* theoretical viewpoint would probably agree with this view. Some scientists, however, would pursue inquiries aimed at the investigation of variables from one level of organization without addressing other levels (i.e., they would adopt a "main effects" approach to science). Others would adopt a reductionistic orientation, seeking to study or at least interpret variables from multiple levels in terms of one level—a level conceived to be the core, constituent, or elemental level. Developmental contextualists would reject both of these approaches as too limited. Instead they would adopt an interlevel-synthetic orientation in which variables from multiple levels are considered, including those reductionists might emphasize, but would emphasize the intralevel and interlevel patterning of variables.

DYNAMIC INTERACTIONISM

This perspective is linked to a second key idea: Variables from the several levels of organization comprising human life exist in reciprocal relation. The structure and function of variables from any one level influence and are influenced by the structure and function of variables from the other levels. This reciprocal influence among levels, this "fusion" (Tobach & Greenberg, 1984) of interlevel relations, is termed *dynamic interactionism* within developmental contextualism (Lerner, 1978, 1979).

As a consequence of the ubiquitous existence of these dynamic interactions, the potential for change is a continuous property of the multiple, interrelated levels of organization comprising human life. Some changes can occur within levels without significant impact on other levels; however, because levels of organization exist in an integrated system, relations between levels of organization and not an isolated level per se become the key focus of developmental analysis, and *changing relations among levels constitutes the primary process of human developmental change.* Another way of saying this is that it is the organization of multiple levels of component structures and processes that makes possible the structural-functional unity of a person.

At the individual level of analysis, developmental contextualism stresses that neither person characteristics (e.g., biological or psychological ones) nor context characteristics (i.e., involving either interpersonal, e.g., peer group, relations or extrapersonal—institutional or physical ecological—relations), are the primary basis—or cause—of the individual's functioning or development. Rather, the structure (or "form"; Pepper, 1942) of the system—the pattern of relations or dynamic organization—at a given point in time (at a specific moment in history; Pepper, 1942) is the "event" causing the person's functioning. Changes in the form of these relations are the cause of developmental change.

Reciprocal or Mutual Causality

We find that this dynamic interactionism view of causality is confusing for some people because it seems to contradict commonsense beliefs about causality so deeply embedded in our language and culture. For example, a typical view is that if A causes B, B cannot simultaneously cause A. In contrast the theory being presented in this book assumes not only that A and B simultaneously influence one another, but also that any change in A or B is a function of the organization of variables within which they are embedded. Because this systemic view of causality is not familiar to some readers, we will briefly try to clarify and illustrate it.

For centuries philosophers and scientists have proposed a diversity of ways of defining causality and of identifying causal relations, with views ranging from spatial and temporal contiguity to the generative causality represented in experimental designs. (See White, 1990, for a recent brief review of the diversity of views.)

The concept of causality reflected in classical determinism and mechanistic models has perhaps been the most influential. Rapoport (1968) discusses the limitations of linear causality conceptions and related research methods for understanding dynamic systems and discusses the need in modern science to understand "the flux of interdependent events" where "all the variables are interrelated in 'mutual causality.' "

Linear causality is defined in terms of the relationships between antecedent events (causes) and consequent events (effects) because time is considered linear with phenomena flowing sequentially from the past into the future (e.g., A → B). What is considered an antecedent (or cause) and a consequence (or effect), however, is a function of the frame through which the events are interpreted. For example, a child (C) swallows a pill (P). One can ask, "What effect does the pill (P) have on the child (C) (e.g., does it increase stomach acidity or blood pressure?), that is, P Ä C. Or, one can ask, "What effect does the child" (C) have on the pill (P)" (e.g., how do digestive processes affect changes in and absorption of the pill?), that is, C → P.

The fact is that both processes are occurring simultaneously, for example, the pill is affecting the child, while the child is affecting the pill (C ↔ P) and the dynamics of their interaction changes over time, that is,

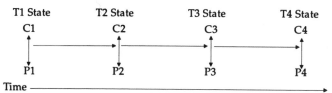

One may choose to examine the relationship between C_1 and P_2, P_3, or P_4, or between P_1 and C_2, C_3, or C_4, or between any other combination of Cs and Ps to make inferences about C causing P or P causing C. Although such information may be useful, it is incomplete. The dynamic interaction or mutual causality view expands that approach by identifying C ↔ P as patterns of organization. The value and organization of these variables at any moment is called a state. Comparison of the state of each variable and its patterns of organization from Time 1 to Time 4 reveals the dynamics of how those changes occur. Murphy (1979) illustrates the multiple patterns of causal relations possible in relationship to genetic analyses of diseases.

Such networks of interdependent variables might be called a *causal field*. In a causal field a change in any variable is understood as a consequence of the operation of the entire field of variables. Causal modeling (Bentler, 1980) and contingency frequency analysis (von Eye, 1990) illustrate data analytic models that attempt to represent patterns of relationships in causal fields. Some examples of the operation of causal fields will help clarify this idea.

Wiener (1961) describes how the organization of a set of electrical power generators regulates the functioning of each generator. Each generator functions as an oscillator with feedback controls to produce a 60-cycle-per-second output, but may vary in a range around 60 cycles. If one generator slows down, the others speed it up. If one speeds up, the others slow it down. The effect on a deviant generator is not "caused" by any other single generator in the system; rather, the effect is a consequence of the organization of the entire system.

Similarly each muscle cell in a heart is an autonomous oscillator displaying rhythmic patterns of contraction. As components of a larger system, a single heart, the cells synchronize their rhythms and the heart beats as a unit. Sometimes that synchronization breaks down for some reason, called fibrillation, and a person will die if the synchronization among individual cell dynamics is not restored (e.g., through an electric shock to the heart). As with the network of power generators, the synchronization results from the influence of the entire organization of heart muscles on component muscle cells, not from the singular influence of individual cells on one another. DeWan (1976) illustrates such systemic causation with examples from control systems.

Such causal fields occur among as well as within organisms. For example, a species of fireflies in southeast Asia may synchronize their flashing as a part of their sexual display activity. Whole bushes of them may flash in unison (Buck & Buck, 1968). Crowd/social conformity behaviors (e.g., the rhythmic movement of the audience at a rock music concert) may be another example of a social causal field.

The idea that variations in any variable are a function of (i.e., are caused by) the organization of the field of variables of which it is a part is not new. For example, it was a cornerstone of Kurt Lewin's (1939) field theory and life space conceptions and of Brown's (1951) proposals to use topological mathematics to study fields of psychological variables. Tobach and Greenberg's (1984) concept of "fusion" of sets of variables is another example. It is our thesis that the person-in-context is best understood as an organization of mutually influential variables, that is, as a causal field. This requires a way of representing persons-in-context as a unit of analysis composed of an organization of subunits or component structures and processes.

THE NATURE-NURTURE ISSUE

Combining the assumptions of multivariate, multilevel organization and dynamic interactionism leads to a key theoretical feature of developmental contextualism. It represents a quite distinct position concerning the core conceptual issue and controversy in developmental psychology (Lerner, 1976, 1986) and, arguably, within psychology as a whole (Anastasi, 1958): the nature-nurture issue. Developmental contextualism proposes that variables from levels of organization associated with a person's biological or organismic characteristics (e.g., genes, tissues, or organ systems) dynamically interact with variables from contextual levels of organization (i.e., involving intrapersonal and extrapersonal variables), within which the biological characteristics are embedded. Therefore biological variables both influence and, reciprocally, are influenced by contextual ones. Accordingly, stances about nature-nurture that stress the primacy of either context (e.g., cultural deterministic views) or biology (e.g., genetic or biological reductionistic or deterministic views) in human development are explicitly rejected by a developmental contextual perspective (Lerner, 1992). Our DST illustrates and describes how biological and contextual factors provide facilitating and constraining conditions that "set the stage" and through different patterns of interaction may produce many different "plays" with a diversity of "plots."

The development of the ideas and evidence associated with the articulation of developmental contextualism have been reviewed by Lerner (1986) and Turkewitz (1988). The contrasts in the stance taken about the nature-nurture issue between developmental contextualism, cultural deterministic views, and biological deterministic views have generated the most debate in the literature as developmental contextualism evolved (e.g., Lerner, 1992). Indeed it is this debate, particularly concerning a genetic reductionistic or biological deterministic stance, that helps bring the distinctive features of developmental contextualism into boldest relief. This is particularly evident with regard to the implications of developmental contextualism for maintaining an optimistic posture about the potential for interventions to enhance human life. Therefore it is useful to present the details and implications of developmental contextualism in relation to its dynamic interactional view of the nature-nurture issue, that is, of the synthetic relation between biology and context that is at the core of human life.

The Fused Influences of Biology and Context on Development

In developmental contextualism influences of biology on human behavior and development are considered important but do not act independently of environment. The influence of genes on development is illustrative.

Genes function neither as the primary nor the ultimate causal influence on behavior and development. Instead genes (heredity) and environment are seen as coequal forces in the determination of development; these two domains function as completely fused in life. Genes always exist in and cannot function without an environment; therefore the functioning of genes is always influenced by the specific characteristics of their context. For example, humans have genes that, under prototypical human environmental conditions, are involved in the development of two arms and two legs. Under different conditions, however, a different result may occur. For example, even a slight change in the chemicals in an unborn baby's prenatal environment can result in an infant born without any limbs at all (e.g., when scores of pregnant British women took the drug Thalidomide in the 1950s).

In turn, the environment would be an empty place without the participation of living systems within it (e.g., compare the moon with the earth). The kinds of influence the environment can exert on development is both made possible and limited by the specific characteristics of the people who live within it. For instance, no known type of environmental enrichment (be it medical or nutritional) can halt the emergence of sickle cell anemia in children possessing the genes for this disorder; and, as far as is understood, no environmental agents (i.e., a virus) can produce this disorder.

The Thalidomide and sickle cell examples also illustrate the relative plasticity of human development. While different kinds of outcomes are possible depending on the genetic-environment interactions, the diversity of possible outcomes is constrained by both the nature of the genome and the context. For example, an infant may be born without arms or legs but not with wings, just as a fly may be born with or without wings but not with hands.

CONSTRAINING AND FACILITATING INFLUENCES OF NATURE AND NURTURE

The fusions of genes and context—of nature and nurture—mean that they are mutually facilitating *and* mutually constraining in influencing behavior. Biology may be associated with more or less of a given kind of development and/or with quite different kinds of development depending on the environmental circumstances within which people exist. For example, a girl may have genes that are associated with the early onset of her menstrual cycle (e.g., about 10 years of age); yet the nutritional and health care she receives will influence whether her cycle begins at this time, later, or, perhaps, even earlier. For instance, the age at which women reach menarche has declined across history in different countries. In Norway, for example, females born in 1840 reached menarche at about 17 years, while Norwegian females born in recent years reach menarche about 4 years earlier than this. Similarly, over the course of about the last 150 years, the average age of menarche has decreased within the United States about 4 months per decade. For example, women born in the United States around 1890 reached menarche at about 14 years; today females in the United States reach menarche between 1 and 2 years earlier.

Such changes in timing of reproductive maturity, called a secular trend, is but one instance of several significant physical changes occurring in males and females over the course of even relatively recent history. For instance, since 1900 American children of preschool age have been taller on an average of 1.0 centimeter and heavier on an average of 0.5 kilogram per decade. In addition, during the growth spurt, which occurs as part of the pubertal changes of adolescence, adolescents have shown increasingly greater increases in height (2.5 centimeters) and weight (2.5 kilograms) across this recent historical period.

These physical and physiological changes have occurred too rapidly to be due to genetic changes across time. Current evidence points, instead, to the role of historical changes in nutritional regimens and resources and in health care practices as the primary basis of these changes.

Similarly the influence the environment may have may vary in amount or kind depending on the specific biological characteristics of the people living in the environment. For example, excellent nutrition and health care may maximize the possible height of people of hereditarily short stature, such as members of pygmy tribes; however, no known diet or medical intervention will result in pygmies becoming as tall, say, as people having hereditarily tall stature.

Thus genes and environment always constrain and facilitate each other through their mutual influence, but these influences are flexible, not absolute. Their interaction constrains development to a set of possible pathways, not a single one, and the size of the set of possible pathways varies with the specific nature of the genes and the environment. For example, the human genome constrains people's ability to see through the skull of another person in order to inspect the brain for lesions or tumors; however, this same genome (by participating in the development of humans' cognitive system, their ingenuity, and their industriousness) contributes to people's ability to peer into the brains of others through the invention and production of X-ray and CAT-scan machines. The geneticist Richard Lewontin (1981) pervasively presents a similar view:

> It is trivially true that material conditions of one level constrain organization at higher levels *in principle*. But that is not the same as saying that such constraints are quantitatively nontrivial. Although every object in the universe has a gravitational interaction with every other object, no matter how distant, I do not, in fact, need to adjust my body's motion to the movement of individuals in the next room. The question is not whether the nature of the human genotype is relevant to social organization, but whether the former constrains the latter in a nontrivial way, or whether the two levels are *effectively* decoupled. It is the claim of vulgar sociobiology that some kinds of human social organization are either impossible, or that they can be maintained only at the expense of constant psychic and political stress, which will inevitably lead to undesirable side effects because the nature of the human genome dictates a "natural" social organiza-tion. Appeals to abstract dependencies (in principle) of one level or another do not speak to the concrete issue of whether society is genetically constrained in an important way ... in fact, constraints at one level may be destroyed by higher level activity. No humans can fly by flapping their arms because of anatomical and physiological constraints that reflect the human genome. But humans do fly, by using machines that are the product of social organization and that could not exist without very complex social interaction and evolu-tion. As another example, the memory capacity of a single individual is limited, but social organization, through written records and the complex institutions associated with them, makes all knowledge recoverable for each individual. Far from being constrained by lower-level limitations, culture transcends them and feeds back to lower levels to relieve the constraints. Social organization, and human culture in particular, are best understood as negating constraints rather than being limited by them. (p. 244)

The development of genetic engineering technologies by humans illustrates that human culture can even negate some of the constraints of genes themselves by direct alteration of genetic material.

RELATIVE PLASTICITY AND DEVELOPMENTAL VARIABILITY

The fusion proposed here of heredity and environment and the resulting mutuality of influence and flexibility of constraints mean that there is *relative plasticity* in human behavior and development. The range of development and behaviors that can occur in an individual's life is certainly not infinite or limitless. For example, females cannot, as a group, be changed to begin their menstrual cycle or "menarche" at five years of age; pygmies, as a group, cannot be changed to have an average adult height of 6 feet. The concept of relative plasticity means, however, that the number of distinct potential developmental pathways for any one individual is quite large given the fusion of heredity and environment because each person has a unique combination of genetic and environmental characteristics and interactions. For example, girls' menarche can begin, within normal limits, anywhere between the 9th and 17th years; the adult height of members of any group can vary widely; and the intelligence, personality, or motivation of people can show an enormous degree of variation.

Relative plasticity results in extensive differences among people. This is the case because genotypes and environments are almost infinitely varied *and no two people in the world have the same fusion of genes and environments across their lives.* Even identical (monozygotic) twins do not share the same environments across life and so their behavior and development will be different. Environments differ in their physical, community, social, and cultural characteristics. Although identical twins have the same genotypes, their respective genes are not likely to be fused with identical environments across their entire life spans. Each twin meets different people, may eat different foods, suffer different accidents or illnesses, may have different teachers, will fall in love with and marry a different person, and, as a result, will construct somewhat different behavior patterns.

Simply, there are multiple levels of the contexts of life, and there are differences that exist within each level. For example, within the physical environment there are differences in noise, pollution, climate, and terrain. Genotypes, in turn, are at least equally variable. The fusion of these two sources of human behavior and development means that, in effect, each person is distinct. The magnitude of individual differences among people underscores the gross errors one makes when characterizing entire groups of people (e.g., based on race, religion, or gender) as homogeneous and undifferentiated in significant ways. Thus it is important to consider how our biology in fact ensures systematic individual differences among people.

Heredity-Environment Dynamic Interactions

A key basis of the doctrine of biological determinism is the idea that the genes' influence on development is relatively unaffected by environmental differences. In other words, biological determinists are, in effect, asking "which one?," nature or nurture, heredity or environment, is the cause of an individual's behavior and development. Their answer is inevitably "heredity." As emphasized by Anastasi (1958), however, the "which one?" question is both illogical and counterfactual.

As indicated earlier there would be no one *in* an environment without heredity but, in turn, there would be no place to see the effects of heredity without environment. Genes do not (cannot) exist or function in a vacuum. They exert their influence on behavior in an environment having specific characteristics at each of several levels (i.e., physical, social, cultural, etc.). At the same time, however, if there were no genes (and consequently no heredity), the environment would not have an organism in it to influence. Accordingly, nature and nurture are inextricably tied together. In life they never exist independent of the other. Therefore *any* theory of the development of living systems, in order to be logical and to reflect life situations accurately (that is, to have ecological validity), must stress that nature and nurture are always involved in all behavior. It is simply not appropriate to ask "which one?" because *both* are completely necessary for any person's existence or for the existence of any behavior. In Chapter 4 the concept of an open system will be described because it provides a model for explaining why this is so.

The proper question one should ask is "how?" that is, "how do nature and nurture interrelate to provide a basis for behavior?" An answer to this question is provided by understanding processes of heredity-environment dynamic interaction.

GENETIC BASES OF INDIVIDUAL DIFFERENCES

Genetic theory and evidence provide substance to the claim that all humans have a unique history of heredity-environment fusions. Estimates of the number of gene pairs in humans typically range between 10,000 and 100,000. If one considers how much genotype variability can be produced by the reshuffling process of meiosis (the division that forms our sex cells—our sperm and our ova) occurring with 100,000 gene pairs, then the potential for variability is so enormous that, as McClearn (1981) states, "it is next to impossible that there have ever been two individuals with the same combination of genes" (p. 19).

Genetic Variability

A conservative estimate is that there are more than 7×10^{17} (or more than 70 trillion) potential human genotypes. Geneticists, in turn, have estimated that each human has the capacity to generate any one of 10^{3000} different eggs or sperm; by comparison, their estimate of the number of sperm of all men who have ever lived is only 10^{24}. Thus considering 10^{3000} possible eggs being generated by an individual woman and 10^{3000} possible sperm being generated by an individual man, the likelihood of anyone ever—in the past, present, or future—having the same genotype as anyone else (excepting multiple identical births, of course) becomes dismissibly small (McClearn, 1981, p.19).

A given human's genetic individuality may be seen to be even greater if we recognize that *genetic* does not mean *congenital*. Says McClearn (1981), the "total genome is not functioning at fertilization, or at birth, or at any other time of life" (p. 26). Therefore the expression of any individual human genotype is a developmental phenomenon, influenced in regard to the turning on and/or off of genes by the internal and the external components of the individual's history of genotype-environment fusions. For instance, different kinds of hemoglobin are produced differentially during different phases of development. For example, beta chain production accelerates at birth and reaches a peak a few months after birth. In turn, alpha chain production rises prenatally and maintains a high level thereafter (McClearn, 1981). A still further indication of the possible variability among humans is the nature of the molecular structure of genes. It is estimated that 6 billion nucleotide bases comprise the DNA of the human genome. The vast number of these distinct chemicals provides an enormous "population" within which mutation—permanent alterations in genetic material—can occur.

Relationship to Environmental Variability

This enormous genetic variability is fused with environments that have at least equal variation, which greatly magnifies the potential for diverse developmental pathways. The explicit recognition that the genes are an integral part of a larger system or a causal field of variables and that the components of this intermeshed system are fused in reciprocal interactions is the most significant feature of this dynamic systems view (Gottlieb, 1991, p.5). In such a dynamic system genes *must* dynamically interact with the environment if they are to be involved in the development of *any* physical or behavioral characteristic of a person (Tobach, 1971, 1972, 1981; Tobach & Schneirla, 1968). In this vein, Gottlieb (1991) explains that genetic activity alone cannot produce human characteristics such as blue eyes or neurons:

> The problem of anatomical and physiological differentiation remains unsolved, but it is unanimously recognized as requiring influences above the strictly cellular level (i.e., cell-to-cell interactions, positional influences, and so forth). . . . Thus, the concept of the genetic determination of traits is truly outmoded (p. 5).
>
> The actual role of genes (DNA) is not to produce an arm, a leg, or fingers, but to produce protein (through the coactions inherent in the formula DNA ↔ RNA ↔ protein). The specific proteins produced by the DNA-RNA-cytoplasm coaction are influenced by coactions above the level of the DNA-RNA coaction. . . . [For example,] an extraorganismic environmental event such as a brief period of exposure to ether occurring at a particular time in embryonic development can alter the cytoplasm of the cell in such a way that the protein produced by the DNA-RNA-cytoplasm coaction eventually becomes a second set of wings . . . on the body of an otherwise normal fruitfly. Obviously, it is very likely that "signals" have been altered at various levels of the developmental hierarchy to achieve such an outcome. (p. 8)

Of course the materials used by genetic activity to produce protein must come from outside the cell, that is, from higher organizational levels, ultimately from substances the organism ingests.

THE DYNAMICS OF DEVELOPMENTAL DIFFERENCES
PRODUCED BY ENVIRONMENTAL VARIABILITY

Given that the influence of genes depends so thoroughly on *when*, in the life of the organism, they coact with the environment, and with *what* environmental factors genes coact at that time, it is important to understand how dynamic integrations of genes (heredity) and environment provide a basis for the relative plasticity of behavior.

To illustrate how these processes function, let us represent hereditary contributions by the letter G (for genes), environmental contributions by the letter E, and behavioral or developmental outcomes by the letter B. As shown in Figure 3.1, it is possible to think of the contribution of heredity to behavior as being "direct," that is, as not being influenced by the environment. This is, of course, the idea found in biological determinism. In this formulation, labeled "a" in Figure 3.1, a particular combination of genes (G_1) will invariably lead to a particular behavioral or developmental outcome (B_1). We have argued, however, that this view is not logical or congruent with the facts of the real world. The alternative, developmental contextual view, illustrated as "b" in Figure 3.1, asserts that the same hereditary contribution (G_1) can be associated with a diversity of behavioral outcomes (B_1 to B_n) as a consequence of integration with a diversity of environments (E_1 to E_n) that could exist.

Examples in Birds and Fish

Numerous examples exist of the dynamic integration of genes and environments illustrated by Figure 3.1(b). For instance, under experimentally altered rearing conditions, it is possible to produce mammal-like teeth in birds, which under their typical conditions of development never have teeth (Gottlieb, 1991).

Another quite striking example of gene-environment dynamic interaction occurs under what are the typical conditions of development for coral reef fish. According to Gottlieb (1991):

> These fish live in spatially well-defined, social groups in which there are many females and few males. When a male dies or is otherwise removed from the group, one of the females initiates a sex reversal over a period of about two days in which she develops the coloration, behavior, and gonadal physiology and anatomy of a fully functioning male. . . . Such sex reversals keep the sex ratios about the same in social groups of coral reef fish. Apparently, it is the higher ranking females that are the first to change their sex and that inhibits sex reversal in lower ranking females in the group. (p. 9)

This example illustrates how the expression of genes at hormonal, physiological, and morphological levels changes as a function of the

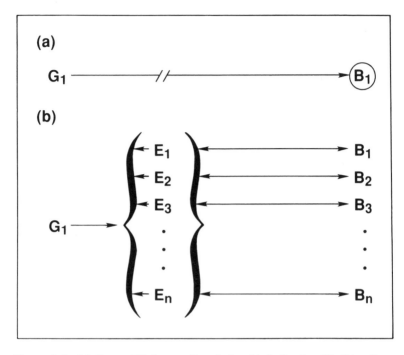

Figure 3.1. (a) Genes (G) do not directly lead to behavior (B); (b) rather, the influence of the genetic level will vary when integrated with; (1) levels of the environment (E) having different characteristics and (2) the behavioral level.

presence of different characteristics within the changing abiotic and biotic levels of the context in which they are integrated. In particular it appears that the changing number of fish in the group affords the different sources of stimulation involved in the occurrence of the changes in sex (Ethel Tobach, personal communication, November, 1990).

Down Syndrome as an Example

A child born with Down syndrome illustrates gene-environment dynamic interactions among humans. The genetic material—the DNA—of genes is arranged on stringlike structures called chromosomes present in the nucleus of each cell. The typical cells of the human body have 46 chromosomes, divided into 23 pairs. The sex cells (sperm in males, ova in females) are an exception. These cells carry only 23 chromosomes, one of each pair. This arrangement assures that when a sperm fertilizes an ovum to form a zygote, the new human so created will have the 46 chromosome pairs appropriate for the species. In a child born with Down syndrome, however, a genetic anomaly exists. There is an extra chromosome in the 21st pair—three chromosomes are present instead of two.

The complement of genes transmitted to people at conception by the union of the sperm and ovum is termed the genotype. At least insofar as the extra chromosome is concerned, the Down syndrome child has a specific genotype. Yet even though the genotype remains the same for any such child, the developmental outcomes associated with this genotype differ in different contexts.

For example, as recently as 30 years ago, Down syndrome children, who are typically recognized by certain physical (particularly facial) characteristics, were expected to have maximum life spans of about 12 years, and to have quite low IQ scores. They were typically classified into a group of people who, because of low intelligence, required custodial (usually institutional) care. Today, however, Down syndrome children often live well beyond adolescence. Additionally, they lead more self-reliant lives. Their IQs are now typically higher, often falling in the range allowing for education, training, and, sometimes, even employment. One quite striking instance of substantial intellectual accomplishment is Nigel Hunt, a child born with Down syndrome, who grew up to author his own autobiography (Hunt, 1967). .

How did these vast differences in the developmental impact of the Down syndrome genotype come about? Certainly the genotype itself did not change; rather, what changed was the environment of these children. Instead of invariably being put into institutions that severely constrained the childrens' developmental possibilities, different and more advanced special education and training techniques were provided, often on an outpatient basis. These contrasts in environment led to patterns of individual development quite different from patterns displayed by other children in previous years despite the same heredity, that is, despite genotypic invariance.

PKU as an Example

That heredity always exerts its effects indirectly through environment in the development of physical as well as behavioral characteristics is illustrated by the disease *phenylketonuria* (PKU). This disorder, involving an inability to metabolize fatty substances because of the absence of a particular digestive enzyme, led to the development of distorted physical features and severe mental retardation in children. It was discovered that the lack of the necessary enzyme resulted from the absence of a particular gene, and, as such, PKU is another instance of a disease associated with a specific genotype.

Today, however, many people—perhaps even some people reading this book—may have the PKU genotype without having either the physical or the behavioral deficits formerly associated with the disease. It was discovered that if the missing enzyme is put into the diets of newborns identified as having the disease, all negative effects can be avoided. Rather than the gene providing the enzyme, the environment did. A change in the environment has changed the outcome, illustrating once again that the same genotype can lead to alternative outcomes, both physical and behavioral, when it dynamically interacts with contrasting environmental settings. The PKU example also illustrates Gottlieb's (1991) point, quoted earlier, that all genetic activity does is to produce basic chemical compounds important in development. Those chemical compounds sometimes may be provided in other ways, thereby altering the course of development.

DNA-RNA Alteration as an Example

More striking than these examples of gene-environment dynamic interactions are those indicating that *environment can actually alter key features of the genotype itself: Environment can alter the functioning of the DNA.* The results of several experiments indicate that exposure to complex and stimulating environments, that is, enriched contexts, as opposed to simple, unstimulating, or impoverished settings, alters the most basic chemical constituents of genes, the carriers of the genetic message itself, the RNA and the DNA.

In a study by Uphouse and Bonner (1974) rats were exposed to: (a) high environmental enrichment (i.e., living in a cage with 11 other rats and having "toys" and mazes available for exploration); (b) low environmental enrichment (i.e., living in a cage with one other rat but no exploration materials); (c) isolation (i.e., living in a cage alone and with no exploration materials).

The brains and the livers of the rats were studied to determine the transcription to DNA by RNA. The RNA from the brains of the environmentally enriched rats showed a level of transcription of DNA significantly greater than that of the other groups. No significant differences were found with liver RNA. Similarly other investigators have found significant differences between the brain RNA of rats reared in environmentally rich versus environmentally impoverished contexts. In addition the total complexity of brain RNA has been found to be greater for normally sighted kittens than for kittens who had both eyelids sutured at birth (Grouse, Schrier, & Nelson, 1979); however, the RNAs from the nonvisual portions of the cerebral cortex and from subcortical brain areas were not different for the two groups. It seems, then, that the normal development of the visual cortex through normal visual experience involves somewhat different genetic processes than occurs in the absence of visual experience.

We should remain cautious about extrapolation of specific findings in animal research to humans. Nevertheless a diversity of evidence indicates that the dynamic integration between genetic and environmental levels can alter both the behaviors that develop across life and the chemical messages involved in the genes themselves. Developmental behavioral genetics research makes it clear that many opportunities exist for genetic change during development (Plomin, 1986). Indeed the data in support of the integrations represented in Figure 3.1 (b) weaken—to the point of complete untenability—any claim that genes represent a "blueprint" for a single outcome of development. Available evidence strongly supports the conclusion that there is no one-to-one correspondence between genotype to phenotype. Thus any such "extreme" genetic determinist claims could not be supported in the face of this evidence.

Similarly even the "weaker" genetic determinist claim that genes directly translate into behavior is not supported by available evidence. For instance, it might be argued that genes are associated with not a single behavioral outcome but, rather, a limited range of outcomes. It might further be argued that for people from genetically different groups (e.g., men, women, blacks, whites), the range of possible outcomes would not significantly overlap, particularly given the "average expected environments" that these different people might encounter. In the genetics literature, for example, it is often stressed that for a given genotype there is an array of outcomes, of phenotypes, that can be associated with the genotype, depending on specific environmental characteristics in which the genotype develops (Anastasi, 1958; Hirsch, 1970; Lerner, 1986; McGuire & Hirsch, 1977). This array of outcomes is termed the "norm of reaction" (see Hirsch, 1970; McGuire & Hirsch, 1977) in the genetics literature. The presence of such a norm of reaction is consistent with the relative plasticity represented in Figure 3.1; however, it is precisely because of this plasticity that the concept of norm of reaction cannot be used to support even the above-noted weaker genetic determinist position.

As stressed by behavior-genetic analyst Jerry Hirsch (1970), for any living form, the norm of reaction remains largely unknown. This is the case because in order to be able to specify exactly the norm of reaction for any living animal (or plant, for that matter), one must be able to reproduce exactly an individual, specific genotype many times and then, in turn, expose this replicated genotype to as diverse an array of environments as possible. The array of phenotypes that developed through this procedure would *at best* provide only an estimate of the norm of reaction for that one genotype because, in reality, it would take an infinite number of genotype replicates exposed to an infinite number of sets of environmental conditions to determine the exact norm of reaction.

Accordingly, to suggest that groups differ in any necessary way because of their genotype is to ignore the fact that the actual norm of reaction, for *any* living organism, cannot theoretically or in practicality be known, and even accurate estimates are difficult. Moreover, any argument that there are "average expected environments" within which genotypes may be expressed and that somehow the presence of such settings represents a necessary constraint on behavioral development is also too narrow. Both the concepts of norm of reaction and available evidence support the view that as the context changes in new ways so too may the outcomes of the integrated processes of human development.

As McGuire and Hirsch (1977) put it:

> There are undeniable genetic differences between individuals in anatomical, physiological, and behavioral traits. The genetic differences are important in determining how any individual develops in a given environment. Observation of development in one environment, however, provides no basis for predicting how the same individual might have developed in a different environment. In fact, it does not give 100% predictability of how a replicate with an identical genotype might develop in the same environment. (p. 25)

THE DYNAMICS OF DEVELOPMENTAL DIFFERENCES PRODUCED BY GENETIC VARIABILITY

Not only does available evidence contradict biological determinism formulation, but it also contradicts environmental determinism as well. As McGuire and Hirsch (1977) note:

Any phenotype is the result of the interactions of the alleles at all loci, the interactions within and between loci, and the interaction of this genotype with environmental variables. A phenotype cannot legitimately be discussed independently of the environment in which it has developed. Similarly, environmental variables (teaching techniques) cannot legitimately be discussed independently of the genotypes they were tested on. (p. 26)

In other words, similar developmental plasticity can be seen when one inverts the information displayed in Figure 3.1 and considers how a given environment may be dynamically integrated with organisms differing in their heredity. Figure 3.2 illustrates this.

As in Figure 3.1, two views of the relation between nature and nurture levels are illustrated in Figure 3.2. First, in part "a" of the figure, we depict the position taken by cultural determinists. Here the contribution of environment (e.g., societal institutions, culture) to behavior is depicted as being "direct." Thus a particular environmental event or set of events (E_1) is seen as directly leading to a particular behavioral outcome (B_1), and any particular biological features of the person are not considered seriously or systematically. The belief here is one of complete malleability, of absolute plasticity. This view, however, is no more tenable than those of biological determinism. Rather, just as the influence of heredity on development is contingent on the characteristics of the environment with which it is fused, environmental contributions to development are contingent on dynamic interactions with characteristics of the biological levels of the organism. From this view, the same environmental event (i.e., contraction of a disease, exposure to a particularly stimulating lecture) or group of events (e.g., those associated with middle-class as opposed to upper-class membership) have different developmental impacts depending on the integrations that occur with the characteristics of the biological levels of the person.

This view is illustrated in Figure 3.2(b). Here the same environment (E_1) can be associated with an array of behaviors or developmental outcomes (B_1 to B_n) as a consequence of dynamic integrations with people having different heredities (G_1 to G_n). This basis of relative plasticity in development may be illustrated in several ways.

Dizygotic Twins as an Example

First, consider a very general set of experiences, those associated with being a child of upper-middle-class parents. Imagine that such

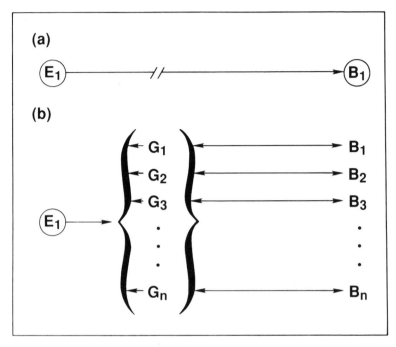

Figure 3.2. (a) Environment (E) does not directly lead to behavior (B). (b) Rather, the influence of environmental levels will vary when integrated with; (1) People having genetic (c) level characteristics that are different, and (2) the behavioral level.

parents had two children who were dizygotic twins, also termed fraternal twins. Such siblings are born of the same pregnancy but are from two separate ova that are fertilized at the same time. Thus although born together, these siblings have different genotypes. If one of these twins was born with the genetic anomaly discussed earlier (Down syndrome), while the other was born with a normal complement of genes, a situation would result wherein children born of the same parents at the same time would potentially be exposed to the same general set of environmental events.

Whatever the experiences encountered by the Down syndrome twin, however, the effects of those experiences could not be expected to result in developmental patterns falling within a range exactly identical to that of the sibling. For instance, despite the advances in special education noted earlier, one still cannot expect a Down syndrome child to attain the same vocation or live as long a life as the sibling born with the normal genotype. Thus the hereditary nature of the organism imposes limits on the possible contributions of environment.

Maternal Stress and Fetal Development as an Example

Developmental outcomes may vary as a function of differences in fetal environments. For instance, if a mother contracted rubella during pregnancy, adverse physical and functional outcomes for the infant might follow; however, this same experience (contraction of rubella) may or may not lead to these outcomes depending on when in the development of the fetus this disease is contracted. If the experience occurs during the embryological period, these negative effects are likely to occur; if it happens in the late fetal period, they are not likely to happen. Similarly excessive maternal stress will be likely to lead to certain physical deformities (such as cleft palate) as a function of the developmental time during which it occurs. Thus here again the biological features of the developing person moderate the influence of experience on him or her.

It may be concluded, then, that even if one is talking about limited sorts of environmental experiences (such as encountering a specific person in a specific transitory situation, for example, a rude passenger on an elevator) or broad types of experiences (such as those associated with membership in one culture versus another), the influences of these environments would have different outcomes when integrated with hereditarily (genotypically) different people, or with the same person at different developmental phases of their life. Moreover, the outcomes would be different even if it were possible to ensure that the different people had identical experiences, because the biological, psychological, and behavioral nature of the person is different. Thus the effects of experience will vary.

SUMMARY

Because of genotype uniqueness, all individuals will interact with their environments in unique, specific ways. Thus the environment always affects development, but the precise direction and outcome of this influence can only be understood in the context of an appreciation of the genetic and developmental individuality of the person. In turn, individual differences in genetic makeup do not in and of themselves directly shape development. Interaction with an environment, itself having a host of distinctly individual features, has to be taken into account.

If, however, the trillions of possible distinct genotypes are difficult to envision, it is no less formidable to conceptualize the potential complexity and diversity of the contexts of human life. Such a task is, nevertheless, necessary in order to appreciate the full meaning of the developmental contextual perspective. Let us now pursue this topic.

Biology and the Contexts of Human Life

One of the core ideas in developmental contextualism is that biology and context cannot be functionally separated; both are fused across life. It is useful, however, to conceptually distinguish among the different kinds of variables involved. The diagram presented in Figure 3.3 can be used for that purpose.

THE INDIVIDUAL AS A COMPLEX ORGANIZATION OF STRUCTURES AND PROCESSES

In the figure we use the circle on the center-left to represent an individual child. Within the child are represented (as slices of a "pie") several of the dimensions of the child's individuality: his or her health, physical, and biological status; personality and temperament; behaviors; and demands placed on others (parents in this figure). All of these dimensions, as well as others (included in the figure by inserting the pie slice "etc."), are represented as existing in a manner contingent on the child's development level, which is a final pie slice within the child figure. This portion of Figure 3.3 shows that a child is a complex and differentiated biological, psychological, and behavioral organism, and that this differentiation is not static; rather, it develops across time.

SOCIAL AND CULTURAL CONTEXTS OF INDIVIDUALS' DEVELOPMENT

Just as genes are embedded within a differentiated, multilevel environment, so too are children. By embedded we mean that children

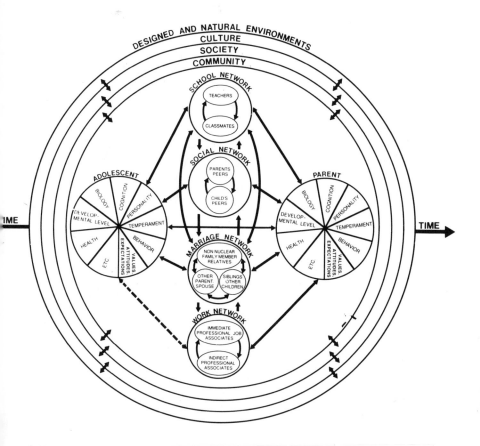

Figure 3.3. A developmental contextual model of human development. People are "fused" with their contexts across life.

function within and as part of, not just in relationship to, their contexts. Accordingly, we have used a circle on the center-right of Figure 3.3 to represent a parent of the child. As is the case for the child, the parent also is a complex and differentiated biological, psychological, and behavioral organism and is, as well, a person who is developing across his or her life.

The mutual influence between child and parent, their fusion with each other, is represented in the figure by the bidirectional arrows between them. It is important to point out that we may speak of dynamic interactions between parent and child that pertain to either *social* or *physical* relationships. For example, in regard to social relationships, the parent's attitudes, values, and expectations might involve demands on the child for attention. If the child does not show attention, this "lights" the parent's "short fuse" of tolerance; he or she scolds the child, who then cries. This creates remorse in the parent and elicits soothing behaviors from him or her. The child is calmed, snuggles up to the parent, and now both parties in the relationship show positive emotions and are happy.

In turn we may illustrate also dynamic interactions that involve not only the exchange of "external" social behaviors, but also biological or physiological processes. For example, parental religious practices, rearing practices, or financial status may influence the child's diet and nutritional status, health, and medical care. In turn, the contraction of an infectious disease by either parent or child can lead to the other member of the relationship contracting the disease. Moreover, the health and physical status of the child influences the parent's own feelings of well-being and his or her hopes and aspirations regarding the child.

Thus the child's internal physiological status and development are connected to the functioning and development of his or her outer, behavioral and social context (in this example, parental). The inner and outer worlds of the child are, then, fused and dynamically interactive. In addition, of course, the same may be said of the parent and, in fact, of the parent-child relationship. Each of these foci—child, parent, or relationship—is part of a larger, enmeshed *system* of fused relationships among the multiple levels that compose the ecology of human life, that is, a larger causal field of variables.

For instance, Figure 3.3 illustrates the idea that both parent and child are embedded in a broader social network, and each person has reciprocal relations with this network too. This set of relationships occurs because both the child and the parent are much more than just people playing only one role in life. The child may also be a sibling, a peer, and a student; the parent may also be a spouse, a worker, a peer, and an adult child. Furthermore, all of these networks of relations are embedded also within a particular community, society, and culture. These "outer" levels of the model are interpenetrated with the "interior" levels. In addition, all levels depicted in Figure 3.3 are dynamically interactive with the designed and the naturally occurring physical ecology of human development. And, finally, all of these relations are continually varying and changing across time, across history. In fact for all portions of the system of biology-environment relationships envisioned in developmental contextualism, change across time is an integral, indeed inescapable, feature.

CONCLUSIONS

Developmental contextualism is an optimistic view of the character of human development. The ubiquitous presence of change is a key feature of the developmental contextual perspective. It is a difference between pessimism and optimism. It is a difference in believing that we must accept and live with our biology, with the purportedly fixed and immutable limits it imposes and that we must accept and live with our environment and its purported fixed constraints; or in believing that we should celebrate and take up the challenge for change and improvement that our biology offers.

As evidenced by the epigram at the beginning of this chapter, the system of person-context relations comprising human development means that at any point in the life span there is some probability that means exist for altering significantly an individual's structural and/or functional characteristics. Because these characteristics are conceptualized in relational terms, such alteration may be possible through interventions aimed at any of the multiple levels of organization of which the person is composed or within which the person is embedded. Of course complete alteration of the person or, more precisely, of the person-context system is not possible. The structure and function of a level influences other levels both through affording or facilitating some changes and through delimiting or constraining others (Lerner, 1984; Ford, 1987).

Humans have two coupled change-related characteristics: a capacity for change and powerful stabilizing processes protecting existing arrangements and capabilities (Ford, 1987). Actual change (as contrasted to the potential for change) results from the interaction of these two coupled characteristics. In other words, *plasticity*—systematic change in structure and/or function—is not absolute, but only relative (Lerner, 1984). Nevertheless, the relational character of human life and or human change means that development is seen as more open to influence and change when considered from a developmental contextual perspective than from one associated with other organismically or mechanistically derived theoretical perspectives.

It is reasonable, then, that we attempt to conceive of, and implement, means through which each person can acquire the resources to capitalize on his or her possibilities for development. How is it that individuals can act as agents in promoting their own enhanced development? The next section of this chapter summarizes developmental contextualism's answers to these questions.

Individuals' Behavior as the Means of Fusing the Influences of Biology and Context on Development

We saw illustrated in Figure 3.3 that across the development of their lives individuals are "fused," are dynamically interactive, with a complex and changing context. This enables people to act to promote their own development.

INDIVIDUALS PRODUCE THEIR OWN DEVELOPMENT THROUGH CIRCULAR FUNCTIONS

Relationships between any given individual and other persons in his or her social world differ from person to person because each of us is distinct. Each of us has characteristics of biological, psychological, and behavioral uniqueness that are associated with our own particular history of biology-context fusions. We each have our particular body builds, facial characteristics, personalities, and beliefs and opinions.

Because of your characteristics of individuality you will evoke particular reactions in the people with whom you interact. Their reactions serve as feedback to you. Because this feedback depends on how your particular physical or behavioral characteristics affected other people, it becomes part of your ongoing history of unique person-context fusions. The special feedback you receive will promote your further development as a unique individual. Because this distinct feedback arises, at least in part, because of your already-established individuality, you act in this manner as a producer of your own continued development.

This ongoing, spiraling process of person-context feedback provides the basis of a *circular function* (Schneirla, 1957) between you and your environment. It is the existence of such circular functions that allow you to be an active agent in your own development. It is, moreover, this circular process that allows scientists to characterize the processes involved in your development as relatively plastic in character.

CIRCULAR FUNCTIONS AND EVOLUTIONARY DEVELOPMENT

The life-long reciprocal person-context relations that allow us to be active agents in our own development appear to have been involved also in human evolution. In other words the circular (person-context) functions in which all human's engage may have acted, across history, to be a source of our own evolutionary development. In Lewontin's and Levins' (1978) words:

> The activity of the organism sets the stage for its own evolution . . . the labor process by which the human ancestors modified natural objects to make them suitable for human use was itself the unique feature of the way of life that directed selection on the hand, larynx, and brain in a positive feedback that transformed the species, its environment, and its mode of interaction with nature. (p. 78)

Similarly Johanson and Edey (1981) summarize Lovejoy's argument that the social relationships that led to brain evolution were themselves altered when larger brained and more plastic organisms were involved in them. Such new social patterns may have extended humans' adaptational presses and opportunities into other arenas, ones fostering further changes in brain, in social embeddedness, and so forth. They argue that such an evolutionary process would require the mechanism of a complex feedback loop, one composed of multiple interrelated feedback loops.

In the case of primate evolution the feedback was not a simple A-B interaction, going forward and backward between two variables. It was multivariate and circular with many features to it instead of only two, and all of them were mutually influential. For example, if an infant was to have a large brain, it needed time to learn to use that brain before it had to face the world on its own. That meant a long childhood. A key way of learning during childhood is through play. That meant playmates, which, in turn, meant a group social system.

But if one was to function in such a group, one had to have learned acceptable social behavior. One can learn that properly only if one is intelligent. Therefore social behavior ended up being linked with three interrelated loops: intelligence, extended childhood, and, finally, with the energy investment and the parental care system that provided a brain capable of that intelligence. Thus the entire feedback loop network was completed.

All parts of this feedback system are cross-connected. For example, if one is living in a group, the time spent finding food, being aware of predators, and finding a mate can all be reduced by the very fact that one is in a group. As a consequence, more time can be spent on parental care (one loop), on play (another), and on social activity (another), all of which embrace intelligence (another) and result ultimately in fewer offspring (still another). The complete loop shows all poles connected to all others (Johanson & Edey, 1981, p. 326).

An illustration of this "complete loop," or system of reciprocal influence, is presented in Figure 3.4. This figure illustrates that the foundations of humans' plasticity evolved in a complex system of bidirectional (indeed dynamic interactional) relationships among social, individual, and biological (e.g., brain) characteristics. Accordingly, it appears probable that the ways in which humans act as agents in their own development were central as well in the history of human evolutionary change. Thus rather than passively and mechanistically enacting social roles specified by our genes, we, as individuals, shape our lives and the social institutions within which we live. Three such processes will be discussed:

1. People stimulate other people.
2. People process their world in unique ways.
3. People select and shape their contexts.

PEOPLE STIMULATE OTHER PEOPLE

For at least two decades some developmental psychologists and psychiatrists have stressed that people can influence those who influence them; that is development involves reciprocal relations rather than only unidirectional (e.g., from parent to child) ones. Moreover, not only do people influence those who influence them, but through "circular functions," people also get feedback as a consequence of their influences on others.

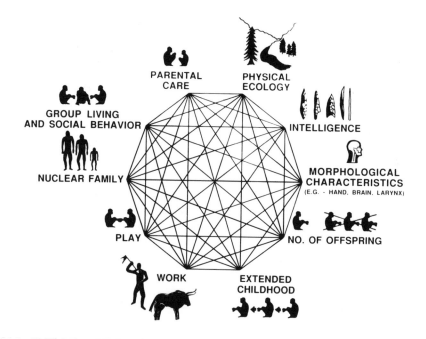

Figure 3.4. Components of the system of individual-level and contextual-level integrations believed to be involved in the evolution of human functioning. SOURCE. Adapted from Johanson, D.C. and Edey, M.A.

Such circular functions arise in relation to characteristics of physical and behavioral individuality. For example, children who differ in body build, physical attractiveness, or whether or not they were born prematurely receive different reactions from their parents, teachers, or friends. Physically attractive and/or average build children are evaluated more positively by adults and other children than are unattractive and/or chubby or obese children (Lerner, 1987). Social feedback is consistent with such evaluations. For instance other children want to come closer to average build children than to chubby children. Similarly premature infants elicit less parental involvement during the newborn period than their full-time counterparts (perhaps because of their fragility); but they receive more attention across their first 8 to 9 months, probably because of the infants' inability to initiate or maintain behavioral interactions with their parents and the parents' desire to have such interactions.

Furthermore there is evidence that the subsequent development of children is consistent with the different feedback they receive. For example, physically unattractive children have more behavioral and adjustment problems than do physically attractive children; and premature infants, probably because of the extra stress they may generate for already highly stressed parents, appear to run an increased risk of being maltreated.

Evidence exists for similar circular functions in regard to characteristics of behavioral individuality as well, such as temperament (Lerner & Lerner, 1987; Thomas & Chess, 1977). Children who differ in their temperament place differing caregiving demands on their parents. For instance, children who are biologically arrhythmic (e.g., who sleep and wake or get hungry at unpredictable times), who are intense and negative, who tend to withdraw from new foods or situations, and who are slow to adapt to any new features of their context (e.g., a change in schedule or routine) are more difficult to deal with than children who are rhythmic, who tend to approach and adapt easily to new situations, and who react with moderate intensity and positive moods. Children with such temperamental differences also behave differently with their parents and other adults, are regarded in different ways by their caregivers (e.g., teachers), and have a differential probability of developing a problem requiring clinical (e.g., psychiatric) intervention. Simply, "difficult" children are more likely than are temperamentally "easy" children to have personal and social problems with family, friends, and other people in their social worlds.

PEOPLE PROCESS THEIR WORLD IN UNIQUE WAYS

One assumption of developmentalists is that people do not remain the same over the course of their life span; rather, in the typical case, physical, cognitive, social, and emotional characteristics undergo systematic changes. The history of developmental research reveals a vast array of scientific information supportive of this assumption.

The fact that individuals undergo developmental changes means that they are, in effect, somewhat different persons at various points in their life spans. It follows that the same experience—for instance the same parental child-rearing strategies (e.g., being "grounded" for misbehavior) occurring in different developmental periods (e.g., late childhood versus the middle of the adolescent years)—may be "processed" by one differently. Because it is processed differently, the same experience could have different effects on development in the different periods.

To illustrate, children in a period of rapid growth may respond to a physical-education program differently than may children in a period of slow or little growth. Younger children, in turn, will be less able to use abstract rules for self-control than will cognitively more advanced children. Similarly children who are in the process of establishing secure social relationships with their parents (i.e., children during their first year of life) are likely to have different sets of social skills than are children who have already established such attachments.

PEOPLE SELECT AND SHAPE THEIR CONTEXTS

A competent person is one who is capable of showing appropriate behavior, thought, and emotions. To behave appropriately in a changing and/or complex world, one cannot always do the same thing. Flexibility is required for dealing with the issues and problems encountered in life. Flexibility, underlain by the relative plasticity of the developing person, allows him or her to change to meet new problems or demands or to change the context in order to better fit personal objectives. Simply, a competent person can modify effectively his or her own behavior and/or the features of the social situation in which he or she is engaged.

People can, for instance, change their topic of conversation if they find they are boring or upsetting others; or if they are bored or upset by what is being said, they can turn the conversation round to more pleasant topics, or terminate it. To indicate how such competency—such efficient self-regulation—is an instance of how one may act as a producer of their own development, it is useful to discuss what has been termed the "goodness of fit" model of relations between people and their contexts.

Goodness of Fit

Just as you bring your particular characteristics of individuality to a given social setting, demands are placed on you by virtue of the social and physical components of the setting. These demands may take the form of: (a) attitudes, values, or stereotyped beliefs held by others in the context regarding your particular physical or behavioral characteristics;

(b) the attributes (usually behavioral) of others in the context with whom you must coordinate, or fit, your characteristics for good interactions to exist; or (c) the physical characteristics of a setting (e.g., the presence or absence of access ramps for the handicapped) that require you to possess certain characteristics for the most efficient interaction to occur within the setting.

People's individuality in differently meeting these demands provides a basis for the feedback they get from the people in their social world. Psychiatrists Thomas and Chess (1977) and psychologists Lerner and Lerner (1983, 1987, 1989) indicate that effective psychological and social functioning is most likely to occur when people's characteristics match (or "fit") the demands of a particular setting.

The precise competencies required to attain a good fit within and across time include one's ability to evaluate appropriately: (a) the demands of a particular context (i.e., you must ask "What is required or expected of me?"); (b) one's psychological and behavioral characteristics (for instance, one must ask "Can I do—physically or behaviorally—what is expected of me?"); and (c) the degree of match that exists between "1" and "2" (i.e., the "fit" between one's answers to the first two questions).

In addition, other cognitive and behavioral skills are necessary. One has to possess the ability to select and gain access to those contexts with which there is a high probability of match and to avoid those contexts where poor fit is likely. For instance, one may want to avoid playing tackle football if one is 5 feet tall, weighs 97 pounds, and has frail bones. In turn one might seek out settings (i.e., small, informal parties) wherein one's particular skills (i.e., conversations about old movies, world events, etc.) would be useful.

In addition, in contexts that cannot usually be selected—for example, one's family of origin or one's assigned work role—one has to have the knowledge and skills necessary either to change oneself to fit the demands of the setting or, in turn, to alter the context to better fit one's individual attributes. As in the earlier example of upsetting or pleasant conversations, one must decide if a good fit is more likely if one changes one's contributions to the discussion or if one tries to alter others' topics of conversation. In most contexts, moreover, multiple types of demands will impinge upon one, and not all of them will provide identical requirements. As such, one must be able to detect and evaluate such complexity, and one must judge which demand it will be best to meet when it is the case that all cannot be met. In other words, "goodness of fit" is a dynamic process, not just a goal to be achieved, because characteristics of both persons and their context vary and change, and a "good fit" on one occasion may not be good on another.

In short, people develop competency in self-regulation across their life. They will be able to become a more active selector and shaper of the contexts within which they develop (e.g., with friends, parents, spouse, co-workers). Through such influences people develop their capacity to be active contributors to their own development. In systems terms, people function to simultaneously create coherent intraperson and person-context organization. Chapters 4 and 5 present an operational model of the content and dynamics of those activities.

Summary

The purpose of this chapter has been to present and to justify a set of basic assumptions—a metamodel for understanding human development. This set of assumptions provides the general framework for Developmental Systems Theory, so this chapter represents the first phase in describing DST. Table 3.1 summarizes the guiding assumptions in a form that displays their internal coherence. It will be referred to periodically in later chapters to show how other aspects of DST manifest different parts of this guiding metamodel. The assumptions in Table 3.1 may be considered "design criteria" that must be met by any adequate theory of development.

Next Steps

The guiding assumptions for Developmental Systems Theory have been presented and justified. What is needed next is to translate those guiding assumptions into an operational model of the nature of humans and their development. That is the purpose of Chapters 4 and 5. Chapter 4 will describe how the component biological structures and biological, psychological, and action aspects of people are organized as open, living systems to enable them to function and develop as structural-functional units within themselves and in relationship to their contexts. Chapter 5 will discuss the processes and dynamics of change and development. It may be helpful to think of Chapter 4 as providing a dynamic representation of the circles labeled child or parent in Figure 3.3 of Chapter 3, with the remainder of Figure 3.3 being represented by the concept of environment in Chapter 4.

TABLE 3.1 A Summary of the Metamodel or Guiding Assumptions for Developmental Systems Theory

1. There are variables from multiple, qualitatively distinct levels of analysis or levels of organization involved in human life and development. These must operate in organized patterns to produce the coherent unitary functioning of the person-in-context on which both life and development depend.

   a. The individual as a dynamic unit is to be understood as a complex, multilevel organization of biological structures plus biological and psychological/behavioral processes embedded and fused in dynamic interaction with multilevel environments.

2. Individuals' functioning and development result from a dynamic interaction within and between levels of organization of multiple, qualitatively different variables.

   a. The dynamic interactions among variables are in the form of reciprocal or mutually causal relationships through which the functioning of and changes in any variable are influenced by the organization of the set of variables in which it is embedded. This may be called a causal field of variables.

   b. The maintenance of stability as well as change and development result from the organization or configuration of variables rather than solely or even primarily through the operation of single variables.

   c. Changes in the dynamic organization of variables between and within levels constitute the basic nature of human development.

3. Each human differs from every other human in his or her genetic endowment, in the environments in which he or she is embedded during his or her lifetime, and in the dynamic interactions through which genetic and environmental variables are fused in their influence on behavior and development.

   a. A person's biological characteristics make possible his or her psychological/behavioral potentials through biological constraining and facilitating influences, but do not strictly determine the person's psychological/behavioral functioning and development. Similarly, a person's environments make possible sets of functional and developmental possibilities but do not strictly determine which are actualized.

TABLE 3.1 Continued

b. The flow of dynamic interactions among environmental and genetic/biological variables promotes and produces individuality in both developmental pathways and outcomes.

4. Human development displays relative plasticity so there is no single, ideal developmental pathway for any person.

a. The dynamic interactions of one's genetic endowment and environments provide constraining and facilitating conditions or boundaries within which one's development occurs. Those boundaries are, themselves, dynamic because both one's environment and the nature of one's genetic processes vary and change across a lifetime.

b. Within those dynamic boundaries there are multiple though not unlimited potential developmental pathways for any individual, i.e., development is multidimensional and multidirectional. The range of plasticity, of potential developmental pathways, may differ within and between components and levels such as biological, psychological, and social (e.g., the development of one's heart may be constrained to fewer possibilities than the development of one's cognitive capabilities).

c. The nature of the constraining and facilitating conditions and of a person's potential developmental pathways change in both predictable and unpredictable ways, making development open ended and probabilistic rather than preordained and rigidly deterministic. Both chance and necessity play a role.

5. Individuals influence their own development through their own functioning in several ways. In that sense, humans are self-organizing and self-constructing.

a. People process their world in unique ways so that the same environmental conditions may have different developmental influences from one person to another and for the same person from one occasion or developmental period to another.

b. People are proactive as well as reactive. They selectively engage specific contexts and specific aspects of those contexts from among their potential environments. Through their actions, they alter their actual and potential environments, thereby influencing the nature of the environmental variables that may influence them.

Continued

TABLE 3.1 Continued

c. Person-context dynamics result from circular functions within and between levels of organization through which the person's characteristics and behaviors influence the feedback the environment provides, which, in turn, influences the person's characteristics and behaviors. This process is continuous although the content of the circular functions will vary.

d. The social context is of special importance in human development, and people influence and stimulate changes in one another through their patterns of circular functions.

6. Individuals not only function to establish and maintain coherent intraperson organization so they can function effectively as a unit, but they also function to establish and maintain coherent person-context patterns of organization so they can function effectively as a component of their larger contexts.

a. Establishing a goodness-of-fit between their personal characteristics and their contexts is a dynamic, continuing process since both persons and environments vary. The extent to which a person successfully matches his or her personal characteristics and functioning to the demands and opportunities of his or her contexts is an indicator of competence and a major influence on the content of the circular functions with his or her contexts.

CHAPTER FOUR

The Person as an Open, Self-Regulating, Self-Constructing System

THE PURPOSE OF THIS CHAPTER is to translate the guiding assumptions or metamodel presented in Chapter 3 into an operational model of the content, organization, and dynamics of individual development across the life span. The focus of this chapter is primarily to answer two questions: "How can the organized nature of individuals as contextually embedded, structural-functional units be represented?" and "What can develop?"

TOWARD AN INTEGRATIVE, OPERATIONALIZABLE MODEL OF PERSONS AS UNITS

Anderson (1978), in his Nobel prize address, described model building as an essential tactic in science for revealing the underlying order in a mass of information, for giving meaning to specific data, and for guiding further work. The mass of detailed information about different aspects of human life is already overwhelming to students (and scholars as well) and is growing exponentially. Sorely needed is some way of simplifying and integrating all of that detail and the multiple theoretical formulations about different aspects of humans.

That is the role of theory and theory construction. The metamodel about the nature of human development presented in Chapter 3 represents the first step in creating an integrative theory, that is, Developmental Systems Theory (DST). The metamodel provides a set of "design criteria" that must be met by any adequate operationalizable model of human development and functioning. Table 3.1 presents a summary of those basic assumptions to provide an accessible reference frame for the operational model of individuals as structural-functional open living systems to be presented in this chapter.

To be adequate DST must also encompass two other sets of design criteria that are related to the metamodel. First, the operational model must reflect the characteristics of the definition of development, restated here for convenience:

> Individual human development involves incremental and transformational processes that, through a flow of interactions between current characteristics of the person and his or her current contexts, produces a succession of relatively enduring changes that elaborate or increase the diversity of the person's structural and functional characteristics and the patterns of his or her environmental interactions while maintaining coherent organization and functional unity of the person as a whole.

Second, the model must be able to accommodate and synthesize existing knowledge about the nature and development of various aspects of human life (i.e., the content of development) from the diverse fields of biological and medical sciences, psychology, sociology, history, and anthropology. For example, it must show how human biological processes, cognition, attention and perception, emotions, and action patterns function in an integrated way and how different aspects of people's social, cultural, natural, and designed environments interact with persons' characteristics in dynamic patterns of mutual causal relationships as outlined in Figure 3.3.

The operational model summarized in this chapter is constructed to meet all of the design criteria summarized above. It seeks to represent the person-in-context as the focal unit of interest, which can be described as an open, self-organizing, self-constructing system, or a "living system." Any model should be compatible with the broader knowledge bases that humans have constructed. A common strategy in scientific model building is to take a model whose value has been demonstrated in other domains and try to transform it to represent the phenomena of interest. Therefore the model represented in this chapter draws upon several well-established ideas in the modern natural and human sciences and transforms the systems models well established in other fields to represent human development (see Chapters 1 through 5 in Ford, 1987, and Miller, 1978, for more detail). Because DST represents humans as a living system, it is first necessary to review the concept of system as a starting point.

Complex Organization and the Concept of System

Many kinds of complexly organized phenomena are sometimes called systems, for example, an economic system, stereo system, legal system, or personality system. That usage makes synonymous the concepts of system and complex organization. We will explain why we believe it is more useful to reserve the term system for a particular kind of complex organization, but first we must define the concept of organization.

ORGANIZATION

Organization is a function of constraining and facilitating conditionalities (Ashby, 1962; Ford, 1987). When two or more components exist, each with multiple possibilities, three types of relationships among them are possible.

1. The states of any one may vary independently of the others (i.e., randomly). They are unrelated; no organization exists (e.g., you cannot have a friendship with a person you have never met).
2. They may be related so that only some of all of their unique possibilities can become actualities. Organization exists because such *constraining conditionalities* limit the components by making variations in the states of each dependent on and limited by the states of the others (e.g., a tire used on a car is constrained from being used as a child's swing).
3. They may be related so that new possibilities emerge from them collectively, possibilities that none of them have individually. Organization exists because such *facilitating conditionalities* link components to produce properties that emerge from the components' relationships (e.g., H_2O = water).

Organizations may differ in complexity based on the number and kinds of components involved and the number and kinds of constraining and facilitating conditions linking the components (see assumptions 4a, 4b, and 4c in Table 3.1).

Mechanistic Organization

In some types of organization, the facilitating and constraining relationships among components are firmly determinate and mechanistic in nature. Components and their relationships are not modified by one another or their history. Mechanistic processes follow fixed pathways; final states are fully determined by initial conditions and the process pathway (e.g., Deutsch, 1951). This is a very useful form of organization because its operations and outcomes are highly predictable. For example, modern technological societies are made possible by machines. The power and utility of mechanistic organization led de la Mettrie in 1747 to apply it to humans in his book *Man, a Machine*. A reflex or a rigid habit such as compulsive smoking illustrates mechanistic organization in humans. Though mechanistic organizations may be complex and very useful, they do not have certain important properties essential for effective living.

Systemic Organization

In some kinds of organization, the functioning of each component is, in part, controlled by their collective state. Weiss (1971) recommends that the concept of system be reserved for such organizations defined as:

> a complex unit in space and time so constituted that its component subunits, by systematic cooperation, preserve its integral configuration of structures and behavior and tend to restore it after such nondestructive disturbances. (p. 14)

All biological entities display such systemic organization illustrated by homeostasis (Cannon, 1939). A person learning to speak again after a disrupting brain injury is an example. This special kind of self-regulating organization we will call a *system*. Cybernetics is the study of such systems.

Open and Closed Systems

Systems differ in terms of whether or not they exchange material, energy, and/or information with their contexts. They are called closed if they do not and open if they do. This is a very important distinction for understanding living systems. *Closed systems* do not gain anything from or lose anything to their environments. Therefore the only change possible is from their internal activities, and they will tend toward a state of nonorganization, termed entropy by physicists. For example, a child locked in a closet and deprived of food, drink, movement, and information from outside will progressively become psychologically disorganized and eventually die. In contrast, *open systems* (sometimes also called dissipative structures, e.g., Prigogine & Stengers, 1984) can become larger, more complex, and more elaborate because they can obtain and use additional resources from their contexts and transmit materials and information into their environments. Through such exchanges, moreover, they can alter the content and organization of their contexts. For example, a child well fed, physically active, embedded in a loving family, and having a diversity of experiences will flower biologically, psychologically, and socially and will enrich the lives of other family members as well. Understanding the dynamics of open systems is a key to understanding developmental processes and outcomes in humans. (See assumptions 2, 2a, 2b, and 2c in Table 3.1.)

CONTROL SYSTEMS

The most familiar kind of self-regulating organization in modern society is the *control system model* manifest in all kinds of technologically useful servomechanisms such as automated controls for many industrial processes. (Atomic power plants could not run without them.) Figure 4.1 is a prototype representation of a control system.

It is important to emphasize that *all functions* in Figure 4.1 *occur simultaneously and continuously so that it functions as a dynamic unit whose states change from moment to moment; that is,* visualize Figure 4.1 flowing through time as depicted in Figure 4.2. Comparison of states of the system across time yields information about system changes and the dynamics of system operation. The labels in Figure 4.1 represent different functional components or processes, and the arrows represent constraining and facilitating (i.e., organizing) relationships

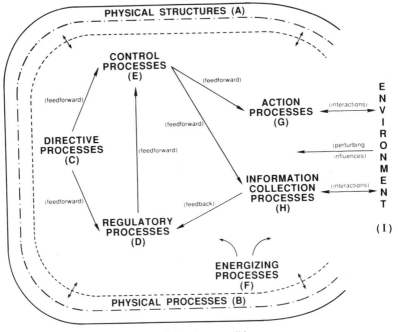

A = physical structures that make all functions possible.

B = physical processes supporting all functions.

C = directive processes that specify the state or consequence that system functioning is to produce.

D = regulatory processes that compare present conditions with specified states and identifies discrepancies.

E = control processes that organize and coordinate functioning of system components to produce specified states.

F = energizing processes that fuel all system activity.

G = action process that can affect environmental conditions and the system's relationships with the environment.

H = information collection processes that selectively collect relevant information about enviromental states, the action-impacts of the system and system-environment relationships.

I = environmental conditions with which the system must interact to produce specified, desired states.

Figure 4.1. A prototypical representation of a self-regulating control system. Some kind of physical structure makes possible a set of self-regulating processes through which the system can produce and maintain specified states against peturbations produced by interactions with the system's environment. Feedforward signals activate and coordinate specific patterns of functioning likely to produce specified states. Feedback signals provide information about current conditions relevant to specified or desired states.

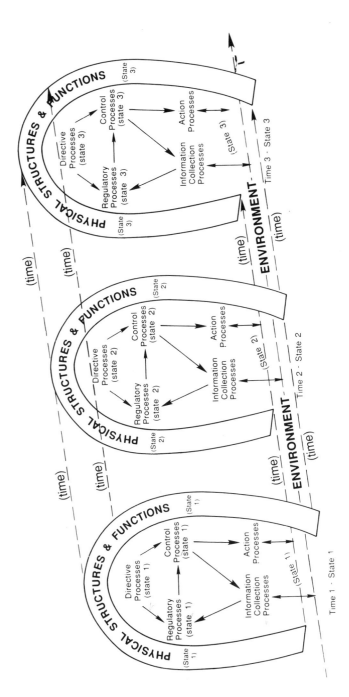

Figure 4.2. A prototypical representation of the dynamic nature of control systems. The component structure and processes are continually interacting among themselves and with their environment. The content of those activity configurations, called states, will vary and change across time as a function of their changing environment and of the internal dynamics of the system.

97

among those components. Notice that no detail is provided about the nature of the structure. That is because the functional pattern called a control system can be created through a diversity of physical structures (e.g., a home thermostat and the computerized controls of a space shuttle are both control systems). *Though the structures may differ, the prototypical functional pattern is always the same.*

To illustrate how to read Figures 4.1 and 4.2, imagine an airplane's "automatic pilot." The plane's computer contains the speed, altitude, and compass heading to be maintained (directive processes). When the automatic pilot is activated (feedforward processes), various measuring instruments continuously collect information about current speed, altitude, and compass heading (information collection processes) and transmit that information to the computer (information feedback). The computer continuously compares the current flight path with the desired one (regulatory processes). If the comparison reveals a discrepancy, a subprogram is activated (feedforward to control processes) that computes adjustments needed to reduce that discrepancy (control processes). The action mechanisms are signaled (feedforward processes) to make the appropriate adjustments, for example, change engine speed or wing or tail "flaps" (action processes). All the processes use energy, so a variable energy source is required. Flight conditions vary in unpredictable ways (e.g., variations in wind), so the guidance pattern just described must be continuous.

Similarly when a person reaches for an object, his or her mind establishes the goal (directive processes), the nervous system organizes the necessary movement pattern (control processes), and the body carries out the movements (action processes). The eye and muscle senses collect information about the accuracy of the action (information collection processes), the mind compares that with the desired result (regulatory processes), and initiates movement adjustments to ensure the desired result.

Notice that it is not necessary for the control system to anticipate, identify, and measure all the factors that might perturb its successful operation. That would be impossible. As long as the control system can compare current with desired states and make adjustments to reduce the discrepancy it doesn't need to know the nature of the perturbing influences. Because perturbations are frequently occurring and there is a time lag between the perturbation and the corrective action, the system will always oscillate around the exact values toward which it is directed. This kind of stable pattern of variability within boundaries is called a *dynamic equilibrium* or *steady state*. (See Chapter 2.) Thus a person's life is never a steady hum (equilibrium), but, rather, it is more like a symphony (a dynamic equilibrium).

A control system's functioning may be quite complex. It may pursue several goals simultaneously (e.g., speed, altitude, or direction). Multiple goals require multiple simultaneous and interacting regulatory and control processes and priority setting to reduce conflicts (e.g., is it more important to maintain speed or altitude?).

FEEDBACK AND FEEDFORWARD

In Figure 4.1 the arrows identifying feedback and feedforward functions represent "signals" by which component structures and processes relate to and influence one another and enable the system to operate as a unit. The circular functions described in Chapter 3 operate through feedback and feedforward processes. (See assumptions 5a, 5b, 5c, and 5d in Table 3.1.) These "signals" may represent different kinds of information (e.g., information about the current speed, altitude, and direction of the plane), or, in biological systems, they may be physical and/or biochemical, for example, cellular components can produce chemical compounds that activate or attenuate intracellular or intercellular activities. For example, genetic functioning is biochemically regulated. In humans both biological and informational "signals" carry out these feedback and feedforward processes. These two processes play very different system roles. Feedback is reactive; feedforward is anticipatory.

Negative Feedback Processes

There are two kinds of feedback processes. The best known is negative feedback. It operates to reduce the discrepancy between desired and current states, so it is a stability-maintaining regulatory process. The "automatic pilot" example used earlier illustrates the operation of negative feedback.

Positive Feedback Processes

Sometimes feedback operates to increase the discrepancy between desired and current states. This is called positive feedback and results in change-producing rather than stability-maintaining dynamics. For example, imagine a couple who marries (their desired state). At first they find ways of resolving their disagreements and of restoring their affectionate relationship (negative feedback stability-maintaining processes). Over time, however, he becomes less responsive and cooperative. She increases demands for his attention and help. This makes him increasingly resentful and avoidant, further escalating her pressure on him. The discrepancy between their desired loving relationship and their actual relationship is growing (positive feedback discrepancy-increasing processes). If that positive feedback process continues, it will lead to significant changes in their relationship, for example, abuse, abandonment, or divorce.

Feedforward Processes

Feedforward is future-oriented and proactive in contrast to the past-oriented, reactive role of feedback. (See assumption 5b in Table 3.1.) Feedforward processes are anticipatory; they prepare the system for future action. They involve predictive processes about how to produce desired results rather than just interpretive processes about current circumstances. For example, when a fly ball is hit in the direction of a ball player, he or she must anticipate the ball's trajectory and run to where he or she predicts the ball will come down. If the ball player only reacts and runs to where he or she first saw the ball, it will be gone when he or she gets there.

Most attempts to use control system models to represent humans have emphasized their negative feedback properties while ignoring positive feedback and feedforward processes. Such incomplete systems models that represent humans solely as reactive, stability-maintaining organisms by including only negative feedback processes have tended to discredit the use of systems models for understanding humans. And appropriately so, because it is feedforward processes that make humans proactive, goal-directed functioning possible, and it is positive feedback processes that play a critical role in human change and development. Therefore both are emphasized in DST along with negative feedback processes.

Even though the importance of positive feedback and feedforward processes is recognized, however, a control system model is still not an adequate representation of humans because it is still only a fancy machine. If it runs into circumstances for which it has not been designed, it cannot deal with them. If its structure becomes damaged, it is helpless. It cannot create its structural and functional characteristics through its own activity. To transform a control system to more adequately represent humans, self-constructing capabilities must be added through which the system can create, construct, and repair its own structures and create and modify its own functional patterns, that is, the model must represent them as living systems.

SELF-CONSTRUCTING LIVING SYSTEMS

A control system is like a neonate who responds to stimuli with its reflexive responses; for example, shine a light in its eyes and its pupils contract, hit its patellar tendon and its leg will extend, stick a nipple in its hungry mouth and it will suck. Control systems (and neonates) react to conditions with a limited repertoire of "built in" response capabilities.

But neonates can grow into adults and can learn many complicated behavior patterns and skills; control systems cannot. In other words, *people are self-constructing; control systems are not.* Using biological processes that are products of their evolutionary history, babies "disassemble" materials they selectively ingest into simpler material components and then "reassemble" those material elements to create, elaborate, and repair the physical parts of their bodies and to produce energy to fuel their functioning. Analogously, through evolutionarily based information processing and learning capabilities, babies can collect, organize, and retain information as well as disassemble and reassemble it to create or elaborate new ideas, knowledge, skills, and behavior patterns. Human living systems literally construct themselves both structurally and functionally through their selective material/energy and informational transactions with their environments and through internal constructive processes. (See assumptions 3a and 3b in Table 3.1.) The term *autopoiesis* has been used for these self-constructing properties (Maturana, 1975; Zeleny, 1981). A sound technical definition of a living system is provided by Yates and Iberall (1973):

> Living systems are autonomous, nonlinear, dissipative, active, open, thermodynamic systems that persist, adapt, evolve, reproduce, and construct themselves. In a number of complex ways, they are hierarchical in both structure and function. (p. 17)

The Person as a Living System

Self-constructing capabilities are a key feature that distinguish living systems from nonliving control systems. Humans are both biologically and psychologically/behaviorally self-constructing. Therefore before transforming Figure 4.1 into a living system, it is essential to explain the foundation for these two kinds of self-construction. Simply stated, the question is "From what could these different kinds of human characteristics be constructed and how are they related?"

BASES OF BIOLOGICAL AND PSYCHOLOGICAL/BEHAVIORAL DEVELOPMENT

Historically many scholars have struggled to understand the differences between inanimate (i.e., material) and animate (i.e., behaving) entities (Toulmin & Goodfield, 1962). A dualism, illustrated by terms such as physical-mental and biology-behavior, has been dominant to reflect the fact that people not only have a body, but they also think, feel, communicate, and act. Intuitively, it has seemed something more than material substance must underlie those qualitatively different attributes. The dualisms have never been very satisfying, however, because individuals function as integrated units so their two "sides" must somehow be related. DST presents a model in which biology and behavior are integrated, based on the following formulation of this "body-mind" issue (see Pribram, 1986, for similar views, as well as Sperry, 1988, and "Comments" in the *American Psychologist*, January, 1990, for recent debate).

Proposition I: The world and humans within it are composed of two kinds of phenomena that are different but related: Material/energy forms and organization.

Material/energy forms have been the primary focus of the natural sciences from the study of nuclear particles to atoms to materials to objects to organisms to galaxies. Anything that exists must have some material/energy form. The human body is a physical (biological) entity that can be understood as an hierarchical organization of physical parts, for example, physiology studies organs and organ systems while cell biologists study the physical components of which organs are composed. Materialists argue that is all there is, and other human attributes such as thoughts, emotions, and actions are simply epiphenomena; once the material/energy forms are fully understood everything else about humans can be derived therefrom.

Organization exists as a pattern of relationships among a set of material/energy components. Therefore different kinds of entities are the product of both the nature of their material/energy components and of their organization. Organization is demonstrably something different than the material/energy components organized. For example, when a person speaks, he or she creates an organized pattern of air pressure waves. When those air pressure waves impinge on the mouthpiece of a telephone, they recreate the same organized pattern in the form of electrical impulses transmitted on a telephone wire. The material/energy components organized are qualitatively different, but the organization is the same. Organization is invariant across such material/energy transformations, so its nature is not dependent on any specific material/energy form! It is something different.

Proposition II: Information represents the properties termed organization or pattern.

Zeman (1962), as translated in Miller (1978), relates information as a measure of organization to measures of basic physical properties:

If mass is the measure of the effects of gravitation, and of the force of inertia, and energy the measure of movement, information is in the quantitative sense the measure of the organization of the material object. . . . Matter, space, time, movement, and organization are in mutual connection. (p. 42)

The more complex the pattern of organization, the more information it contains.

Proposition III: The growth, health, and functioning of the human body as a physical entity requires the ability to collect and use appropriate material/energy forms and to protect against potentially damaging ones.

Humans' lives requires a regular flow of raw materials into their physical bodies. This is accomplished primarily through the ingestive functions of eating, drinking, and breathing. In addition there must be

processes for utilizing the raw materials in the construction, maintenance, operation, and repair of their bodies. This is accomplished through
a host of interacting biological processes. Finally, protection against
damaging substances is essential. This is accomplished through eliminative and protective (e.g., immune system) processes. There must be
a way of integrating all of the biological processes so the entire body
can function as a biological unit, and that is accomplished through
the circulatory system. This complex of capabilities is what is meant
by the phrase biologically self-organizing and self-constructing.

Proposition IV: The organization of humans' functioning to carry out
essential and effective transactions with their complex and variable
environment requires the ability to collect and use information representing the organization of their environment, themselves, and
their relationships to the environment.

The raw materials essential for humans' lives can only be obtained
through transactions with their environment and, unless these materials are universally available (e.g., oxygen), that requires discovering
where and when they can be obtained and obtaining them. Finding a
mate imposes similar requirements. In other words, the evolutionary
demands of survival and reproductive success required the use of
information representing the spatial-temporal organization of the
environment and the person's relationship to it. Humans obtain the
relevant information through a set of sensoriperceptual structures,
each capable of collecting different kinds of information, and the
nervous system that can use that information to construct, maintain,
elaborate, and use different patterns of psychological/behavioral
functioning. Moreover, humans create new organization (and information) through their actions on the environment. The human brain
can dissemble, combine, and reorganize information to create new
information (ideas) and action patterns. This capability separates the
information from the organization it originally represented and therefore frees humans from dealing solely with entities and their organization in the here and now.
    To understand how this is possible, it is necessary to understand
the distinction between *information codes* and *carriers*. Recall that
information represents the organization of some material/energy
substance (e.g., a tree or dog). The organization may be dynamic (e.g.,
a dog sniffing a tree). When a person sees the entities and events, the

organization of the actual phenomena is rerepresented in the organization of neural activity in the visual portions of the brain and its sensory apparatuses. When a blind person hears the organization of the same entities and events described, the actual organization of the phenomena is represented first in the verbal description and then in the neural activity of the auditory portions of the brain and its sensory apparatus. Conscious perception converts these neural codes into "mental" representations.

In other words, the same information is represented in the organization of two different kinds of material/energy forms, that is, the organization of the actual entities and events on the one hand and the neural activity on the other. In information theory the material/energy form that manifests the organization is called the carrier; the form in which the organization is represented is called the code. (See Miller, 1978, for a more extended discussion of codes and carriers.) For example, actually seeing entities and their interactions is represented in a visual-perceptual code, while hearing them described is represented in auditory-linguistic codes. Both, however, use the same kind of carrier, that is, patterns of neuronal activity. Because the carrier is the same, it is possible to relate the two codes to one another, and that is the basis of the interface between "brain" and "mind." Human thought involves the manipulation and combining of various information codes (mental activity) through the dynamics of the neural activity carrier (brain activity); however, the meaning lies in the code itself and cannot be derived solely from the neuronal functioning.

The nervous system links all parts of the body to make possible information-based psychological/behavioral unity. This complex of processes is what is meant by psychological/behavioral self-organization and self-construction.

Proposition V: For a person to function as a unit within himself or herself and in relation to his or her environment, the person's biological and psychological/behavioral self-organizing and self-constructing aspects must be coordinated and operate in synchronous fashion. This is accomplished through interfaces between the circulatory system serving material/energy-based integration and the nervous system serving information-based integration.

The nervous system has two subsystems: the central nervous system (CNS) and the autonomic nervous system (ANS). The CNS collects information about the dynamic organization of the person's contexts, his or her interactions with those contexts, and his or her own functioning, and uses that information to construct representations of and ideas about the person's world and the person, and to organize and guide his or her behavior. That is why the CNS reaches every sensory and skeletal-muscle component in the body.

The ANS coordinates internal biological functioning. Through its connections with smooth muscles and glands, it collects information about and orchestrates the operation of the person's biological processes to coordinate that with the requirements of his or her behavior as organized by the CNS. Through its links to the circulatory system, the ANS can activate the manufacture and distribution of chemical compounds to any part of the body. Of course the neurons that provide the material carrier for information-based functioning are also nourished by the circulatory system. Therefore through the links between the integrating functions of the nervous and circulatory systems, psychological/behavioral functioning can influence biological function and vice versa. Such interfaces exist at multiple levels in the human body. Through these interacting material/energy-based and information-based integrative capabilities, humans can create and alter organization within themselves, within their environment, and in their relationships with their environment. (See assumptions 1 and 1a in Table 3.1.) Through these arrangements human's biological and psychological/behavioral self-organizing and self-constructing capabilities operate in synchrony to ensure unitary functioning.

The operational model to be described next seeks to represent this dynamic biological and psychological/behavioral unity. The form of the relationships among the actual biological components is not modeled here because that is available in the literature on human physiology and developmental and cell biology; however, it, too, could be represented as a complexly organized set of self-organizing and self-constructing components.

STRUCTURAL AND FUNCTIONAL COMPONENTS

Because the DST model of development is composed of hierarchical and systemic organization of structural and functional components, the concept of components must be defined so one can be recognized when it is seen.

A *component* is defined as a semiautonomous entity that displays unitary functioning. Its internal dynamics are separated from its contexts by a *boundary* that enables its internal functioning to occur relatively unaffected by influences from its contexts. Boundaries separate intracomponent dynamics from intercomponent dynamics and permit only selective interactions across the boundaries, thereby limiting the influence components can have on one another within levels of organization as well as between levels. (See assumption 4b in Table 3.1.)

A living cell is a good example. The cell membrane encloses the internal dynamics of cell metabolism and is dynamically selective about the substances it permits to enter or leave the cell. A cell is more influenced by cells in the same organ or tissue than by cells in different organs or tissues. Therefore processes occurring at one level of organization may differ from those occurring at another.

As the number and diversity of specialized components increase, the need increases for coordination among components to maintain the unity of the whole, because if each component functioned unilaterally chaos would reign and organization would be destroyed. Therefore *componentization* (i.e., specialization) and *coordination* are coupled requirements through which increased complexity, efficiency, and flexibility of structural-functional patterns can be simultaneously achieved. (See assumption 1 in Table 3.1.) The separation of intracomponent and intercomponent dynamics makes coordination much easier because a simple input or signal from outside a component can trigger a complex pattern of intracomponent functioning synchronized with that of other components in the unit.

An American football team provides an example. In the huddle the quarterback may say "32 right, on 3." Each player privately recalls the play and his specific assignment. Each goes to the appropriate place on the field and, "on 3," carries out his assignment varying his actions as necessary to meet unexpected events and to coordinate with his teammates. This results in a complexly choreographed pattern of activity as a team that produces a 20-yard gain. Eleven persons' (components') actions were coordinated into a larger unit, "the play," by five words! Through such coordination, different complex patterns can be produced with the same components, for example, different plays with the same football players.

Structural Components

We define structural components as *physical parts of the body*. The concept of structural components is easily grasped because physical entities are clearly identified by a physical boundary, like the threads composing a piece of cloth. The human body is an hierarchical organization of structural components. Gross anatomy is the study of the large structural components such as the skeletal bones and joints, muscle groups, sensory mechanisms, and organs such as the heart, lungs, and stomach. These largest components are organizations of smaller components made of specialized tissue. Histology or microanatomy study such tissues. The smaller components (i.e., tissues) are organizations of cells, and cell biology studies the properties of cells and their components such as organelles. Structural development is manifest in changes within and between each of these hierarchically organized structural levels (see assumption 2c in Table 3.1).

Functional Components

We define *functional components* as recognizable, coherently organized patterns of activity that occur as a unit and that retain their pattern and identity across time and contexts. Such persistent functional patterns or components exist and develop at each structural level. Examples include cell metabolism, respiration, body temperature control, habits of thought, speech, or motor behavior, and patterns of social behavior. For example, the study of coordination of motor behavior is a domain in which there is extensive examination of functional components (Turvey, 1990).

Functional boundaries are a less obvious concept and are not as easily recognized. They are sometimes called activity boundaries because they are manifest in activities that differentiate the behaviors within the unit's organization from other behaviors. Functional boundaries also operate to protect the internal coherence of a functional component. For example, a skilled gymnast concentrates on her routine and tries to exclude any influences that might affect that well-practiced and somewhat automated performance.

Because structures make functions possible, and functioning maintains and develops structures (Gottlieb, 1976; see assumption 2a and 3a in Table 3.1), some functional units may be produced by certain structures, for example, talking using the mouth and respiratory structures. Moreover, the operation of functional components may modify their related structures (e.g., changes in bones and muscle cells as a function of activity or inactivity; modification of neural connections through visual functioning or lack thereof) (Gottlieb, 1976). Though structural and functional components are reciprocally related, they are different because often the same function can be performed with different structures, for example, a person can "talk" with their hands using American Sign Language. Concepts such as reflexes, habits, concepts, attitudes, and schemas represent proposals about different kinds of functional components.

Organizations of Components

The development of the hierarchical structural organization of body parts is controlled by each human's genes dynamically interacting with his or her environments (Gottlieb, 1991). Because the environment in which most humans develop is prototypical of that in which their genome evolved, the resulting structural body organization is essentially the same for all humans. Some deviations from the species-typical structural organization sometimes occur, however, when environmental conditions deviate too far from the species norm. Usually such deviations are the result of some biochemical disruption during particular embryonic phases (e.g., a baby born without limbs; a heart located somewhat differently; twins whose bodies are joined at some point) or some trauma during development.

Similarly there are a set of species-typical functional components with which most newborn infants enter the world. For example, they can breathe, cough, sneeze, suck, swallow, regurgitate, digest, and assimilate certain kinds of food, and eliminate urine and feces; they can react to strong light, loud sounds, heat, cold, pressure, painful stimuli, and loss of physical support; they can cry, turn their head, move their arms and legs, perform a variety of reflexes, and display some patterns of emotional arousal. In contrast to structural/biological development in humans, however, the diversification and elaboration of functional components is primarily a result of the information-based self-constructing activities of individuals. And, because there are wide individual differences in experiences, great diversity in the functional components humans construct is to be expected.

The principle of hierarchical organization also operates in functional componentization to produce efficiency and flexibility in functional capabilities (Werner, 1957; see assumption 1a in Table 3.1). In motor behavior, for example, simple motor components such as sitting and standing develop first in infants. Later these simpler motor patterns are combined to construct more complicated functional components such as jumping, climbing or running. These can be combined into even more complicated patterns such as playing basketball.

Similarly, cognitive constructions are hierarchical. For example, Einstein's famous equation, $E=MC^2$, is an abstract cognitive construction in which each component (symbolized by E, M, & C) is itself a complex concept. So hierarchically organized functional components can develop within each of the process domains represented in Figure 4.3 as well as among them. Those component functions, however, do not operate in isolation from one another, so we need a way of representing person-environment level organizations of these specialized functional components.

Figure 4.3 transforms the control system model of Figure 4.1 into a person as a living system by equating different kinds of basic control system components with different kinds of human biological, psychological, and behavioral characteristics functioning in continuous patterns with their contexts and by adding biological and psychological/behavioral self-constructing capabilities. Figure 4.3 converts the circles labeled "child" and "parent" in Figure 3.3 into a living system model. Each component in Figure 4.3 will now be briefly discussed to illustrate its content, organization, functioning, and interrelationships as a dynamic, structural-functional unit. (See assumptions 1 and 2 in Table 3.1.)

Humans are complex living systems composed of organizations of subsystems. To simplify consideration of human complexity and for ease of reference, the discussion of Figure 4.3 will be divided into three parts labeled the biological person, the psychological person, and the action person. The reader should keep in mind, however, that all of these aspects operate together in integrated fashion. Humans are complex entities, and space limitations require that a great deal of information be omitted to simplify matters as much as possible. A more detailed examination of each aspect may be found in Ford (1987) and Ford and Ford (1987).

System Component Structures and Functions

THE BIOLOGICAL PERSON

The biological aspects of humans are represented by components A and B (biological structures) and processes in the bands around the outside of Figure 4.3. Notes A and B below Figure 4.3 provide a diversity of examples of the components through which biological self-organization and self-construction operate. (See assumptions 3a and 4a in Table 3.1.) Only a few biological components are considered next. Many more could be mentioned. Humans are very complex biological organisms.

Boundaries

Every living system is separated from its contexts by a permeable boundary, so the dark border line symbolizes the boundary that, structurally in humans, is their skin. Figure 4.3 is open to the environment on one side to convey that humans are open systems whose existence, functioning, and development is dependent upon continual selective material-energy and informational exchanges with their environments. Therefore *a person's functioning and development cannot be understood separate from the environments in which his or her life is embedded.* (See assumption 1a in Table 3.1.)

The word selective must be emphasized. The function of boundaries is to protect and make possible the semiautonomy of the internal dynamics of the system from external influences. Yet these internal dynamics require a continual supply of diverse materials and information that can only be obtained from the environment. Some materials could damage the system and must be excluded, just as waste products produced by biological functioning must be disposed of or the system will smother in its own waste. Moreover, through physical actions and emitting information, people relate to and manipulate their environments. The two-headed arrows connecting the biological structures and processes with the action, communication, and information-collection processes in Figure 4.3 symbolize these selective transactional processes that serve the biological person.

How material/energy forms and information get through the boundary to serve the system's internal dynamics and how they enable the

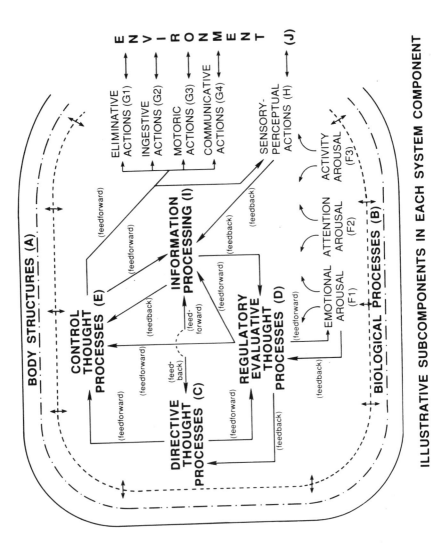

ILLUSTRATIVE SUBCOMPONENTS IN EACH SYSTEM COMPONENT

A = body structures such as skeleton, joints, muscles, tendons, tissues, cells, genes, glands, organs, chromosomes, arteries, veins, heart, stomach, colon, anus, mouth, throat, vocal cords, teeth, taste buds, genitals, skin, torso, legs, feet, arms, hands, tongue, nose, hair, ears, eyes, and touch receptors.

B = biological processes such as digestive & respiratory processes, growth & immune system processes, cell metabolism, neural & hormonal processes, body repair processes, DNA-RNA processes, waste elimination processes, blood circulation and biochemical balances, and sensory and muscular processes.

C = directive thought processes such as specifying purposes, intentions, or goals, prioritizing goals, and formulating preparatory anticipations.

D = regulatory evaluative thoughts such as evaluating current performance, personal agency beliefs and evaluations, standard setting, moral values and valuations, and evaluating environmental responsiveness.

E = control thought processes such as reasoning, problem solving, planning, decision making, and implementing, coordinating, and revising action plans.

F1 = emotional arousal process that both energize behavior and provide evaluative information such as anger, affection, satisfaction, fear, depression, disgust, sexual excitement, and interest.

F2 = attention arousal processes that selectively activate neural patterns both for selective information collection and processing and for selective organization and coordination of action patterns.

F3 = activity arousal processes that provide variations in the production and utilization of energy by various parts of the body to fuel all other processes.

G1 = eliminative actions such as urination, defecation, sweating, heat dissipation, vomiting, and sneezing.

G2 = ingestive actions through which materials and energy are taken into the body such as eating &, breathing.

G3 = motoric actions by which a person moves around in or manipulates their environment such as walking, jumping, running, sitting, lying down, manipulating objects, and using tools.

G4 = communicative actions through which a person attempts to influence and interact with their environment through information processes such as talking, writing, singing, and various kinds of gestural forms.

H = sensory-perceptual information collection actions that selectively scan for and selectively collect information about person-environment characteristics and states relevant to the system's operation and its impacts on the environment.

I = information processing activities that make possible information-based self-regulating and self-constructing characteristics of humans such as remembering, concept and proposition formation, knowledge construction, schema-script construction, goals-values construction, self-representation construction, and action pattern construction.

J = environmental conditions that provide facilitating and constraining conditions for a person's functioning such as heat, light, gravity, oxygen, food, animals, and other people and social institutions.

Figure 4.3. A transformation of a prototypical control system into a model for representing a person as an integrated structural-functional unit in continual transaction with an environment. It illustrates the diverse biological, pyschological, and behavioral characteristics that compose a person and the elaborate feedforward and feedback patterns that provide both dynamic flexibility and unity. An information-processing component provides information-based self-construction capabilities, and biological processes provide material-based/self-construction capabilities that distinguish humans as living systems from mechanical control systems.

system to relate to its contexts represents a set of very important issues. Fields such as nutrition and dietetics, gastroenterology, urology, gynecology, and dermatology illustrate specializations focused on different aspects of material/energy exchange processes. Fields such as the biology and psychology of sensation and perception, communication disorders, ophthalmology, otolaryngology, and speech illustrate specializations focused on different aspects of information exchange processes.

The complex, unitary, structural organization of the human body cannot be fully conveyed in Figure 4.3, but it is an elaborate, embedded heterarchical organization. We use the term *heterarchy* to identify an hierarchical organization in which influence flows not just from "top down," but also from "bottom up." (See assumptions 2 and 2a in Table 3.1.) For example, genes are organized into chromosomes, which are embedded in cells and regulate cellular functioning; cells are organized into tissues, tissues into organs, and organs into organ systems; and organ systems are integrated with one another to create a body that can function as a unit.

The biological processes made possible by this elaborate structure are similarly complex and complexly organized to support unitary functioning. For example, cell metabolism depends on material exchanges between each cell and the circulatory system; the biochemistry of the circulatory system is a function of ANS and hormonal functioning, of exchange processes with the gastrointestinal and respiratory organ systems, and of the functioning of other organs. The circulatory system provides the integrative material distribution arrangement that integrates all aspects of this elaborate but harmonious arrangement.

The two-headed arrows between the biological structures and processes in Figure 4.3 symbolize the mutual dependence of biological structure and functional components. The two-headed arrows between the biological structures and processes and the psychological and behavioral processes symbolize the constraining and facilitating conditions each provides the others, resulting in their interdependence (see assumptions 2b and 2c in Table 3.1).

Some living systems, such as plants, have only a physical existence. They are typically immobile and deal only with their immediate environment. This simplifies biological existence considerably, and so evolutionary processes could eventuate in "built-in" adaptive processes sufficient to deal with limited environmental variability (e.g., the curling of a plant's leaves to restrict moisture loss in dry periods). The rigidity in such "hard-wired" processes makes an organism vulnerable, however, because if the environment changes in a way for which there is no built-in adaptation, then the organism cannot adapt to the change.

Therefore, over the course of evolution, complex, mobile organisms that must deal with complex and highly variable contexts (such as humans) have evolved a synthesis of "coupled" and "decoupled" processes (Lewontin & Levins, 1978). *Coupling* (integration) of processes allows the organism to meet contextual demands in an organized, coordinated manner (e.g., the integration of CNS and ANS processes). *Decoupling* of processes allows the organism to alter only one or a few processes to deal with variations in demands (e.g., to think before acting).

The Advantages and Limitations of
"Built-In" Adaptations

"Hard-wired" adaptations are mechanistic in form; they reliably always work the same way. Their efficiency and reliability are useful for conditions with high repetitiveness; however, they are not effective under highly variable conditions. As increasingly mobile organisms evolved, and as the environment became more diverse, the variability with which organisms had to cope became exponentially more complex. Space, time, movement, and environmental complexity became linked.

Evolutionary processes appear to have forged a more flexible strategy. Biological structures and psychological/behavioral functions evolved that made it possible for humans to take into themselves and to retain the organizational properties of their environment and their interactions with it (i.e., to link past, present, and potential futures at any moment) and to use that to behave in anticipation of or to create future conditions and outcomes. Information-based self-organizing and self-constructing capabilities make this possible and have evolved to their highest level in humans. These capabilities are typically called cognitive or psychological processes, and their operation is often called learning.

THE PSYCHOLOGICAL PERSON

Just as people a few centuries ago thought of their bodies as a home for "spirits," so today many of us think of our bodies as something "we" live in. For example, people frequently complain that some bodily deficiency is interfering with what "they" want to do. There is a certain validity to this subjectively sensed difference. The structure and functioning of one's body only puts boundaries on the possibilities for one's psychological and behavioral development. Biology and behavior influence one another in a diversity of ways, but psychological and behavioral development involve primarily information-based self-construction rather than material-energy based self-construction. Therefore *human behavior cannot be reduced solely to biological causes* (Washburn, 1978). (See assumptions 3a and 3b in Table 3.1.)

Figure 4.3 summarizes the characteristics of the psychological person as cognitive and arousal processes identified as components C, D, E, F, and I in Figure 4.3. *Cognitive processes* perform the system-governing functions summarized in Figure 4.1 and are made possible by the Central Nervous System (CNS). *Arousal processes* perform the system-energizing processes in Figure 4.1 and also participate in regulatory governing processes as will be described later. Arousal processes bridge the central and autonomic nervous systems and therefore link the biological and psychological person. (See M. Ford, in press, for an extensive discussion of how cognitive and arousal processes combine to create patterns of motivation.)

Cognitive Processes and System-Governing Functions

Information-based self-construction is most evident in cognitive processes. Knowledge is power. Cognitive capabilities free people from being completely controlled by present events. They enable people to conceive of objects, entities, environments, and events that have never existed and to combine such conceptions with memories of the past, expectations of the future, and current perceptions to guide actions that actually create imagined future possibilities. People use information-based constructions to maintain their unity as a person, to orchestrate their behavioral interactions with their contexts, to influence and alter their environments, to influence one another, and to construct and maintain social organizations and cultures. (See assumptions 4a, 5d, 6, and 6a in Table 3.1.) The elaborateness of these capabilities and the consequences they produce is the most distinguishing characteristic of humans.

Sections C, D, E, and I, labeled "thought processes" and "information processing" in Figure 4.3, represent these information-based capabilities. The three thought processes are directly analogous to basic control system functions represented in Figure 4.1, that is, the directive, control, and regulatory functions. The fourth, information processing, adds the information-based self-constructing capabilities not present in control systems.

Directive Cognitive Processes

Directive thought processes are illustrated in note C of Figure 4.3. Cognitively, the directive process is manifest in thoughts that specify the consequences the person would like to obtain or anticipates occurring as a result of his or her activity. Concepts such as goal setting, purposiveness, and intentionality refer to the operation of directive cognitive processes. Because people usually try to produce multiple results simultaneously, directive and regulatory cognitions must combine to set priorities among multiple goals, intentions, and anticipations.

Directive thought processes give human behavior its future-oriented properties. Without beliefs in desirable and possible futures, there can be no coherent organization of the flow of one's behavior and no reference against which to evaluate one's activities and experiences. Without direction, life is like a ship on a stormy sea without someone steering it. One gets pushed around by the winds and waves of life until the ship sinks to oblivion. Without goals and hopes for a better future with which to guide their current behavior, people experience the devastating conditions called loneliness, depression, helplessness, and hopelessness, and health and life are jeopardized (Antonovsky, 1979). This is dramatically demonstrated by studies of people in Nazi concentration camps during World War II (Frank, 1968; Frankl, 1963; Gil, 1988); of people during the siege of Leningrad during World War II (Salisbury, 1969); and of people who display thoughts of and attempts at suicide (Farber, 1968). Research by Klinger (1977) demonstrates that the very "tenor and tempo" of people's thoughts and feelings depend on their success in achieving and enjoying goals they value.

Currently operative directive thoughts exert constraining and facilitating influences on all other aspects of behavior to organize them to try to produce the intended/desired future conditions. The content of such personal guiding goals can be very diverse. They can be simple and very short term, such as tying your shoe laces or preparing a meal, or long term and grandiose such as becoming president of the United States. They can represent potential future environmental consequences (e.g., getting a raise in salary) or potential future personal states (e.g., achieving inner peace). They can represent desired consequences to be produced (e.g., get an A in a course) or an undesirable consequence to be prevented (e.g., avoid developing cancer). Personal goals are often hierarchically organized with some shorter-term goals serving as means or instrumental goals to achieve longer-term or terminal goals (e.g., see Winell's 1987 research on retirees and Ford & Nichols [1987]).

Such *intentions* and *personal goals* are cognitive constructions that result from the flow of one's perceptual, cognitive, and affective experiences. Their construction relies upon other basic cognitive capabilities for perceiving, recognizing, remembering, and anticipating things and events. Their construction also relies upon valuing processes that give a good-bad or desirable-undesirable valence to perceptions and conceptions (which will be discussed under regulatory processes). Because living occurs in a continual flow of variable environments, activities, and experiences, there is always the potential for constructing new personal goals as well as relinquishing old ones. (See assumptions 4c, 5a, and 5b in Table 3.1.) *Once activated, personal goals provide the reference frame for organizing the other cognitive functions as well as the arousal and transactional processes.*

Regulatory Cognitive Processes

Regulation involves an evaluative comparison. Therefore *evaluative thoughts* perform this process in humans. Regulatory thought processes, illustrated in note D below Figure 4.3, represent the "How am I doing?"; "How might I do?"; and "Is it good or bad?" aspects of current behavior as well as general and anticipatory evaluations of oneself and potential future conditions.

There are several kinds of evaluative thoughts. Some thoughts directly regulate the flow of current behavior by comparing current with desired conditions and by evaluating the extent to which they match. This is sometimes called *performance evaluation*. Such thoughts include the *setting of standards*, that is, the level of goal achievement considered acceptable. Because desired consequences may be achieved in varying degrees, (e.g., a student may pass a course with an "A" or a "C,") a person establishes some satisfactory level of accomplishment (e.g., some students will settle for a "C" while others will demand an "A" performance of themselves).

A second type involves comparing different potential means of achieving ones goals in terms of their social implications. This is where *good-bad evaluations* and *moral judgments* come into play. For example, people disagree over whether abortion or the death penalty is moral or immoral. Measures of moral reasoning examine this aspect of cognitive regulation (e.g., Kohlberg, 1976).

Social/moral evaluations are of special importance in regulating social relationships. People function not only as individuals but also as component members of larger social systems, such as families, work or school groups, communities, and societies. Regulatory processes are necessary to ensure that the functioning of individuals serves not just their personal interest but also the interests of others and the larger social systems. (See assumptions 6 and 6a in Figure 3.1.) Shared cognitive representations of social and moral values and their formal representations in laws serve this social regulatory function.

A third kind of evaluation emphasizes the potential relative effectiveness of different means rather than their social implications, that is, which one will "work best." One form of such *efficacy evaluations* uses feasibility and resource criteria (e.g., which will take the least time, use the least resources, or appears most feasible under current environmental conditions). A fourth type evaluates possibilities in terms of ones' personal capabilities. Bandura's (1986) research on self-efficacy is focused on this kind of *self-evaluative cognition* and its regulatory influence. M. Ford (in press) refers to efficacy evaluative thoughts as *personal agency beliefs* and summarizes evidence concerning the critical role they play in both the regulation of current actions and the evolving of developmental pathways. He emphasizes the importance of distinguishing between *capability evaluations* (i.e., beliefs about personal capabilities) and *context evaluations* (i.e., beliefs about the extent to which the environment is likely to constrain or facilitate one's efforts). He also stresses the need to understand the *patterning* of these two kinds of evaluative thoughts with regard to particular goals. For example, people are unlikely to pursue goals for which they believe they do not have the capabilities or for which they believe the environment will be unresponsive or unsupportive.

Because several different kinds of evaluative criteria may be applied at the same time, the possibility exists that they may conflict (e.g., the most effective means may be morally unacceptable). Therefore *regulatory thought processes must also set priorities within specific behavior episodes among simultaneously applicable evaluative criteria.*

Moreover, because of the probability of conflicts among simultaneously operative evaluative cognitions and the psychological disturbances such value conflicts may lead to, they are a primary focus of many forms of psychotherapy (e.g., see Ford & Urban, 1963; Burke, 1989). The role of emotions in regulatory/evaluative processes, and therefore in intrapsychic conflicts, will be discussed later.

Control Cognitive Processes

Control thought processes, illustrated in note E below Figure 4.3, represent the "how to do it" or "means" aspects of behavior. Within the "design criteria" established by directive and regulatory cognitions and the facilitating and constraining conditions of current body and environment states, cognitive control processes *construct plans for producing the intended consequences and organize, coordinate, and revise behaviors to carry out the plans.* Research on human intelligence, reasoning, problem solving, planning, cognitive influences on motor behavior, and selective perception examines control cognitive processes. Most intelligence tests focus on control process cognitions. In fact Sternberg (1982) asserts that reasoning, problem solving, and intelligence are such interrelated concepts that it is often difficult to tell them apart.

As with regulatory process evaluative thoughts, there are several types of control process thinking. For example, *reasoning* is the study of thinking that involves organizing information and drawing conclusions in a rule-governed way, and formal logic is one kind of rule-governed thinking (e.g., Braine & Rumain, 1983; Revlin & Mager, 1978). *Decision making* refers to thought processes targeted to produce outcomes that can then organize and guide actions (e.g., Janis & Mann, 1977). Decision making may involve *simulated episodes* in which potential alternative courses of action are imagined and evaluated as a basis for choosing one alternative to implement.

Problem solving combines both reasoning and decision-making approaches. Computer simulations (e.g., Kleinmuntz, 1966; Simon, 1978) and other research have identified several aspects of problem-solving thought processes. *Problem formulation* or *definition* involves identifying relevant characteristics of current and intended future states and relevant constraining and facilitating conditions. *Problem solving* and *plan formulation* includes conceiving of and evaluating optional plans for trying to achieve one's goals. This involves weighing information about environmental conditions and one's capabilities and resources and utilizing conceptions of cause-effect relations (e.g., MacCrimmon & Taylor, 1983). *Plan execution* involves organizing, coordinating, and revising action patterns designed to produce the desired/intended consequences.

It is important to recognize that *all of this is one integrated process in which the subprocesses interact.* For example, feedback from plan execution activities may lead to revised problem formulations or revised plans. Cognitive control processes are most directly related to environmental conditions because they must organize behavior that will "work" within current environmental constraints and opportunities.

Integration of Governing Functions

Although different kinds of thought processes perform the directive, regulatory, and control functions, it is important to emphasize that they operate together dynamically in coherent behavior episodes (the nature of those episodes will be discussed later). If they did not, the system could not function as a unit. It would be like a corporation's board of directors specifying the production and marketing of one set of products, the employees trying to produce a different set of products, and the accounting office evaluating company performance in terms of criteria unrelated to either. The goals, values, knowledge, and methods that provide the content of the governing functions come from the operations of humans' information-based self-construction capabilities.

Information Processing: Information-Based Self-Construction

These processes are illustrated in note I under Figure 4.3. Humans begin in utero to use perceptual data for information-based self-construction. The evolution of human perceptual capabilities provided the ability to gain accurate information about humans' terrestrial environment, their own functioning, and their interactions with their environment (Gibson, 1979). Because all perceptions arise from the person's observational vantage point, there is a self-referent aspect to all perceptions. Therefore *perceptions are direct representations of specific spatial-temporal instances of some phenomenon observed from one's personal vantage point.* Perceptions may be of static (e.g., "What is it?") or dynamic (e.g., "What's happening?") conditions.

In humans all sensoriperceptual systems are continually operating so that all perceptual experiences are multimodal, that is, they combine sights, sounds, tastes, odors, touch, temperature, pressure, and bodily experiences of movement and affect (Abravanel, 1968; Birch & Lefford, 1963); however, one modality is often the focal point around which the other information is organized, for example, vision. In addition, individuals' sensoriperceptual capabilities and functioning display both developmental and decremental changes (Schaie, 1979).

Because a person is continuously behaving in some way, the perceptual content of consciousness occurs in a flowing, variable "stream" (James, 1890) whose content is a function of the operation of selective attention in the service of current directive, regulatory, and control cognitions. Therefore perceptions are not cognitive constructions. *Perceptions are conscious representations of the organized pattern of sensory stimulation of each sense organ; they are accurate representations of what one attends to; they function to provide accurate information about "what's there" and "what's happening."*

Perceptions, though, only provide information about current circumstances, for example, "That is a red, round object with a smooth surface." For the information in a perception to be personally meaningful it must be combined with information (concepts and propositions) constructed from previous experience, for example, "That round red thing is a tomato, and it is good to eat." Therefore people *interpret* the meaning of perceptions, and their interpretations may be inaccurate. For example, one may see a familiar figure on the street, recognize them as a friend, approach them with a greeting, and then realize with embarrassment that the person is a stranger. Strictly speaking, the percept was of a figure with certain characteristics in a specific context; labeling that perception a friend is an interpretation of its meaning, not a perception.

This distinction between perceptions and their interpretation is very important in understanding and dealing with many human misunderstandings and psychological disturbances. For example, a child may say she "perceived" that her mother or father was angry with her and she became upset. In fact she could not perceive anger. What she actually perceived was the parent's loud voice, abrupt movements, and scowling face. She interpreted it as anger. Alternate interpretations are possible, for example, the parent may be ill or telling a story. The scientific method as well as effective psychotherapy rests upon careful distinctions between perceptions (what one actually observes) and interpretations (the inferences made from these observations).

The human brain operates to construct generalized representations of the flow of their perceptions and of their cognitive constructions and then uses those generalized representations to interpret the meaning of specific perceptions. These generalized representations or conceptions are in three types of codes: imagistic, abstract, and linguistic.

Imagistic Representations

Perceptions, as conscious representations of patterns of sensation, provide the initial "raw data" that is the starting point for humans' cognitive constructions. Each perceptual instance, however, is a unique, transitory event whose utility for a person is severely limited, and perceptions occur in a continuous flow. Therefore the human brain abstracts redundancies from a flow of similar sensoriperceptual instances and thereby constructs a generalized imagistic representation of those similar percepts. These may be called *first-order imagistic concepts*.

The representations are termed *imagistic* because they are in the same information code as the perception itself (e.g., visual or auditory). For example, 2-year-old Kevin meets and plays with Scooter, a beagle. Later he meets and plays with Winston, a sheepdog. Kevin forms a generalized image of Scooter and of Winston, and when he sees (perceives) either of them again he can "re-cognize" which it is (i.e., accurately interpret the meaning of the percept) by comparing that specific percept with his imagistic concepts. This usually happens so automatically that a person is not aware of that interpretive process, and so people often label their interpretations as "perceptions." Under some circumstances, however, they are aware of the differences. For example, one may answer the phone, hear a voice that sounds familiar, and actively perform a quick cognitive search for a match between images of people constructed from past experience and the current perception to try to "remember" who it is.[1]

Once formed, imagistic concepts become tools for further cognitive construction. First, they are used to interpret the meaning of new perceptual instances (e.g., to "re-cognize" something) and may be revised and elaborated as a result. It is important to reiterate that perception is an integrated multimodal experience, so imagistic representations are also multimodal or multidimensional. For example, Kevin's imagistic representation of Scooter will include what Scooter looks like, sounds like, feels like, smells like, what Scooter does, and the feelings Kevin experiences with Scooter.

Such imagistic representations become *functionally autonomous* from the objects in the "real" world that they represent. As a result, imagistic concepts can become reconstructed in consciousness as percept-like experiences through cognitive processes called remembering, imaging, dreaming, and hallucinating. These reconstructed images can influence current behavior (e.g., Kevin may remember and try to find Scooter). Moreover, imagistic representations can be combined in various ways to construct new images representing something one has never perceived or that may not even exist. For example, Kevin might dream of the sheep dog, Winston, as having wings and flying.

Abstract Representations

The human brain can also operate on and combine these functionally autonomous imagistic representations in various ways to create *second-order* or *abstract concepts*. They are called "abstract" because the information form in which they are coded is different from sensoriperceptual codes and therefore cannot enter consciousness imagistically as a percept-like experience. For example, Kevin may identify similarities in his imagistic concepts of different dogs and construct a cognitive representation of dogs in general; but only specific dogs exist and can be perceived. For example, if he dreams of a dog, the dream image will be of a particular dog. Therefore the generalized concept of dog must be a mental construction in a code different from imagistic concepts. This is true for all abstract representations, often called concepts or ideas.

Such second-order or abstract conceptions also become functionally autonomous from their original sources and can be mentally manipulated to construct still more abstract representations that can then be manipulated to create still other abstractions (e.g., third-, fourth-, or fifth-order abstract concepts). *Human abstract cognitive constructions include not only information about what things are or the nature of things and events* (i.e., *conceptual knowledge*) *but also about what they do, how they work, and how they relate to other things or events* (i.e., *propositional knowledge*). Thus, through their ability to construct imagistic and abstract concepts, humans are not only freed from the here and now and from their history of experience, but they are also freed from sensoriperceptual reality. They can imagine possibilities that:

1. Have never been observed or do not exist and then try to arrange conditions so they can be observed or created; and
2. That do not exist and that can have no material and therefore no sensoriperceptual existence (e.g., an angel).

Linguistic Representations

The inability to represent abstract concepts in perceptual form creates a problem. If a person constructs a grand abstract idea, how are others to know about it if it can be given no perceivable form? Is it doomed to die with the conceiver? This dilemma is resolved by the use of the third form of representation or code called language. A language is a set of arbitrary but agreed upon perceptible symbols and rules for organizing them that can be used as surrogates for representing anything, including the conceptual abstractions individuals create. Language, whether in written, spoken, or gestural form, can be perceived as visual (e.g., written words), auditory (e.g., spoken words), or tactile images (e.g., braille); but those images have no intrinsic meaning as do other perceptions, that is, they carry almost no information directly.

If the language image can become a part of an abstract representation, however, it can be used to manipulate the abstraction of which it is a part, just as the tuning buttons on a radio can be manipulated to hear a particular station. Consider the analogy of an iceberg. If it is totally beneath the sea, a sailor has no way of knowing it is there; but attach a floating buoy with a bell to the iceberg in a color signifying the size of the iceberg, and the presence and size of the iceberg become indirectly perceptible to the sailor as long as he understands the meaning of the buoy.

If different individuals have the same linguistic images linked to similar abstract representations, then they can communicate meanings to one another by using language to activate one another's abstract and imagistic representations. Because of language, each person doesn't have to "reinvent the wheel," but, rather, can quickly acquire the ideas others have already created and can build upon those. And, that is a basis for the creation of cultural products.

And so, while information-based self-construction starts in utero, such self-construction rapidly transcends perception and first-order imagistic concepts and elaborates sensoriperceptual functioning into a tool for testing the utility of conceptual abstractions that are far removed from any sensoriperceptual base. These human capabilities not only enhance adjustment to the demands of "reality" but are also used to help create new realities. The relationship of cognitive processes to action patterns will be considered in the section on "the action person."

Arousal Functions

There are three kinds of arousal processes that are illustrated in notes F1, F2, F3, below Figure 4.3. Living requires energy. The body functions as an energy system (Duffy, 1962), or as a dissipative structure (Prigogine & Stengers, 1984), collecting, storing, and releasing energy in various ways. This capability enables individuals to swim upstream against the eroding tide of entropy. Humans have evolved their own built-in energy-generating capabilities. This is a fundamental function of cell metabolism. Humans have two related but somewhat different energizing problems. The first is to provide energy to fuel biological and motoric activity that deal with the material-energy processes of life. This will be considered under the headings of activity arousal and emotional arousal. The second problem is to selectively energize the nervous system in support of the information-based processes of life; this is labeled attention arousal. In Figure 4.3 arrows link all arousal processes to biological functions because that is where the energy must be produced.

Activity Arousal

All activity uses energy. Variations in energy production and use to support activity are so pervasive and automatic a part of daily life that they often escape notice. For example, one may sit lazily in the sun, stroll casually down a street, or go from immobility to a dead run in a second when playing tennis. Energy production and utilization vary in amount and body location as a function of the vigor, kind, and duration of activity being performed.

The *amount* of energy needed can vary extensively. For example, in deep sleep a person burns approximately 65 calories per hour; dressing in the morning uses about 118 calories per hour; climbing stairs consumes about 1,100 calories per hour. Variations in activity level require coordinated alteration of energy-producing biological processes. For example, vigorous exercise can increase cardiac output 5 to 7 times normal rates, blood flow to the muscles more than 20-fold, and the blood concentration of free fatty acids for fuel as much as 10-fold.

The *distribution* of energy needs by various parts of the body also varies with the nature of activity. For example, although skeletal muscles constitute about 40% of a person's body weight, they receive only about 15% of the blood flow when they are at rest. A seated person doing intensive thinking uses energy in a different way than a person out for a jog. Selective energy production and use require selective resource distribution so that parts that need more energy get more raw materials, and parts that are not as active get less. For example, vasodilation occurs in active muscles to increase their blood supply, while vasoconstriction continues in inactive muscles. Blood flow increases in active parts of the brain, and some technologies for studying brain organization and functioning are based on that fact.

Meeting these variable energy demands is orchestrated by an elaborate, continuous flow of feedforward and feedback influences within and between governing levels, utilizing both biochemical and informational signals. These influences regulate the energy production, distribution, and utilization functions (Winegrad, 1965). (See assumptions 1 and 2 in Table 3.1.) Cognition plays a part, and preparatory arousal is determined by the degree of effort required by the circumstances "as interpreted by the individual" (Duffy, 1951). For example, imagine bracing yourself to lift a large carton of books. Unknown to you, the box is empty. You may fall over backwards because, guided by your expectations (feedforward), the effort you exert far exceeds that necessary to lift the empty box.

Emotional Arousal

Life is not like the steady pace of a long distance runner where a steady-state balance between energy consumption and energy production can be established. The search for food, competing for a mate and mating, protecting oneself from attack, overcoming obstructions, fleeing from danger, and working and playing illustrate the need for major and often sudden variations in the rate, amplitude, and intensity of behavior. There is great adaptive value in being able to mobilize energy resources rapidly to meet changing environmental conditions as one struggles to accomplish personal objectives. Emotional arousal processes help provide energy for such special demands and are illustrated in note F1 below Figure 4.3.

Emotional arousal represents a complex pattern of psychological, neural, physiological, and expressive responses that functions to temporarily augment and amplify or attenuate activity arousal patterns as summarized in Figure 4.4. Emotions function to prepare bodily processes to support different levels of activity and approach or avoidant behavior (Grinker, Korchin, Bosowitz, Hamburg, Sabshin,

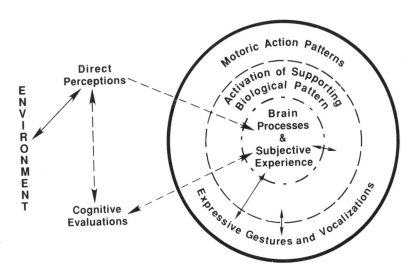

Figure 4.4. A representation of the prototypical form of all kinds of emotional arousal patterns. Direct perceptions and evaluative thought processes interact to selectively activate different patterns of limbic system brain functioning and related effective experiences. These, in turn, activate supporting biological and motoric/expressive patterns, further broadening the effective experience.

Persky, Chevalier, & Borad, 1956). The evolution of qualitatively different patterns of emotional arousal (e.g., affection or fear) facilitated dealing with different kinds of prototypical adaptive problems with different kinds of action patterns that require different kinds and distribution of energy (Plutchik, 1980). For example, you may be leisurely strolling home at night when you are confronted by a strange person. A sudden surge of fear mobilizes you for a quick dash to the safety of your home to escape what you interpreted as a threat to your welfare.

This example also illustrates the role of emotions in regulatory processes. Figure 4.4 shows that emotions enable humans to behave more selectively in three ways so as to deal more effectively with varying environmental conditions:

1. By altering physiological processes to prepare for and to support the execution of different patterns of behavior;

2. By facilitating actions and communications to selectively influence the environment to produce desired consequences; and

3. By providing evaluative information about one's interactions with the environment.

Different kinds of emotional arousal patterns produce qualitatively different kinds of perceptible feeling states that regulate continuation, termination, or alteration of current behavior patterns. The subjectively experienced hedonic qualities of emotions provide a primitive regulatory process that operates before a person constructs a repertoire of evaluative thoughts and provides one source of information for the construction of values, preferences, and personal goals. Therefore in Figure 4.3 emotional arousal and regulatory evaluative cognitions are shown as influencing one another. (M. Ford, in press, discusses the motivational properties of emotions in more detail.)

Attention Arousal

People are composed of many kinds of components. For a person to function as a unit, there must be some way to dynamically orchestrate the organization of structural and functional components to produce smoothly coordinated and integrated behavior patterns (see assumptions 1, 1a, and 2b in Table 3.1). The nervous system provides the structural basis for such integration, but to produce different organizations of behavior the nervous system must be selectively activated or energized in different patterns. The phenomena of attention and consciousness can best be understood as an "essential property" of the nervous system related to the "functional unity" of our bodies (Chauchard, 1979). Or, as Angell (1907) put it, consciousness should be regarded functionally as primarily and intrinsically a "control phenomenon." Attention and consciousness arousal selectively energize information-based functions as illustrated in note F2 below Figure 4.3.

The subjective experience of *consciousness*, or being awake, indicates that the nervous system is sufficiently activated to carry out its information-processing and information-based self-constructing functions. The substance of the information-processing activity is represented in the contents or states of consciousness and action patterns. When generalized nervous system activation (i.e., consciousness) exists, then attentional processes can selectively activate relevant neural circuits to produce targeted, coordinated behavioral functioning. Consciousness is essential for learning. Learning requires some investment of attention arousal and cannot occur in deep sleep or a coma (i.e., when a person is "unconscious").

THE ACTION PERSON

The biological person represents the complex, integrated biological structures and processes that provide the material-energy base that make possible all other functions. The psychological person represents the elaborate information-based, cognitive self-regulating and self-constructing processes that produce integrated, effective action patterns and that orchestrate biological processes to support those action patterns as well as the arousal processes that selectively energize the flow of activity. But the existence, functioning, and development of open systems, such as humans, requires continual exchanges with their contexts. It is the action person that carries out the actual environmental transactions that make individuals' life, learning, and accomplishments possible. (See assumptions 5, 5a, 5b, 5c, 5d, 6, and 6a in Table 3.1.) Notes G1, G2, G3, G4, and H below Figure 4.3 illustrate the transactional capabilities of individuals.

Human Transactional Functions

Figure 4.3 represents two interrelated forms of transactional capabilities. One form, guided by psychological processes, *operates on the environment to influence it.* The environment and one's relationships with it can be influenced in two ways:

1. By direct physical action, labeled motoric, ingestive, and eliminative actions in Figure 4.3; and
2. By emitting information aimed at influencing the environment, labeled communicative actions in Figure 4.3.

The second form, also guided by psychological processes, *selectively searches for and collects information* from the environment and provides this "informational nutriment" to the psychological processes for use in constructing, organizing, and coordinating one's knowledge and effective behavior patterns. The elaboration of a person's action repertoire results from information-based, self-construction processes within the constraints and possibilities of his or her biological structures and capabilities. For example, a quadriplegic will have to construct somewhat different transactional capabilities than would be typical of a nonparalyzed person.

Information Collection

The evolution of human sensoriperceptual capabilities made possible the collection of information useful for constructing and guiding practical action in humans' complexly organized and dynamically varying terrestrial and social environment. To be effective, humans must be able to coordinate their internal functioning with their environmental interactions. Sensoriperceptual structures and processes enable humans to collect information about: (a) internal states (e.g., affective and movement experience, pain); (b) the environment; and (c) the person's relationships and interactions with the environment.

A person is continuously bathed in a flow of different kinds of material phenomena (e.g., light; chemical compounds in the air; air pressure waves; mechanical pressures and temperature variations on different parts of their body), all of which can be organized as material carriers of information about different aspects of the environment (e.g., sights, odors, tastes, sounds, touch, temperatures, and movements). Sensory structures and processes transduce these different kinds of information from diverse material carriers that serve different sensory modalities onto one common carrier (i.e., neuronal processes), making possible the combining of different sources and kinds of information into unitary, multimodal perceptions.

The information flow across sensory receptors is continuous and highly variable and would be adaptively useless in that form; however, the nature of human sensoriperceptual processes is such that they actively abstract two types of invariances from the patterns of stimulation produced by this flow. *Topographic invariants* represent stable properties of objects and their relationships. *Dynamic invariants* represent consistencies in patterns of variability such as duration and rate of change or trajectories of motion. Moreover, all perception is anchored to a perceiver so topographic and dynamic invariants about self-functioning are also abstracted and perceived. In addition, information about self and context relationships is abstracted, for example, touching something simultaneously provides information about the object touched and the act of touching.

Information collecting must be selective for two reasons. First, the amount, diversity, and spatial-temporal variability of information within and around a person is always extensive, and a person would be overwhelmed if they had to deal with it all at once. Second, at any moment not all of the information bathing a person is of potential use to them; only that relative to the current content of his or her directive, regulatory and control processes is useful, that is, to the person's current objectives, concerns, values, and efforts. As symbolized in Figure 4.3 by the feedforward arrow between cognitive processes and information collection processes, what a person is trying to do "tunes" the information collection activities through *selective attention* to focus on certain kinds of relevant information and to give less attention to others. To ensure that a person does not ignore particularly important events unrelated to his or her current purposes, however, certain kinds of events such as sudden, loud sounds or an earthquake can *preempt attention* and activate a different pattern of functioning.

Motoric Actions

Action patterns are the means by which people physically interact with their environment. Through them, people find and ingest foods, find and relate to other humans, explore unfamiliar situations, protect themselves, use tools, create objects, and shape their environments to serve their purposes. Entertainment fields such as dance, music, and athletics have made the cultivation of high levels of motor skills a road to fame and fortune.

Motor behavior is made possible by the body's skeletal-muscle components along with the loose connective tissue. Together they give the body strength, structural stability, and flexibility of movement. Action patterns must be coordinated dynamically with a flow of environmental events, requiring both behavior-behavior and behavior-environment coordination. Psychological processes and the central nervous system orchestrate these complex, dynamic patterns. (See assumptions 1 and 1a in Table 3.1.) That orchestration is accomplished by combining conceptually constructed information (e.g., representations of goals to be achieved; knowledge and expectations about the environment and how it can be affected by or may affect a person) with the "current news" of perception representing both environmental dynamics and the movement experience itself.

Frequently repeated action patterns (e.g., sitting, standing, walking) are similar although never identical. Prototypical action pattern representations of the consistencies in such repeated actions are constructed and have been labeled *sensorimotor schemes* or *schemata* (e.g., Piaget, 1950, 1960). Once constructed, such sensorimotor schemes can be activated when useful and performed as a unit without much thoughtful guidance. For example, a 2-year-old concentrates hard on the task of learning to walk, while a healthy teenager does so easily while talking with his or her friends and thinking of other things.

Material Ingestion and Elimination

Motoric actions involved in the ingestion of materials essential for life and health and the elimination of unneeded materials or potentially damaging waste materials are of special importance. Eating, breathing, and drinking, along with the digestive and respiratory processes that make possible the absorption of materials into the bloodstream, are the primary forms of material input. Sweating, urination, defecation, and respiration are the primary forms of material elimination. Ingestion and elimination processes cooperate in maintaining appropriate balances of different materials in the body (e.g., water). Disruption of these special motor capabilities is life threatening (e.g., paralysis of breathing capabilities through polio).

Communicative Actions

Motoric actions influence the environment directly through physical processes; for example, hitting a ball with a bat; moving oneself through space. *Communicative actions are designed to influence the environment indirectly through information-based processes*, for example, attracting help by emitting a scream or by asking for something to eat.

Communicative actions are also motoric actions, but in this case the motor behavior serves as the material carrier on which information is coded. Because different kinds of motor behaviors are possible, information can be coded onto different actions, such as facial expressions, hand gestures, writing, or speech. *Intentional communication*, however, requires knowledge of some symbolic code and skill in performing actions that convey that code (e.g., being able to speak a particular language). Moreover, another person cannot understand an act as a communication unless he or she knows the symbolic code being used, for example, the meaning of the gestures or the language being spoken. A person can simultaneously communicate contradictory messages by simultaneously coding one message on one action pattern (e.g., a facial gesture of anger) and a different message on another action pattern (e.g., a friendly statement). Cross-cultural misunderstandings often result from lack of knowledge about the meaning of one another's communicative codes (e.g., an up-and-down head nod may mean different things in different cultures).

Communicative actions provide the "glue" for creating interpersonal relationships, societies, and cultures. Therefore damage to or destruction of the motor capabilities on which communicative actions rest can severely restrict a person's ability to fit into and to influence his or her environments. Fortunately the same information can be coded on different kinds of carriers. Therefore if the motor behavior capability is destroyed on which some communicative act depends, it may be possible to substitute a different motor capability to perform the same communication. For example, if a person cannot speak, he or she may substitute the motor capability for hand gestures and communicate using American Sign Language.

Environment

The final component of the DST operational model is the environment illustrated under J in Figure 4.3. Every facet of human life is shaped by environments. They provide the resources, demands, constraints, and opportunities within which people construct their lives. Concepts such as poverty, middle-class, abuse, school, attachment, and work illustrate the view that life and development occur in relationship to different kinds of environments.

Sophisticated study of person-environment dynamics and development requires some clear conceptualization of what environment is, classification systems representing its different aspects, and methods of measuring them. Recently there have been a growing number of efforts to address the environmental side of the equation in a more rigorous way (e.g., Ittelson, 1978; Magnusson, 1980; Studer, 1980). Developmental researchers are giving increased emphasis to the importance of environmental factors (e.g., Altman & Wohlwill, 1978; Bronfenbrenner, 1979).

Phenomena of such basic importance, however, require more rigorous and intensive theoretical and empirical examination than has yet been mounted. One need is for a clear formulation of shared classification systems for specifying environmental variables as units of analysis. This would make it possible to make more accurate comparisons across studies of environmental influences on development. Four broad categories of variables that are implicit in how different disciplines divide the domain might be a useful starting point. Natural environments are aspects considered the product of nature (e.g., rain, land, gravity, and plants). Designed environments are physical aspects constructed by humans (e.g., homes, cars, eyeglasses, and telephones). Human environments are represented by personal interactions with others (e.g., family members, lovers, coworkers, and friends). Sociocultural environments are humanly created means for creating and maintaining coherent, large social groups (e.g., languages, laws, religions, and schools). Units representing typical environmental patterns may also be useful, such as the concept of behavior settings (e.g., Barker, 1968; Wicker, 1979).

What Can Develop?

Human development begins the moment a sperm fertilizes an ovum. As Figure 4.3 conveys, a person is an environmentally embedded complex, unitary organization of biological, psychological, and action components and processes. Moreover, as an open system, people's existence, functioning, and development rests upon continuous material-energy and information exchanges with their environments. This means that every component structure and process and their organization into complex patterns must be subject to change because they are all influenced by these material-energy and information exchange processes. In other words, everything can change. This includes both the person and environment components. (See assumptions 4a, 4b, and 4c in Table 3.1.)

Not all human changes, however, are developmental change (see Chapter 2). We have defined the subtype of change called development as enduring elaborative change; but there are decremental changes as well. Therefore, at any point in time, a person's characteristics are the result of combinations of developmental and decremental change.

It is important to distinguish between decremental and performance changes. For example, when children learn to walk they typically give up crawling as a mode of movement; however, this does not mean that they have lost the capability for crawling. They can still crawl if circumstances warrant it (e.g., in a game or to get under a fence).

There is a performance change but not a decremental change. They haven't lost a competence; they just don't use it much.

Simultaneously the person's environment is changing in diverse ways. The family may add members; they may move to a different geographic locale; death or divorce may alter the family; children are required to go to school; new tools are created as are new means of obtaining and communicating information; belief systems, laws, and social institutions change; wars, economic recessions, and droughts begin and end. One can never step into the same river twice.

Because each person is embedded in and must "fit into" his or her environments, dynamically changing environments mandate dynamically changing persons. (See assumptions 6 and 6a in Table 3.1.) Moreover, because a person is a complexly and hierarchically organized structural-functioning unit, change or development in any one component structure or functional capability typically will be accompanied by changes in other components so that the organizational unity of the person in his or her contexts can be maintained. So not only must the development of the parts be understood, but the development of the person as a complex organization of those parts, embedded in larger contexts, must also be understood. (See assumption 2c in Table 3.1.)

Lewontin and Levins (1978) speak of a synthesis or *coupling* (integration) of processes and *decoupling* (separation) of processes so that both parts and wholes contribute to human functional flexibility. This is true socially and environmentally as well as personally. Koestler (1967) refers to this as the "Janus effect"; like the Roman god Janus, humans have two faces simultaneously looking in opposite directions. One is the face of the "master"; as an autonomous unit, a person can function "independently." The other is the face of the "servant"; as a component of social groups and the environment, a person functions "dependently" to fit within the group or environment. Ford and Nichols (1987), following Koestler (1967), refer to these two kinds of social relationships as *self-assertion* (e.g., social "decoupling") and *integrations* (e.g., social "coupling"). It is important to reiterate that these are not separate processes; as the metamodel in Chapter 3 emphasizes, they are "fused," occur simultaneously, and the dynamics of their balance varies (see assumption 5d in Table 3.1).

Any complete and adequate theory about how development occurs must simultaneously encompass this diversity and represent its organizational unity and differentiation; however, no existing theory of development does that. For example, Piaget's (1950, 1970) theory is based primarily on the study of cognitive control processes. Kohlberg's (1976, 1979) theory deals solely with one aspect of regulatory processes: moral reasoning. Freud (1949) and Erikson (1968) focus primarily on the motivational aspects of life. Other fields such as embryology and developmental biology emphasize the biological aspects of persons, while still others, such as exercise and sports science, focus on motor development. How our integrative theory relates to other theories of development will be considered more fully in future work. Suffice it to say here that our objective is to create a framework within which such "part theories" can be related to one another to provide a more comprehensive representation of a Person-in-Context.

In our Developmental Systems Theory, we are attempting to provide a more comprehensive model that simultaneously identifies key person and context structural and functional components and proposes a form of dynamic organization (i.e., a self-regulating, self-constructing open system) that shows how those components form a coherent, dynamic, relational unit, that is, a person-in-context one.[2]

DEVELOPMENT THROUGH DIFFERENTIATION, ELABORATION, AND COMBINATION OF EXISTING COMPONENTS

The evolution of complex organisms has occurred through the successive development of intermediate forms of organization. These are sometimes called *subassemblies* or *subsystems*; we have labeled them *components*. Simon (1969) demonstrated that if there exists a hierarchy of potential "stable subassemblies," a complex entity can evolve in a much shorter time by utilizing and combining existing simpler components than if it were to start "from scratch." He concluded that the reasons hierarchies predominate in the complex forms found in nature is that of all possible forms, hierarchies are the ones that have had the time to evolve. For example, scientists now agree that components of human (and other) cells, such as mitochondria, evolved from algae and bacteria that were incorporated into cells long ago; that much of humans' genetic substance is like that of other animals; and human cell metabolism is basically the same as in other animals. Our biological structural and functional components have evolved from already available sub-components.

We are proposing that individual development also proceeds through a process of creating an increasing diversity of specialized components, by elaborating on those components, and by organizing them in increasingly complex and diverse ways. Models of complex organization are sometimes criticized because they seem to imply that every component influences every other component. Componentization and hierarchical organization avoid that impossibly complex arrangement by restricting the kinds of influences components have on one another.

Moreover, because a person must function as a coherent unit in relationship to his or her environment, it is necessary to be able to represent the development of complex behavior patterns that depict different organizations of component structures and processes that "fit" dynamically with different kinds of environmental conditions. Our model provides a way of doing that. The approach rests on the concepts of behavior episode (BE) and behavior episode schema (BES).

PERSON PATTERNS: ORGANIZATIONS OF ENVIRONMENT-RELEVANT BIOLOGICAL, PSYCHOLOGICAL, AND ACTION COMPONENTS

Living is a continuous process until a person dies. Awake or asleep, at work or at play, in isolation or social interaction, a person is always functioning or behaving as a unit in some context. He or she is always doing something somewhere. Therefore to adequately represent the dynamics of a person's living, it is necessary to visualize Figure 4.3 flowing through contexts and time (as illustrated in Figure 4.2) and to visualize the content of the component functions or processes varying and changing during that flow.

A person always functions as a unit in a context, so all component functions are always occurring in some form in a variable but organized flow of different kinds of behavior-environment events. For example, a person may be driving a car (called an instrumental episode), watching someone else driving a car (called an observational episode), or sitting quietly thinking about driving a car (called a thinking episode). In each of those episodes there are biological, cognitive, arousal, and transactional processes occurring, but their content, organization, and context are different. For example, the nature of the perceptual and motoric activities will be quite different.

The variations and changes in the content of the components or the organization of the flow itself are not random or capricious. The content is selected and selectively organized at any point in time to serve some aspect of the person's existence and life within the opportunities and constraints of his or her body and environment at that moment. At different points in time, each person's functioning is organized to serve different aspects of his or her life in different kinds of environments. Therefore the stream of a person's life is organized into natural, internally coherent "chunks" or units. Bain (1855) asserted that units of constructive activity require: (a) a feeling of the end to be served, (b) command of the elements to be used, and (c) good judgment of when the end is satisfactorily attained.

These natural units of human functioning have been labeled action cycles (Bruner, 1982), transactive or behavior cycles (Gibbs, 1979), personal projects (Little, 1983), social episodes (Forgas, 1979), acts (Tolman, 1932), and behavioral episodes (Petrinovich, 1979). Much experimental study of behavior (e.g., research on learning) designs specific action cycles to elicit the behaviors of interest, frequently called experimental trials. We have chosen to call these natural units *behavior episodes* to convey two meanings. We use the term behavior to connote that they include all aspects of human functioning; not just overt actions. The concept of episode connotes an internally coherent event occurring in identifiable contexts that is distinctive and separate although part of a larger series (like an episode of a television series; cf. Kuo, 1967). Moreover, the concept of episode has been used with a similar meaning in the study of some aspects of human functioning (e.g., episodic memory).

Behavior Episodes

A behavior episode (or BE) is a time-limited pattern of behavior occurring in a particular context and has the following defining five attributes:

1. It extends over a period of time and has an identifiable beginning and end.
2. It is cognitively organized and guided by some intention(s) or personal goal(s).
3. It involves a variable pattern of biological, perceptual, cognitive, arousal and action functions selectively organized to try to accomplish the intentions.

4. There is a specific set of environmental circumstances toward which and/or within which the behavior pattern is directed.

5. The pattern terminates when either: (a) the intended consequences occur, (b) some internal or external event preempts attention and activates a different guiding intention, or (c) the evaluation of progress leads to the conclusion that the intended consequences are unobtainable on that occasion.

For example, a grocery shopping trip is a common BE. It begins when the goal of grocery shopping starts organizing ones behavior and ends when one returns home with the groceries. If one is stopped on the way to take an injured person to the hospital, the grocery shopping episode is preempted by a more important goal.

Behavior episodes may be *nested*, that is, complex episodes may be composed of interrelated briefer episodes. For example, the shopping episode is composed of subepisodes such as deciding what store to shop at; getting there; shopping for produce, then meat, etc.; checking out; returning home; and putting the groceries away. Both research and clinical experience reveal that people find it easy and meaningful to represent their daily life in terms of sets of behavior episodes indicating that these are indeed natural units (e.g., Corneal, 1989, 1990; Cornwall, 1990; C. Ford, 1987).

Each behavior episode is a temporary occurrence. If the flow of behavior is organized in terms of such episodes, it follows that such episodes must provide the context for the construction or development of all functional components. The nature of the basic type of generalized functional component will be described next.

Behavior Episode Schemata

As indicated earlier, through information-based self-construction people create a diversity of ideas, knowledge, goals, plans, values, and action patterns from the flow of their experience; however, for these diverse constructions to be of future value, they must be organized in adaptively useful forms. Otherwise they would be like a library with books shelved randomly: much that was potentially useful would be there but efficient access to it would be impossible. To solve this adaptive problem, the behavioral repertoire each person constructs or learns is organized around general types of similar adaptive tasks as manifest in similar behavior episodes (BEs). *BEs may* be considered similar to the extent that they are directed toward similar goals in similar contexts although they may vary considerably in how the person goes about achieving the goals.

During any period of life a person's behavior is guided by a limited set of intentions or goals in a limited set of contexts; for example, attending church, eating in a restaurant, going to the dentist, driving his or her car someplace, or carrying out work tasks. One of the efficiencies of human development is that through repeated experience people construct generalized approaches to accomplishing repetitive episodes. These are not rigidly detailed scripts, but, rather, are broad formats for conducting such episodes with subroutines that permit some variability in the specifics. The old concept of habit is a similar but narrower version of the idea that humans develop a repertoire of relatively automated, complex patterns of functioning to deal effectively with repetitive and routine episodes of living.

Bartlett (1932) and Piaget (1950, 1960) labeled such generalized representations "schemes." Miller, Galanter, and Pribram (1960) used the terms "plans" and "images." Fowler (1977) and Neisser (1976) used the term "schema." We have chosen the term schema because it has been used to refer to more than cognitive processes (e.g., motor schema). Schema is singular and refers to one generalized pattern; schemata is plural and refers to a set of such patterns (see Arbib, 1989, and Arbib & Hesse, 1986, for an extended discussion of schema theory).

Therefore the concept of *behavior episode schemata* (BES) refers to organized, generalized representations of all the basic components of Figure 4.3 as they are relevant to different sets of similar behavior episodes. BES are composed of more than cognitions of which one can become conscious; they combine what are often separately labeled as motor schema, cognitive schema, and affective schema. Moreover, they also include biological components.

For example, driving to work is a repetitive BE for me; I've gone to the same place by the same route for years. As a result I have constructed a highly automated BES (or complex habit) for carrying out that BE. I don't have to plan or think about it. I get in the car and it happens. In fact the BES is so automated that I sometimes find myself driving to work when I started to go somewhere else. It takes a conscious effort to interrupt that BES once it is started.

All patterns start their development from existing components. BES are products of humans' self-regulating, self-constructing functioning.

Therefore the only ones present at birth are those that prototypically develop through interactions of the human genome with the prototypical fetal environment (e.g., reflexes). BES are constructed through differentiating, elaborating, and combining those initial programs and through adding new constructions. When a new BE begins, some existing BES relevant to that episode is activated (e.g., walking, car driving, or attending church services). If the activated BES fits the episode well, the person can carry out the BE efficiently with much less investment of attention and thought than would be necessary with an unfamiliar episode.

When an unfamiliar BE begins, some BES in one's existing repertoire will be activated, tried, and revised to make it "work." For example, imagine that you have been lost and have not eaten for several days. You find a cottage, but the people there do not understand your language; therefore you cannot verbally ask for food. How could you construct an alternate BES that would work in that situation?

BES are organized hierarchically, so complex BES can be constructed from component BES. In addition, because BES components are to some extent functionally autonomous (e.g., certain movement patterns; concepts), new BES can be constructed by selecting and recombining components from existing BES. For example, to deal with the above eating BE, one likely approach would be to activate an "eating BES" and pantomime eating, which is a universal kind of human BE. In addition, one might point at visible food or locations where food might be stored. In other words, one would combine relevant components from several BES.

BES IN PRACTICE: UNDERSTANDING PERSONALITY

So the "what" of development includes not only development of the component structures and functions represented in Figure 4.3, but also the development of generalized, flexible, efficient, somewhat automated complex behavioral "programs" (i.e., BES) representing the functioning of a person as a unified entity. The study of the development and operation of a person's BES repertoire provides a basis for the study of personality.

Personality theory seeks to understand the nature of consistencies and changes across time and situations that gives persons their individual identities. The concept of trait has been the dominant form for representing personality. In fact, Buss (1990) asserts "if there is to be a distinct field of study called personality, its central and defining characteristic must be traits." (p .1387). The traditional concept of trait has three serious limitations. First, it is typically defined solely in terms of properties of the person independent of contextual differences, although context features are considered very important in the functioning of traits. Second, its content typically has been limited to cognitive and affective processes. Third, it connotes a relatively fixed or invariant form.

The concept of BES expands upon the concept of trait to overcome all three of those limitations. It includes context characteristics in the unit itself (i.e., it is referenced to a set of similar behavior episodes), and it includes sensoriperceptual, motoric, and biological processes as well. Moreover, it is anchored to a specific, observable functional unit—the behavior episode—that can be defined and observed in naturalistic settings or experimentally designed and manipulated. Finally, it encompasses the typical flexibility of human behavior by including optional subroutines within the general form. By elaborating the concept of trait to be similar in content, form, and function to the concept of BES, the fields of personality theory and development could be linked, providing significant strength to both.

When Does Development Occur?

The just completed summary of what can develop makes it clear that some kind of development probably occurs throughout life; but we need a more precise answer to the question of "when?" Figure 4.3 represents a person as a complex, dynamic organization of many kinds of structural and functional components. The components do not all develop at the same time or rate, although they must develop in harmony with one another. So a more precise form of the question "when" would be to ask when different aspects of each component develop and when various kinds of complex patterns (e.g., organ systems; BES) develop. In fact most past research on development is organized around the study of component structures and processes (e.g., physical growth and maturation; cognitive development). Figure 4.3 could be used as a useful heuristic for future efforts to review and synthesize existing evidence concerning different aspects of development. That task is beyond the scope of this book. Distinguishing between material-energy-based development and information-based development and how the two interact would also be useful.

Material-Energy-Based Development

Because biological structures and processes make psychological and action functions possible, they have to develop prior to or in synchrony with psychological/behavioral development; and they do, as revealed by the study of embryological and fetal development. The embryo and fetus are connected to the mother's blood supply but not her nervous system because embryological and fetal development rests primarily on material-energy exchanges rather than information exchanges with the environment. While there is growing evidence that the fetus can respond somewhat to information (e.g., sounds), information transactions have limited influence on basic fetal development.

Anatomical development and development of basic biological processes continue after birth but are essentially complete after approximately 2 decades, except for some elaborations of the basic structures and processes that can occur in the adult years. For example, dendritic elaboration can continue to occur in significant ways, even in the advanced years of adulthood (Greenough & Green, 1981). Once biological maturity is reached, the major role of material-energy transactions is to maintain and repair biological structures and to fuel the functioning of biological and behavioral processes.

Information-Based Development

Information-based development, that is, psychological and action capability development, begins immediately after birth (although some minimal development of this kind may take place during fetal development); however, this kind of development accelerates rapidly, and a child's behavioral repertoire displays explosive growth during the first 6 years of life.

Information-based development can continue throughout life as long as the biological structures and processes necessary for those behavioral functions continue to operate. An "old dog" can learn "new tricks!" (Baltes, Dittman, Kapli, & Dixon, 1984); however, we have much to learn about how the development of different kinds of behavioral repertoires may facilitate or inhibit further behavioral development. For example, are some kinds of BES relatively so rigid that they greatly restrict potential future learning (e.g., BES with major fear components)? To what extent do arousal processes affect such development? For example, there is some evidence that learning and performance decrements in elderly people are, at least in part, a function of declining efficiency in attentional processes (Schonfield, 1980; Woodruff, 1985). People can use their behavior construction capabilities to build functional components that compensate for damage or deterioration of structural components. For example, a paraplegic artist learned to paint by holding his brushes in his toes rather than his hands.

Development can continue throughout life, but not all kinds of development can have "equal opportunities" for equivalent degrees of change. As Baltes and Baltes (1980) assert, there is, with aging, *selective optimization with compensation*. In other words, people use their self-constructing processes to make the most of what they have and to construct substitutes for the capabilities they have lost. Rehabilitation services and the creation of prosthetics illustrate ways in which the promotion of selective optimization with compensation is accomplished. Similarly neuropsychologists Greenough and Green (1981) stress that with aging only some neural systems are "selectively preserved" for continued growth and dendritic elaboration. We need a clearer understanding of whether there are optimal times for different kinds of behavioral development to prolong different kinds of developmental plasticity as long in life as possible. We hope Developmental Systems Theory will provide a more adequate framework for pursuing such issues concerning developmental possibilities across the life span.

Next Steps

In this chapter we have provided a model representing the content and organization of a person-in-context and have used that model to address questions of "what" can develop and "when" it can develop. In Chapter 5 we will examine the basic issue of the processes of development. We will present proposals about principles of change and use those to deal with the question of how development occurs.

Notes

1. Piaget's (1950, 1960) concept of *sensorimotor schemes* includes a form of imagistic representations; however, the content of *motor schemes* themselves are not represented in forms that can appear as conscious cognitions, as can imagistic concepts constructed from sensory processes.

2. The task of representing patterns of development in different component domains (e.g., motor development, cognitive development) is not addressed in this book. That task remains to be done.

CHAPTER FIVE

Processes and Dynamics
in Developmental Systems Theory

IN A BOOK presenting her structural/behavioral model of development, Horowitz (1987) states "The overarching scientific question about behavioral development is: 'How is the behavioral repertoire of the human organism acquired?' " (p. 62). This chapter addresses that question by identifying and describing basic change processes and dynamics that can generate the diverse developmental outcomes observed in humans. To begin our discussion we present several examples of human development and functioning, chosen to represent various phases of life and aspects of persons. These examples will be used later to illustrate the operation of developmental processes.

An otherwise normal baby is born without arms. A malnourished, growth-stunted child is adopted, receives love, healthy nutrition, and care, and, in a few years, is of normal size and health compared with children of similar age, gender, and background.

A talented, young athlete in an impoverished, illiterate family was unable to read. A teacher who also coached the basketball team took an interest in her and told her that unless she learned to read, she could not be on the team. She learned to read, became a star player, and graduated from high school. She went to college, became an all-American basketball player, earned a degree in business, and became a successful business executive. She married and had a child. Her husband and child were killed in an auto accident. She became angry and depressed, performed badly on her job, and was fired. She was hospitalized for treatment of a suicidal depressive episode and, when discharged, moved back to live with her husband's parents. She briefly tried three other jobs. She sought out, dated, and became engaged to a old boyfriend, but broke it off. She moved to an apartment with a Catholic girlfriend who talked her into attending an Easter mass. During the service she was deeply moved and felt a peace come over her she had not experienced for years. She decided to give her life to Christ, became a Catholic, entered a nunnery, became a nun, a skilled teacher, and nurse, and devoted much of her life to helping the homeless.

A white man with strong racial prejudices was assigned to a work team with several African-American men and women. These men and women consistently produced superior work performances. Two of them covered for the prejudiced man when he "fouled up" on the job. Moreover, when his wife was ill, they brought food and ran errands to help the family through that difficult period. Despite all of that positive evidence, the man stubbornly maintained his prejudiced views.

Development Described as a
Sequence of Outcomes

Professional practitioners and theorists typically discuss change and development in terms of outcomes, as illustrated above, rather than in terms of the processes by which such outcomes are generated. For example, when psychotherapists discuss the process of therapy they usually refer either to outcomes (e.g., "reduce anxiety") or to therapist methods for producing outcomes (e.g., psychoanalytic or nondirective interviewing). They seldom identify the processes by which such methods produce change (Ford & Urban, 1963).

Similarly most theories of development focus on the substance or content of what develops (i.e., patterns of outcomes) rather than the "how" of development (Horowitz, 1987). For example, they may describe "stages" of development (cf. Lerner, 1989), or normative patterns of developmental outcomes (e.g., Gesell, 1946; McGraw, 1935).

Sometimes developmental theorists focus on changes in organizational form, regardless of content. For example, Werner's (1957) orthogenetic principle of development asserts that "development proceeds from a state of relative globality and lack of differentiation to a state of increasing differentiation, articulation, and hierarchic integration" (p. 126), and this applies to all aspects of a person. If development is defined as change from a less organized to a more complexly organized entity or state, then change outcomes that reduced organizational complexity would not be considered developmental change. Terms such as differentiation and integration can also be used as labels for processes, but then their operation must be described, and the orthogenetic principle, for example, does not do that.

Developmentalists also discuss factors that influence development such as family life and socioeconomic conditions (Horowitz, 1987); however, they seldom discuss the processes by which those factors exert their influence on developmental outcomes. A few do. For example, Piaget (1950, 1970) proposed three interrelated processes: assimilation, accommodation, and equilibration; and Bijou and Baer (1978) discuss developmental processes in terms of Skinner's (1938; Ferster & Skinner, 1958) operant conditioning principles.

A full understanding of human development requires not only a framework for understanding the content or outcomes of development, but also one for understanding the processes and dynamics by which developmental outcomes are generated. Chapters 3 and 4, in discussing DST's metamodel and operational model for human development, make it clear that developmental outcomes can vary among people. Therefore no attempt is made here to catalogue all the possible developmental outcomes. Rather, this chapter's purpose is to present DST's proposals about the processes of development. The proposed processes must operate at the level of component structures and functions and in terms of complex person-environment patterns.

Outcomes, Processes, and Dynamics

Because the distinction between outcomes and processes has been emphasized, it is essential that the meaning of those concepts be specified. We propose an analogy between the concepts of *statics* and *dynamics* in the physical sciences and the concepts of *outcomes* and *processes* with regard to human development.

In physics *statics* is the study of the conditions under which bodies remain stable, that is, either at rest or in consistent movement, such as the trajectory of a bullet. It is the study of stability or constancy rather than of change. In living systems such as humans, biological structures that remain stable (e.g., stop growing) or functional patterns that are relatively stable, persistent, and recurring (e.g., are habitual) are referred to as *steady states* (as discussed in earlier chapters). *Developmental outcomes are new steady states that have resulted from some kind of change processes* (Featherman & Lerner, 1985). Therefore the study of developmental outcomes (steady states) is analogous to the field of statics, that is, it is the study of stable conditions. Much developmental research is the study of the"statics" of the human condition in the form of trying to identify the normative steady-state structural or functional characteristics of people of different ages. Presenting an age-graded sequence of developmental outcomes (e.g., as do typical "stage" theories) still does not deal with developmental processes because it does not describe the dynamics by which one steady state is changed to become the next steady state.

In physics *dynamics* is the study of bodies as they move and change and the way these changes are influenced by applied forces. Thermodynamics considers the relationship of heat to energy and the ways heat may be transformed into mechanical work and vice versa. Therefore, in contrast to statics, dynamics is the study of processes of change, for example, change in spatial position, rate of movement, or organization of material entities. *A process is a pattern of activity that produces some outcome.* Thus a process is a description of the dynamics by which particular outcomes are produced. *Developmental processes, then, would be those material/energy-based and information-based activities that operate on and within existing steady states to produce different steady states through modifications, elaborations, or transformations.*

Understanding the dynamics of change provides the essential knowledge base for understanding how people may change (e.g., how developmental outcomes are or can be generated), and for designing ways of helping people change and develop (e.g., for designing socializing, educative, or therapeutic interventions). Therefore a specification of developmental processes dynamics is essential. That objective is addressed next.

Three Types of Change-Related Processes

DST proposes that there are three basic change-related processes: stability maintenance, incremental change, and transformational change. All three are derived from systems theory and supported with knowledge in the developmental sciences. If there are some basic processes underlying human development, then one would expect that different disciplinary approaches to understanding development would converge upon the same ideas. That convergence was found to exist in the fields of evolutionary biology and genetics, developmental biology, and psychological and behavioral development and learning. (See Ford, 1987, Chapters 4 and 5, for a more extended discussion). Table 5.1 summarizes the discipline-based concepts in relationship to each type of process. Each process and illustrative discipline-based concepts will be briefly discussed.

STABILITY MAINTENANCE

In the DST operational model summarized in Chapter 4, stability maintenance is accomplished through negative feedback processes. All fields in Table 5.1 agree that any organism must maintain its integrity as a structural-functional unit if it is to remain alive and adaptive. (See assumptions 1 and 1a in Table 3.1.) The more complex the organism, that is, the greater the number of component structures and functions and the more elaborate their organization, the more complicated is the task of maintaining unity. The processes of living (e.g., energy expenditures, obtaining food, and social interactions), along with the environmental transactions that serve them, have as one consequence perturbations of the existing states or organization of the organism. Because such perturbations threaten the unitary integrity of the organism if permitted to elaborate themselves unchecked, every organism has processes by which it defends itself against, overcomes, or adapts to such perturbations. These processes maintain or restore the organism's internal organizational coherence and environmental relationships so that it can continue to function as a unit. Relevant concepts in each field will be briefly described.

TABLE 5.1 A Summary of the Three Kinds of Change-Related Processes Identified in Each of Several Fields Studying Development of Organisms and Illustrative Concepts in Each Field That Represent Each Kind of Change Process

Disciplines or Field	Stability Maintenance	Incremental Change	Transformational Change
Evolutionary Theory	Morphological Stasis	Gradualism Doctrine	Punctuated Equilibrium
Developmental Biology	Homeostasis	Differentiation Elaboration	Metamorphosis Critical Period
Learning and Development	Habit Assimilation Defense Mechanisms	Conditioning Accommodation Motor Skill Development	Insight Emotional Decomposition Faith Healing

Morphological Stasis

In evolutionary theory, stability-maintaining processes are referred to as morphological stasis. Fossil evidence indicates that many species remain relatively unchanged structurally throughout their history despite considerable environmental change and stress on the species (Eldridge & Gould, 1972; Stanley, 1979). Fossils provide direct evidence of stasis only with regard to the skeletal elements and their organization, but do not provide evidence about the evolutionary stability of both structural and functional unity. Breeding experiments (Jackson & Cheetham, 1990), however, reveal that fossil evidence provides a sound indicator of both structural and functional species stasis.

Homeostasis

In biology *homeostasis* refers to the body's propensity to maintain basic biological processes (e.g., body temperature) at a relatively constant level despite perturbing influences (e.g., changes in room temperature). *Developmental homeostasis* refers to the fact that embryonic and fetal development can proceed in a species-typical way despite considerable variation in the organism's environment. For example, it takes a fairly major deviation in the prototypical in utero developmental niche to produce some developmental anomaly in a human fetus.

Habit and Assimilation

In the literature on learning and psychological and behavioral development, the concept of habit refers to a heavily practiced functional pattern that occurs relatively automatically when activated despite variations in the conditions under which it occurs. Developmental theorists such as Baldwin (1894), Pascual-Leone (1976), and Piaget (1950, 1970) use the concept of assimilation to label circumstances in which new information is interpreted so that it fits within existing cognitive and behavior patterns just as food is transformed to serve the existing structure and dynamics of body cells. Thus the nature and organization of the existing functional units are maintained. For example, a child perceives a small, furry animal and calls it "kitty," thereby assimilating the current percept into an existing concept rather than altering the concept or creating a new one.

Defense Mechanisms

Freud's (1949) concept of defense mechanisms refers to behaviors by which a person protects existing psychological behavior patterns in the face of conditions that might disrupt them. For example, rationalization is a method for justifying or defending existing attitudes, traits, habits, behavior patterns or their sequelae by withholding, misrepresenting, or falsifying relevant information, by blaming an incidental cause, or by comparing oneself with others in ways that excuse one's behavior or its consequences.

INCREMENTAL CHANGE THROUGH SELF-CONSTRUCTION

In Chapter 4 the DST operational model proposes that biological and psychological/behavioral self-construction processes are the source of incremental change. If all an organism could do was to protect the status quo, its adaptive flexibility would be limited to its initial states. Change would not be possible. Therefore system processes have evolved for altering initial states, and they differ among different kinds of living systems. In humans both biological growth through differentiation and elaboration and learning through repeated experiences produce changes that are incremental in character. They occur by starting with some existing characteristic(s) and then refining them to make them larger and/or more complex or combining and/or transforming them to create more elaborate characteristics. The relevant concepts in Table 5.1 will be briefly described.

The Gradualism Doctrine

Darwin's (1859) gradualism doctrine represents incremental change processes in evolutionary theory. It proposed that occasionally some random change occurred in an organism that gave it a survival and reproductive advantage in its environmental niche. Its offspring then retained that advantageous characteristic. Succeeding generations experienced additional random, advantageous changes. Such changes gradually accumulated until the old species was transformed into a new one. Growing knowledge of genetics led to an elaboration called the modern synthesis. It proposed additional ways, besides mutations, that new characteristics might occur, but did not change the principle that new species emerge gradually through the progressive accumulation of particular changes.

Differentiation and Elaboration

As knowledge grew in developmental biology, it became apparent that organisms developed biologically through successive changes in existing structures that preserved their basic nature and organization. Through differentiation during development there is an increase in amount, complexity, and organization of existing cells, tissues, and their functional capabilities. Through anabolic processes, new structures and functional capabilities are elaborated by transforming primitive raw materials (e.g., food) and using them for new construction.

Conditioning

Some learning theories propose that incremental changes occur through processes labeled conditioning (e.g., see Bijou, 1978; Bijou & Baer, 1961). There are two types:

1. Through temporal contiguity, existing behavior patterns may come to be elicited by different stimuli, a process called classical conditioning.
2. Existing behavior patterns may become modified, elaborated, combined, or extinguished (i.e., "shaped") as a result of their contingent relationship to consequences, a process called instrumental or operant conditioning.

The conditioning process requires multiple "trials" to produce permanent behavior change, so the permanent functional change emerges gradually through a series of similar experiences. In practical applications conditioning approaches are often termed behavior modification.

Accommodation

Baldwin (1894) proposed that some process was necessary to alter old habits when they were not sufficiently effective. He called that process accommodation, and both Piaget (1950, 1970) and Pascual-Leone (1976) adopted it in their developmental theorizing. When new information or experiences cannot be assimilated into existing cognitive or behavior patterns, then the only alternative is to change the behavior pattern to accommodate the new information or circumstances. This is proposed to occur through a series of efforts in which different possibilities are tried until a new, more effective pattern that will accommodate the discrepant circumstances is constructed.

Motor Skill Development

Specialists in motor behavior (e.g., physical educators, dance instructors, musicians, and athletic coaches) have constructed considerable understanding about how skilled movement patterns are developed. In general they are constructed through *practice with feedback*. Three types of amendment-producing feedback are involved:

1. kinesthetic or response-produced feedback results from movement of muscle fibers and joints;
2. feedback among neural components involved in movement, such as the motor cortex and cerebellum, sometimes called corollary discharge; and
3. knowledge of results of behavior-environment interactions.

Practice utilizes such feedback to change motor patterns in three ways:

1. it eliminates unneeded movements and increases the fluency so that the movement unfolds at the right rate with precision and accuracy and without wasted motion;

2. it improves the rhythm, timing, and varying intensity of the movement components; and

3. it increases generative flexibility, which means the performance can be smoothly altered in a variety of ways to appropriately deal with variability in the performance context.

TRANSFORMATIONAL CHANGE

Not all change occurs in a continuous, incremental way. Some kinds of change involve a relatively rapid transformation of an existing state or pattern into a qualitatively different pattern through some reorganization of existing states, often accompanied by further elaboration. Therefore new states resulting from transformational change are sometime called discontinuities in development. Once the reorganized pattern is established, it may be protected with stability-maintaining processes or differentiated and elaborated through incremental-change processes. The DST operational model in Chapter 4 describes positive feedback as one potential source of transformational change. Transformational change may occur in some component structure or process (e.g., transformation of a belief) or may involve many system components (e.g., personality transformations). Relevant concepts in Table 5.1 will be briefly described.

Punctuated Equilibrium

Transformational change is represented in evolutionary theory by the concept of punctuated equilibrium (Eldridge & Gould, 1972). A growing body of evidence indicates that many species remain relatively unchanged during long periods of time and then new species appear relatively suddenly, without signs of the successive incremental change that should be present according to the gradualism doctrine (e.g., Williamson, 1981). In other words, discontinuities appear to exist in evolution. Earlier, Goldschmidt (1940) had argued that the first step in macroevolution required some other evolutionary method besides "sheer accumulation of micromutations," and Deutsch (1951) asserted that evolution should involve the possibility of "sudden change and genuine novelty" involving both internal change within the system as well as its interaction with the environment. Several theorists argued that some form of developmental homeostasis had to account for the morphological stasis of most species, and that speciation probably started with some developmental disruption and instability during speciation events (Levin, 1970; Mayr, 1963; Waddington, 1976).

Metamorphosis

In biology there are many kinds of physical transformations that occur relatively suddenly in various organisms during biological development, such as the transformation of a tadpole to a frog or of the caterpillar to the butterfly. The concept of metamorphosis represents such transformational changes in form or function.

Critical Period

The concept of critical period has been used with regard to many aspects of human development, but it was borrowed from biology (Colombo, 1982; Kagan, 1966). In biology it is a time when a condition or event has maximal influence on developing physiological processes, but negligible effects at other times. Times of transition from one form of organization to another appear to be particularly critical periods. For example, in embryonic development the transformations of the fertilized ovum to the morula, the morula to the blastula or blastocyst, and the blastocyst differentiation into three tissue layers, called gastrulation, are times of danger. The highest death rate among humans occurs during these embryonic periods when small perturbations can have drastic impacts. As organ systems begin to differentiate out of the three tissue layers, additional vulnerable transition periods occur. For example, the ingestion of certain kinds of substances by the mother can distort fetal development if they are present at times when the embryo or fetus is preparing for or making the transition to some different form; these same substances may have no significant effect on the fetus if present at other times.

Insight

This is a form of learning in which a problem solving activity involves: (a) a period of framing the problem and identifying elements that need to be brought together to form a solution; (b) interruption of activity while there is attention to and examination of relevant elements; (c) a period of struggle to create coherent relationships among previously unrelated elements; (d) a sudden solution in which all the elements are combined into a new pattern that solves the problem, often accompanied by positive emotion ("Aha!"); and (e) easy repetition of the newly discovered pattern and its use in new situations. In effect, the elements are first seen as a disordered array, but after a period of struggle a coherent, useful pattern of organization among the elements is suddenly recognized or created.

Emotional Decompensation

Not all transformational change yields elaborative results. For example, in psychopathology the concept of emotional decompensation represents a relatively sudden transformation from a coherent pattern to a disorganized pattern. If a person has been in a persistently high state of emotional arousal, such as fear, additional instigators of that emotion may precipitate a sudden disorganization of typical behavior patterns. A panic attack is a classic example. It is characterized by extreme fear and purposeless, highly varied, frantic, often uncoordinated actions, frequently accompanied by physiological disruptions such as loss of bladder and bowel control.

Such disorganized states are intolerable to the person, and they are typically resolved by a sudden and often dramatic reorganization into a new pattern, sometimes called a "crucial shift" by psychopathologists. For example, a woman had been experiencing great distress for months because her mother was dying of cancer, she was overloaded on her job, there was continuous and often extreme conflict and discord in her work situation, and her interpersonal relationships were disrupted. One day she "came unglued," accidentally bumped her head, and suddenly was unable to remember who she was, did not know her mother or husband, and could not remember her job skills. The emotional distress, however, was relieved by this personality reorganization. She "lost her memory," but she was no longer miserable. In general the form the reorganized state will take when such disorganization occurs is unpredictable. In this example the reorganization produced a dissociated state or amnesia, but it could have produced a suicide, a psychotic episode, or a religious conversion experience and the start of a new life.

Faith Healing

Intense positive emotional states may also precipitate sudden reorganizations in functional patterns as illustrated by the phenomenon of faith healing. Such "spiritual healing" involves a person with some bodily, behavioral, or psychological difficulty deeply believing that they can be cured through divine intervention and participating in some situation, ceremony, or ritual that is personally very moving. When successful, the result is an often sudden reduction of a person's symptoms, at least for a period of time. Some form of faith healing rituals has existed in many cultures and religions as illustrated in the Christian Bible by descriptions of the astonishing ministries of Jesus and his apostles. Another version of the transforming power of deep faith and emotionally charged religious experiences is the relatively sudden transformation in individuals' life-styles when they experience a new and intense religious commitment, that is, they are "saved" or "born again."

Conditions That Facilitate and Constrain
Change and Development

The preceding discussion demonstrates interdisciplinary consensus among developmental sciences about three basic kinds of change-related processes: stability-maintaining, incremental-change, and transformational-change processes. The operational model of DST will now be used to describe more fully the three kinds of processes. The explanation will lean upon the concepts of organization and disorganization, system perturbations, negative and positive feedback, feedforward, steady states, componentized and hierarchical organization, environmental transactions, behavior episodes (BE), and behavior episode schemata (BES). These concepts have been discussed in Chapter 4 (for a more complete discussion see Chapters 3 and 5 in Ford, 1987). First, however, a set of propositions, summarized in Table 5.2, will be reviewed concerning the conditions that both limit and make possible change and development.

Change and development always occur in something, some place, at some time. Therefore, to put the discussion of change-related processes in

TABLE 5.2 A Summary of Six DST Propositions About Characteristics
That Constrain and Facilitate Change and Development

I. Biological, psychological and behavioral functioning is continuous and
always occurs in the present.
II. A person always functions as a unit in a context.
III. Organismic boundary conditions define current developmental possibilities.
IV. Environmental boundary conditions define currently available develop-
mental pathways.
V. Development always starts with what currently exists.
VI. Changes in current states are always constrained by a hierarchy of selection
operations.

---

context, it is necessary to summarize certain facilitating and constraining characteristics of person, place, and time. More detailed
support for these propositions may be found in Chapters 3 and 4 of
this volume and in Ford (1987).

Proposition I: Biological, psychological, and behavioral functions are
continuous and always occur in the present.

It is not necessary to ask why a person is behaving because behaving
is a property of life. (Here behavior refers to all biological, psychological,
and action functions and their organization in complex patterns.) Awake
or asleep, at work or play, alone or with others, in motion or at rest, a
person is always functioning as long as he or she is alive. Therefore the
basic question is "Why is the person behaving one way rather than
another in a particular set of circumstances?"

In Chapter 3 it was emphasized that to influence one another
directly, objects or events had to interact. That requires spatial-temporal
contiguity, that is, entities have to be at the same place at the same time.
Temporally separate conditions called past and future can only influence a person's behavior through surrogates in the present (e.g.,
through memory or imagination). Similarly, spatially distant conditions
can influence a person only through spatially present surrogates (e.g., a
letter or telephone call from a loved one, the rays of the sun impinging
upon a person). Therefore understanding a person's behavior requires
understanding current states of functioning in his or her current
contexts and identifying consistency or change requires comparing
sequential states. All learning theories emphasize spatial-temporal

contiguity as a necessary condition for learning. Culture influences behavior and behavior change through its proximal manifestations in a person's immediate environment because culture "is a profound and pervasive organizer" of patterns of social interaction or other environmental stimulation and of definitions of appropriate goals and values (Horowitz, 1987).

Proposition II: A person always functions as a unit in a context.

In Chapters 3 and 4 a person was represented as an interdependent hierarchical organization of specialized structural-functional components that must function as a unit to survive, behave adaptively, and develop. Because a person is an open system, his or her unitary nature and dynamics are necessarily a function of continual material/energy and information transactions with the environment. Therefore the content and dynamic unity of the flow of a person's behavior is best represented as a series of internally coherent behavior episodes (BEs) in varying environments.

It follows that *the conditions that produce change must occur within specific BEs.* For example, Glaser and Bassok (1989) reviewed the literature concerning learning theory and instruction and found that all instructional approaches agreed that learning occurs in the context of working on "specific problems." There was agreement that knowledge is not acquired as a set of general propositions, but, rather, that personal knowledge grows through "active application during problem solving" in relationship to "specific goals." Similarly, Case (1985) asserts that development is a process in which strategies are first mastered in "highly contextualized" and "socially facilitated" situations. The development of motor skills requires repetitive practice of the skill in relevant situations (Gallistel, 1980; Shaffer, 1980). In other words, development occurs in the context of specific BEs.

Proposition III: Organismic boundary conditions define current developmental possibilities.

The way a person can function and change in any BE is constrained and facilitated, but not fully determined, by his or her personal characteristics at that time. (See Chapter 4.) The state of the person's body and biological processes, the behavioral repertoire he or she has available, and his or her objectives at that moment facilitate some potential ways of behaving and constrain others. For example, a person paralyzed from the waist down cannot walk, so that method of movement is constrained as a behavioral possibility. A person who has learned to drive a car has elaborated his or her mobility possibilities. The design of training programs for producing complex skills emphasizes that meaningful practice depends on the learner's readiness to learn, including both maturational/physical and psychological readiness, for example, the person's understanding of what is to be learned and his or her commitment to try (Singer, 1975). As emphasized in Chapter 3, each person differs from every other as a result of his or her genetic, environmental, and experiential histories. Therefore people differ in their organismic boundary conditions, and those conditions change for individuals across each of their life courses.

Proposition IV: Environmental boundary conditions define currently available developmental pathways.

The environment in which a person is behaving supports and facilitates some possibilities and constrains others. (See Chapter 3.) For example, an astronaut can "fly" through the air in the gravity-free environment of space, but cannot do so on earth. A child in a well-to-do family will have opportunities available that a child from a poverty-level family will not have and vice versa. A child in a fatherless family has a somewhat different set of opportunities and constraints than does a child living with both parents. The evolution of characteristics with which human infants enter the world facilitated an adaptive person-environment fit in the pervasive properties of earth's terrestrial and humans' social environment (e.g., gravity; water; cycles of light and darkness; plant and animal life; other humans). Other aspects of the environment are not universal (e.g., cultures and families differ).

Therefore many aspects of individuals' environments vary both from moment to moment and across the life course, both contingent upon and independently of peoples' actions. As a result the timing of different kinds of environmental conditions in the developmental pathway of a child may vary, and this variation can facilitate or constrain different kinds of development. For one child the environment may provide opportunities before the child has the characteristics to utilize them, but for another it may occur at a time when it makes a major difference. For example, a set of encyclopedias given to a child who cannot read will have little effect, while it may significantly facilitate the development of a child who reads well.

In short, the *match* or *fit* between organismic and environmental boundary conditions is important in shaping a person's developmental pathway (see assumptions 6 and 6a in Table 3.1); however, both kinds of facilitating and constraining conditions vary and change, both as a result of and independently of a person's own efforts. This results in a dynamic flow of new opportunities and constraints throughout life. Therefore new developments are possible in every phase of life (Baltes, 1987; Brim & Kagan, 1980), but the nature of the possibilities will differ as organismic and environmental boundary conditions change (Lerner, 1984).

Proposition V: Development always starts with what exists.

How is it possible to change something while still retaining its unity? Evolutionary processes operate so that change always occurs by elaborating, revising, or reorganizing what already exists. Individual development operates in the same way, and this is true from conception to death. For example, it is species-typical of newborn humans that they perceive the sensory world "discriminatively and preferentially," have information processsing capabilities that are species-typical "in their operation, selectivity, and organization," have arousal mechanisms that activate selective "attentional and search behaviors," and have an array of "hard-wired" sensorimotor responses through which they can interact selectively with the environment (Horowitz, 1987; see also Mussen, 1983).

Proposition VI: Changes in current states are always constrained by a hierarchy of selection processes.

In ontogeny only changes that permit continued coherent organization can occur. This means that for any temporary variation in a person's structural or functional characteristics to become a permanent change it must meet the tests of a hierarchy of selection processes. First, the variation must somehow fit the biological person. Second, it must fit the psychological person. Third, it must fit the action person. Fourth it must also fit the context. Some patterns that develop may look maladaptive to an "outsider," for example, compulsions or neurotic states, but such atypical patterns have an internal coherence and some functional utility as illustrated by the example used earlier of the woman with amnesia and the various defense mechanisms identified by Freud.

Because of the componentized, hierarchical, structural-functional organization of a person, the set of tests occurs hierarchically. For example, in embryonic/fetal development, changes in cellular specialization must first be acceptable to the cell itself, then to the tissue of which it is a component, then to the organ and organ system of which it is a part, and finally to the organism in its developmental context. Similarly, a cognitive change must first be acceptable to the belief system of which it is a part and then to the other aspects of behavior episode schemata (BES) of which it is a component.

There are four possible outcomes of any specific change, depending on how it traverses the hierarchy of selection operations:

1. A person may die because he or she cannot accommodate the change (e.g., cancer or suicide).
2. A person or his or her body may reject or suppress the change and thereby maintain existing organization (e.g., an infection may be overcome; new coworkers may be rejected to maintain prejudiced beliefs).
3. Aspects of a person may change so that the change is compatible with other aspects of the person, thereby producing a revised state (e.g., a person who becomes blind may learn to read Braille).
4. A person's relationships with his or her environment may be altered, and through such changes disruptions may be accommodated (e.g., a paralyzed person may become mobile with a wheelchair).

Outcomes 3 and 4 often must occur together. For example, as a child becomes a young adult, others must alter their views and actions toward them. Or a person who becomes a quadriplegic can only survive if his or her social environment assumes responsibilities for him or her that the person is no longer competent to assume (e.g., personal cleanliness; obtaining food).

The six propositions in Table 5.2 make it clear why a person cannot and does not develop in unlimited directions, that is., there is only relative plasticity. (See assumptions 4, 4a, and 4b in Table 3.1.) Development results from the shaping or transformation of the existing system-in-context and must conform to its basic continuing components, organization, and "rules."

Mechanisms of Change and Development

A person may somehow be or behave differently on some specific occasion. For such changes to be manifest in future occasions, however, there must be some kind of mechanism(s) by which the change is transported from one occasion to another. There are two types of such mechanisms: one is material/energy-based or biological and the other is information-based or psychological and behavioral.

BIOLOGICAL MECHANISMS

Some changes are a function of material/energy transactions between persons and their environments or between biological components within a person. For example, changes may occur because of what a person eats or drinks, because of some physical trauma, because some gland increases or decreases its output of essential hormones, or because of use or disuse of some components. Material/energy-based changes can be transported to future BEs only through material/energy based mechanisms. These are either changes in biological structures (e.g., a child grows taller or loses an eye) or changes in biological processes (e.g., a person's steady state blood pressure changes to a new level or the kinds or amounts of hormones being produced change).

PSYCHOLOGICAL-BEHAVIORAL MECHANISMS

Some changes are a function of information-based processes. For example, learning new motor skills, creating new ideas, or acquiring new social-emotional patterns are information-based changes, that is, they result from "experience" and thought processes. Information-based changes can be transported to future BEs only through information-based mechanisms or "structures." In cognitive and developmental psychology, the concept of structure refers to a "unit of organization" that exerts "functional control" over behavior (Horowitz, 1987). As described in Chapter 4, behavior episode schemata (BES) provide that mechanism in humans. A diversity of cognitive theorists have made similar proposals (e.g., Bain, 1855; Fowler, 1977; Kreitler & Kreitler, 1976; Neisser, 1976). In his theory of cognitive development, Case (1985) called learned behavior-organizing schemata executive control structures.

The concept of *scheme* or *schema* has been used by a diversity of scholars to refer to an organization of certain aspects of humans. For example, cognitive schema refer to habitual patterns of cognitive functioning (Baldwin, 1894; Piaget, 1950, 1970), and motor schema to habitual patterns of sensorimotor functioning (cf. Stelmach & Requin, 1980). Some other definitions imply a broader conception (e.g., Pascual-Leone, 1976), but most do not. In contrast the concept of BES described in Chapter 4 represents an organization of all the component process in Figure 4.3, including the biological ones, to deal with certain types of tasks in certain kinds of contexts.

This distinction is important because it means that BES are composed of both "explicit knowledge" (the cognitive and affective aspects) and "tacit knowledge" (the sensorimotor and biological aspects). The former can be consciously dealt with, but the latter cannot appear in perceptible form in consciousness, except for the observable outputs. It is the integrated combination of all these aspects of a person that makes possible individuals' unitary functioning in their contexts. Some might think that sensorimotor components are not present in some habitual patterns such as sleeping or thinking, but that would be incorrect. For example, sensorimotor functioning must occur to maintain postural stability while sitting and thinking or to permit lying down and sleeping. (In fact, some sleep-related problems are sensorimotor in character, such as teeth grinding or snoring.)

Behavior episodes may be similar but they are never identical. Therefore the BES constructed as a generalized approach to dealing with similar BEs will include both a prototypical functional pattern and optional components representing variations relevant to differences in the set of BEs from which the BES was constructed. This is because more than one pattern of behavior can produce the desired outcome. Therefore each BES includes a set of possible strategy and performance combinations rather than just one "best way." In computer programming such alternate components are sometimes called subroutines. The ability to shift from one action option to another in the same BES is called *generative flexibility* by motor behavior theorists. Also, as discussed in Chapter 4, several "smaller" BES can become combined to create a more elaborate BES.

Types of Behavior Episodes and Behavior Episode Schemata

It is useful to classify the diversity of human BEs into three basic types, based on the aspects of Figure 4.3 that are emphasized. They are called instrumental, observational, and thinking episodes. (See Ford, 1987, for more detail.) All episodes include every component of Figure 4.3 in some form; however, they differ in the nature of the content of each component.

Instrumental episodes involve the use of actions and communications to influence the environment to produce some desired consequence. In *observational episodes*, the information collection functions are emphasized, while motoric and communicative actions are restricted. The primary focus of observational episodes is to collect and understand information from the environment, rather than to influence the environment. Years ago Heidbreder (1924) referred to instrumental and observational episodes as "participant" and "spectator" behaviors, respectively. In learning theory the construction of BES from observational episodes has been referred to as latent learning, modeling, imitation, and social learning. In *thinking episodes* both information collection and motoric and communicative actions are inhibited. The primary focus is on manipulating and organizing existing cognitive representations. Thinking episodes might be thought of as *simulated* in the sense that cognitive problem-solving activity often involves imagining possible actions and their possible contingencies and consequences before actually selecting and implementing a course of action.

Complex behavior episodes are often composed of subepisode combinations of these different types. For example, a child may watch a parent do something (an observational episode) and then later try to remember how he or she did it (a thinking or simulated episode), and then try to do it himself or herself (an instrumental episode). Of course the BES constructed from sets of BEs will manifest the same three types. In summary, for any change to manifest itself in future BEs it must either occur as an enduring change in biological structures or processes or in a generalized functional pattern called a BES. Changes in biological processes may be general (e.g., changes in height and weight as an infant grows; the hormonal changes that occur at puberty) or specific to a particular BES (e.g., the sweaty palms, dry mouth, and racing heart whenever the person has to speak in public).

Operation of BEs and BES

When a new BE occurs that is similar to previously experienced BEs, one or more BES previously constructed from similar BEs are potentiated for use in organizing behavior in the current BE. Lashley's (1942) neurological version of this same idea asserts that "a complex of stimuli" produces an "organization of nervous activity" in which some components become "dominant for reaction" while others become "ineffective."

Because people's behavior occurs in a continual flow from one BE to another, and because BEs vary in the extent to which they are similar to one another, the different BES constructed by a person will have some similar properties. Therefore, in any new BE, several somewhat similar BES are likely to be potentiated for possible use. This means that if the dominant BES doesn't work in the BE, other relevant ones are often readily available as alternatives, or components of others can be combined with the dominant one.

Of course the two types of mechanisms interact. Because psychological and behavioral functioning are made possible by biological structures and processes, any change carried on a biological mechanism can affect behavior in future episodes (e.g., certain changes in neurochemical functioning precipitated by a brain tumor can precipitate a depressive episode). Similarly, any change in BES may precipitate changes in biological structures and processes through the demands placed upon them by the behavior the BES organizes (e.g., weight lifting can increase muscle size).

So far in this chapter we have distinguished change outcomes from change processes, identified three basic kinds of change-related processes supported by diverse empirical and theoretical evidence, described key facilitating and constraining conditions under which they operate, and described mechanisms of development. We will now combine this set of ideas with those summarized in Figure 4.3 to discuss in more detail how each process operates.

Living Systems Dynamics and Developmental Processes

The LSF model of a person summarized in Chapter 4 provides the framework for discussing developmental dynamics. Figure 5.1 is a simplified version of the DST model summarized in Figure 4.3 and will be used in this discussion. Enduring elaborative and decremental changes occur through the operation of the same basic processes. While the primary focus here is on developmental changes,

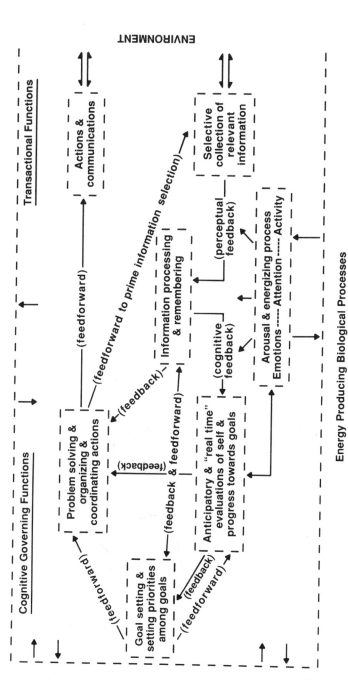

Figure 5.1. A simplified protoypical representation of a person as a self-constructing living system. Cognitive processes perform governing functions to organize and regulate the flow of selective action and communication processes to produce intended and desired consequences from the environment. These processes are influenced by arousal processes, and monitored with perceptual processes, to regulate the flow of the behavioral episode.

169

the processes should be understood as applying to decremental changes as well.

The key idea underlying DST's proposals about change processes is that change is a product of efforts to deal with and resolve disruptions of, discrepancies in, or conflicts in existing structural or functional patterns. Because humans are open systems, there are continual exchanges of material-energy forms and of information-based forms both within the person and between them and their contexts. Thus the very dynamics of daily living necessarily produce disruptions of and discrepancies and conflicts in existing intraperson and person-context patterns.

Other theorists have built their ideas about development on a similar view. For example, Piaget's (1983) proposals, which emphasize feedback (regulation), feedforward (operation), and self-regulation (equilibration), have many similarities to DST:

> What is more important, though, is that coordination of actions involves correction and self-regulation: in fact, we know regulatory mechanisms characterize all levels of organic life. (This is true for the genetic pool as well as for behavior.) But regulation is a process of retroaction (negative feedback), which implies a beginning of reversibility; and the relationship between regulation (which is correction of error with semireversibility in the retroaction) and operation, whose full reversibility allows for precorrection of errors (i.e, for "perfect" regulation in the cybernetic sense) becomes apparent. Thus it seems highly probable that the construction of structures is mainly the work of equilibration defined not by balance between opposite forces but by self-regulation: that is, equilibration is a set of active reactions of the subject to external disturbances, which can be effective, or anticipated, to varying degrees. (p. 122)

Similarly, in his discussion of instruction and learning theory, Glaser (1990) concludes that all instructional strategies view learning as problem solving and agree that learning results from practice that *reduces and minimizes error* (i.e., discrepancies). Case (1985) asserts that a problem exists when there is a discrepancy between a current state and some preferred future state, and that "problem solving" is the person's response to "disequilibrium."

EQUILIBRIUM-DISEQUILIBRIUM AND
ORGANIZATION-DISORGANIZATION

Material/energy disruptions or discrepancies have been extensively studied in the natural sciences. *Equilibrium* is a concept borrowed from physical dynamics where it refers to a state of balance between opposing forces. *Disequilibrium* is a state in which opposing forces are unbalanced, freeing some energy to do "work." Biologically, humans may be thought of as thermodynamic physical systems (Yates & Iberall, 1973). Through metabolic processes, energy is continually produced to do the "work" of fueling the construction of body parts and all behavior, but this uses up resources that must be replaced for metabolic processes to continue. This means that as an energy system humans' physical states are never in equilibrium because their operation continually produces imbalances, so they operate some distance from equilibrium and function to create and maintain dynamic steady states (e.g., Prigogine & Stengers, 1984).

It is misleading, however, to try to characterize the operation of the information-based psychological and action aspects of persons in terms of opposing forces or energy imbalances as Freud (1905) did, for example, in his initial theorizing (Ford & Urban, 1963). What is needed is some nonmaterial/energy-based analogy to the concepts of equilibrium and disequilibrium, one related to information. Developmental Systems Theory (DST) proposes that the concepts of *organization* and *disorganization* provide such an analogy.

Whitehead (1925), in his attempt to understand the nature of life, described nature as a "structure-evolving process"; that is, life processes create organization. Similarly, DST emphasizes the principles of self-construction and of unitary functioning. Humans must be coherently organized so that they can function as a unit. (See Chapter 4 for discussion of the concept of organization.) Any disruption of the regular or systematic relationships among the structural and functional components of a person interferes with unitary functioning, that is, introduces intraperson disorganization. Similarly, any disruption of the regular or systematic relationships between the person and his or her environment introduces disorganization because, as an open system, the person-in-context must compose a structural-functional unit. Any degree of intraperson or person-environment disruption or disorganization reduces functional effectiveness and extensive disorganization threatens the existence of life.

Disruption, Disorganization, and Change

It is a property of all living systems, from cells to societies, that they function to create organization and to prevent or overcome disruptions of organization. Insofar as life is concerned, nature abhors disorganization (Brent, 1978; Prigogine, 1976).

But disruptions of humans' structural and functional organization are properties of life itself because life, development, and functional effectiveness in a variable environment are products of the dynamics of an open system. That is, as a result of environmental variability and change and of the continual requirement of using and replacing material/energy resources and of reconciling new information and action requirements with old habits, the psychological and behavioral organization of a person as well as his or her relationships with the environment are continually being disrupted, producing varying degrees of disorganized states.

It follows that undisrupted life is as impossible as a pure energy equilibrium in the natural world. So on the one hand a person can only exist as a coherently organized, structural-functional unit in a supportive context, and on the other hand the very processes of living and development continually disrupt that organizational coherence. Across evolution this dilemma has been solved: Processes have evolved for continually maintaining, restoring, and creating coherent intraperson and person-environment patterns of organization. *All stability, change, and development in humans must be, therefore, a product of processes that deal with disruptions or discrepancies by maintaining, restoring, or creating coherent organization.*

Two Strategies for Dealing With Disruption and Disorganization

There are only two ways in which disorganization can be dealt with to maintain organizational unity. One is to maintain the existing organization either by preventing it from being disrupted or by restoring the original organization after disruption. The stability-maintaining processes identified earlier in this chapter represent this strategy. The second is to eliminate the disorganization by creating new organization. The incremental and transformational change processes illustrated earlier in this chapter represent this strategy. Therefore the dynamics of change and development must be understood in terms of processes of disruption, disorganization, and organizational elaboration or reorganization to overcome the disorganization. This process may occur at any organizational level from cells to person-context relations. The disruption-disorganization may be small and accommodated by incremental elaboration of existing organization, or it may be major and require significant reorganization of existing patterns. Change may occur by evolution or revolution. Development may be continuous or discontinuous.

In the remainder of this chapter we seek to explain each of DSTs three basic types of change-related processes in terms of the dynamics involved in dealing with disruption and disorganization of existing structural and functional patterns. While each type of change-related process will be discussed separately, it is important to emphasize that they are not mutually exclusive processes; they interact with one another. Horowitz (1987) asserts that:

> It is reasonable to assume that there is a multiple set of processes that are involved in behavioral acquisition. Imitation, observational learning, association by contiguity, reinforced learning, each partially constrained by innate factors characteristic of the human species, are all involved. (p. 14)

We will attempt to show how these traditional concepts about change processes (and others Horowitz did not mention) can be encompassed in the three types being proposed here. We will attempt to demonstrate that the three types of processes are all manifestations of the basic dynamics of our DST operational model of a person. While the same processes operate in biological and psychological/behavioral change, most of the emphases and examples in our discussions will focus on the latter.

Stability-Maintaining Processes

Coherent organization must be maintained for life to exist and effective living to occur. Stability-maintaining processes operate to serve that crucial objective.

NEGATIVE FEEDBACK PROCESSES

Three processes operate in all kinds of control systems, including living systems, to resist changes in existing steady states or to overcome disruptions to restore such steady states, that is, to maintain or restore structural-functional organization. A person is a complex, hierarchical organization of structural and functional components. Negative feedback processes operate both at the person level and at component levels. The way the processes are carried out varies with different components and levels, but the prototypical form of the process is the same, for example, whether at cellular, organ system, cognitive, or person levels. (See Ford, 1987, and Miller, 1978, for a more detailed discussion.)

Individual control systems may be organized so that they are interdependent (i.e., are components of a larger system). By relating them so that the outputs(s) of each may also serve as feedback or inputs for others, it is possible for them to operate together as a larger unit by virtue of the feedback regulatory influences they exert on one another. (See Miller et al., 1960, for more detailed discussion of this idea.)

For example, the heart functions as a unit because of the mutual entrainment of the cells through their combined operation; synaptic interactions among organizations of neurons are regulated by neurochemical feedback and feedforward processes.

The Dynamics of Negative Feedback Processes

Negative feedback was defined and briefly described in Chapter 4. Its operation will be examined more fully here. Figure 5.1 can be used to describe the dynamics of negative feedback processes. First, to understand their dynamics, it is necessary to recall that a person is always functioning and to imagine Figure 5.1 flowing continually through environments and time with the content of each of the components varying during that flow (e.g., see Figure 4.2). Negative feedback involves a comparison between current and preferred (desired; intended) states. This requires some standard of comparison or some comparison rule. The regulatory comparison rule (or standard) may take many forms. For example, it may say "reduce the discrepancy to zero" or "maintain the discrepancy within some range around zero." (See Ford, 1987, for more detailed discussion of the diversity of possible regulatory comparison rules.)

As summarized in Figure 5.1, the dynamics operate as follows. In any BE some existing BES is (are) potentiated by current environmental conditions interacting with currently operative personal goals. That BES begins to organize activity to produce the desired consequences within the constraints and possibilities provided by current bodily and environmental states. Directive processes specify a preferred state. Regulatory processes compare the system's current state with the preferred state. If there is no discrepancy or the discrepancy is within appropriate limits as defined by the operative comparison rule, the system continues operating as is. If there are multiple goals operating in the same BE, there must be multiple interrelated evaluative processes interacting to regulate the flow of behavior.

If there is a nontrivial discrepancy, regulatory processes will activate cognitive control and instrumental action processes from the person's relevant BES repertoire to try to reduce the discrepancy. Any changes in current states will be detected by monitoring processes and will be relayed by feedback processes to the regulatory processes where further comparisons occur. If a discrepancy continues to exist, further efforts to reduce it will be triggered. If the discrepancy is sufficiently reduced, then the system continues with steady-state operation. All of the processes in Figure 5.1 are continuous and interrelated. For example, the regulatory process of using feedback information to compare current with preferred states does not occur occasionally; it is continuous.

Stability Maintenance Through Negative Feedback Processes

When there is no significant discrepancy between current and preferred states, that is, when the current state is the preferred state, the system is operating within its steady state parameters and will continue to do so. When, however, a current steady state is disrupted, then control, transactional, and arousal activities will be triggered to prevent or overcome the disrupting influence so as to restore the preferred state.

For example, imagine a normal, healthy person. She or he is invaded by some infectious disease (a material/energy-based disrupting influence). As that disease process begins to disrupt some aspects of normal biological functioning, negative feedback discrepancy-reducing processes are set in motion. For example, immune system functioning is altered and body temperature may increase to fight the invaders.

Gradually these processes overcome the invaders until they are no longer disrupting normal biological functioning. Then the temporary changes in immune system functioning and body temperature revert to normal steady state functioning. In this example the dynamics are regulated and controlled by biochemical feedback and feedforward processes, for example, the "signals" that temporarily alter immune system and body temperature functioning are biochemical in nature. But they could also be informational in nature. Consider the example of the racially prejudiced man presented at the beginning of this chapter. He had an existing, preferred, steady state belief system about all African-Americans that characterized them as less capable, less trustworthy, and less adequate than white people. Information representing their work performance as superior to the white workers would disrupt his habitual prejudiced belief system (i.e., increase the discrepancy between existing and preferred states). To maintain the preferred state (remove the discrepancy) he must somehow ignore or alter the discrepant information so his existing beliefs are not disrupted.

Several maneuvers can do this. For example, he could avoid attending to or ignore the information about their superior performance; if he is not aware of it, his beliefs cannot be disrupted. Or he could interpret the information to make it fit his prejudices; for example, he could attribute it to luck, to a conspiracy among the African-Americans to make the white workers look bad, or to favoritism by an African-American supervisor. Similarly, their covering for his mistakes or their kindnesses during his wife's illness could be interpreted as maneuvers to "get something on him" that they could use to manipulate him in the future. The mental acrobatics that humans can perform to make discrepant information fit existing beliefs is astonishing, as Sigmund Freud (1949) demonstrated in his revelations about psychological defense mechanisms, and as social psychologists have demonstrated in their research on attitude change (e.g., Brown, 1988).

These stability-maintaining processes may also be focused on disruptions of person-environment relations. For example, imagine a situation in which a child, whose parental relations are loving, stains his or her clothing with ink while at school. He or she goes home, and the parent starts yelling at him or her for ruining the clothing. The child's preferred relationship with the parent is one of positive regard and affection. The stain produces a discrepancy between the preferred and actual relationship. The child will typically try to reduce the discrepancy, that is, to restore the positive relationships. Several strategies are possible.

One strategy is atonement. The child may apologize for his or her carelessness, promise to be more careful, and offer to clean his or her room as evidence of his or her sincerity, hoping that will cause the parent to forgive and forget. A second is deflection. The child may deny responsibility and blame someone else, for example, "Joey threw it on me." If it works, the parent is then mad at Joey instead. A third is to plead ignorance. The child may allege that he or she did not know the stain was there and that he or she has no idea how it happened. A fourth is diversion. The child may cry and express his or her love for the parent to divert the parent's behavior from being critical to caring. Children can be very creative in the ways they try to mend disrupted relationships.

Anticipatory Stability Maintaining Processes

Feedback processes are *reactive*; they deal with what is happening. Feedforward processes are *proactive*; they function to prepare the system for selective action and to make things happen. They are the processes that give human behavior its future-oriented properties. Most human behavior is designed to influence future occurrences based on "predictions" about possible or probable future conditions rather than solely to react to what's happening now. Through feedforward processes people can imagine possible disrupting events and can behave so as to prevent their occurrence. Inoculation to prevent the occurrence of an infectious disease or frequent hand washing to try to avoid "catching a cold" from others are illustrative. In such instances the discrepancy being reduced is cognitive in character, that is, it is imagined rather than currently occurring.

The prejudiced man can be used as another example. There are several ways in which the prejudiced man might prevent exposure to experiences that could contradict his prejudiced beliefs. He might: (a) quit his job and seek another; (b) ask his supervisor for transfer to a white-only work group; (c) define a role in the work group where he can work alone most of the time; or (d) to forestall possible friendly gestures, tell the African-Americans he does not want them around his family.

Similarly, the child with the ink stain could anticipate parental disapproval and pursue preventive actions. For example, he or she could: (a) try to clean the stain off before going home; (b) hide the stained clothing in the wash and hope it will wash out before the parent sees it; (c) throw the clothing away and hope the parent will not notice it is gone; or (d) forge a note from a teacher apologizing for having given the child a leaky pen to use.

Incremental-Change Processes

Stability-maintaining processes operate when the preferred and current state are the same and some event(s) alters the current state, thereby creating an unacceptable discrepancy. They protect existing patterns through the operation of existing habitual capabilities. Therefore they produce stability rather than change; however, negative feedback processes can also be harnessed to produce change.

INCREMENTAL CHANGE THROUGH NEGATIVE FEEDBACK PROCESSES

Under some circumstances stability maintaining processes may result in incremental change in the BES that is typically potentiated to organize that type of BE. If none of the strategies or methods that are currently part of the operational BES are effective in protecting or restoring the preferred state, then new strategies and methods may be invented and tried. If they work (i.e., succeed in restoring the preferred state) they are "reinforced" and become an elaboration of that BES (i.e., they are learned). Thus existing patterns can be differentiated and elaborated through the operation of negative feedback processes.

For example, suppose the prejudiced man's usual methods do not work in protecting his beliefs from disruption by current perceptions. He might then try some alternate strategy. For example, he might antagonize his African-American coworkers and thereby elicit retaliative behavior from them which he could then interpret as support for his prejudiced beliefs. This new component of the habitual BES might be an inventive creation (using his information-based self-construction capabilities), or it might be a component of some other BES in his repertoire that he "borrows" to apply in this new way (e.g., he may have an observational BES constructed from watching TV that has such a component in it). Young children often learn such maneuvers through observation of older siblings or even parents. Thus one way incremental behavior change in an existing BES may occur is through adding to it elements already available in some other BES. This is sometimes called generalization or transfer of training and will be further discussed later when we distinguish between performance and capability change.

There are three other ways in which disruptions of current states can occur and that produce system dynamics that result in incremental change processes. They are goal setting, positive feedback, and biological maturation.

Goal Setting and Negative Feedback Processes

Humans' ability to cognitively construct representations of potential future states was discussed in Chapter 4. (See also Ford, 1987, Ford & Ford, 1987, and M. Ford, in press, for more detailed discussion.) People may use desired imagined states, usually called goals, purposes, wants, or intentions, to organize current functioning in anticipation of, or in preparation for, the imagined events. This is called "modeling of the future" by Bernstein (1967).

When any such imagined valued future state is activated in a particular BE through the directive processes in Figure 5.1, it creates a discrepancy between current and preferred states, and negative feedback processes will then operate to remove the discrepancy. How does this differ from the operation of negative feedback to maintain stability? In stability maintenance the current state *is* the preferred state and negative feedback operates to prevent or overcome disruptions of that state. Goal setting, however, creates exactly the opposite situation, that is, the current state *is not* preferred. It represents a discrepancy from the imagined, preferred state that does not now exist. Therefore goal setting harnesses negative feedback processes to produce rather than prevent change because the processes operate to remove the discrepancy by creating the new preferred state rather than by protecting the existing state. And success in removing this kind of discrepancy often involves differentiating, elaborating, combining, or revising some existing BES, that is, involves new learning.

In effect, by personal goal setting, individuals disrupt their status quo or disorganize themselves and then organize their behavior to try to resolve the disruption or create new coherent organization, thereby becoming, as Lerner (1982) states, "producers of their own development" (p. 342). Thus in goal setting negative feedback also operates to reduce a discrepancy, but it does so by altering the system through incremental change rather than by ignoring, eliminating, or assimilating a disrupting influence.

Where do personal goals come from that function to organize a current BE? This may occur in two ways. First, a goal may become active as a result of processes *inside* the system. One that appears to have arisen across human evolution is represented by the term "curiosity." From birth onward exploration of the environment to discover what is there, how it may affect one, and how one may affect it seems to be a pervasive "outcome" people seek, and such exploratory patterns can only be blunted by aversive experience. Because life depends on successful environmental interactions, the evolutionary utility of such exploratory behavior seems obvious. Constructing accurate knowledge about one's environment (i.e., incorporating environmental organization within ones self) is a necessary precondition for effectively proactively organizing one's transactions with the environment.

Curiosity provides one basis for imitation and observational or latent learning. Starting at birth infants' days are filled with many observational BEs from which they begin constructing representations of their world, themselves, and how the two domains relate. New information is disrupting until one can "make sense" out of it. The construction of observation-based BES is one basic way of doing this. Of course all observation is from the observer's vantage point, so regardless of the content of any observations they always have some self-referential aspects to them.

Most goals are more specific and are constructed from experience, sometimes influenced by biological processes as well. For example, an adolescent boy reaches puberty. This biological change, in concert with his social interactions with boyfriends in a similar state, results in increased interest in girls. This changed evaluation of the desirability of boy-girl relationships typically leads to the construction of a hierarchy of new goals, such as getting dates and learning to dance. In this case the imagining of the preferred future state is partly a by-product of changed biological processes. (Biological transitions will be discussed later under feedforward and transformational processes.)

In addition, through some happy childhood experiences with a father whom the boy admires and loves and through observation of successful baseball players, the boy may construct for himself the goal of becoming a baseball star. That imagined outcome then organizes behavior episodes designed to produce that outcome, that is, to remove the discrepancy between his current and desired circumstances. The boy may start lifting weights to increase his strength and size. He may seek participation on the high school baseball team. He may read books about how to be a good baseball player. He may go to a baseball camp to get special training. He may watch televised games and study the techniques used by excellent players. How much effort and time he invests is a function of how much he values that future possibility. M. Ford (in press) explains how these directive/regulatory and arousal/energizing processes have become the key defining attributes of the concept of *motivation*.

This example illustrates another relevant characteristic. Humans often pursue several goals in the same BE and organize their behavior with hierarchies of goals. For example, the "big" goal of becoming a baseball star can only be achieved by accomplishing a set of "little" subgoals such as becoming larger and stronger, becoming a good hitter, developing endurance, becoming a good defensive player, and getting lots of playing experience. Somewhat different BES will be activated to organize functioning for each subgoal. Moreover, the same behavior pattern may help achieve more than one important goal. For example, this boy may discover that being a successful baseball player helps him impress girls and may simultaneously earn his father's regard, thereby serving two other important "big" goals.

A second source of goals is the environment. Personal goals may become defined through contextual demands and constraints. For example, parents impose goals on their children, schools on their students, and employers on their workers. Thus the adolescent may be told by his parents that he cannot be on the baseball team unless he earns a B average in school. Schoolwork may not be intrinsically valued by the boy, but he adopts his parents' imposed goal of a B average because it serves (i.e., is a subgoal for) two other personally valued goals: being a baseball player and maintaining his parents respect and love. Thus in DST *a goal cannot truly be imposed on people.* They must adopt it as a personal goal for it to perform a directive function. They often do so because it becomes a subgoal for some other personally valued goal, that is, it either helps them produce some other result they want or helps them avoid some other result they do not want. For example, prisoners of war often perform personally distasteful tasks to avoid possible death or some severe feared punishment.

Once again Figure 5.1 can be used to describe the dynamics of incremental change processes. Activation of some personal goal(s) in a current environment begins the process. That triggers the beginning of a BE designed to achieve the goal (i.e., reduce the discrepancy between current and preferred states). Information processing and control cognitive processes define the problem to be solved, collect information about current environmental conditions, examine what personal capabilities one has or needs that might "work," formulate an action strategy, and begin to implement it. This involves starting with one or more existing BES and trying progressive modifications. Information is collected about the progress and fed back to the regulatory processes. This may lead to modifications of strategy and tactics (e.g., to trying a different approach). This is what Baldwin (1894) called circular reactions, one of many Baldwin concepts that Piaget (1950, 1970) and others adopted (e.g., see Schneirla, 1957).

Selection and Retention of Incremental Changes

What determines which among all of the strategies, tactics, and skills tried are retained for future use (i.e., are learned or become part of the new BES)? How do these circular reactions produce change? It is through a process that Skinner (1981) labeled *selection by consequences*, a change process that he asserted was a "causal mode" unique to living systems. In DST this is the discrepancy-reduction process, that is, one learns what "works." Both the concepts of selection and consequences must be examined.

Selection is an operation by which some things, events, or characteristics are given special status or preference over other possibilities. For example, selective attention means a person attends to some things and ignores many others. In the context of a behavior episode (a circular reaction process), a person does something to try to produce a desired consequence. This might be called a "provisional try" (Hilgard, 1948). If that does not work he or she may try something else and then something else again until something "works" (i.e., produces the intended/desired consequences and reduces the discrepancy between current and preferred states). Each such "provisional try" may be considered a sample selected from a population of potential behavior patterns that might produce the desired consequence in that context. Learning or change must involve: (a) the selection from a set of possible ways of producing the desired consequence the one(s) that are effective; and (b) making them permanent parts of relevant BES: that is, learning selects from among a set of "provisional tries."

But how is this selection accomplished? What determines which "tries" will be "selected in" and which "selected out?" Skinner's answer is the *consequences*. "Tries" followed by "positive reinforcement" will be learned, and "tries" followed by "negative reinforcement" will be extinguished. But how can one know what will be a positive or negative reinforcer? Skinner (1981) provides two criteria:

1. A reinforcing stimulus must be a behavior contingent event; and
2. It must increase (positive reinforcement) or decrease (negative reinforcement) the probability that particular behavior will reoccur in future similar circumstances.

There are always many things going on simultaneously within and around a person, however, and at any particular time only a few of them function as reinforcing consequences. What determines which do and which do not? Skinner's criteria can only provide after-the-fact answers.

The DST and the behavior episode unit do provide a way of predicting in advance which consequences will perform the selection operations involved in learning in any BE (or learning trial). Simply stated, something functions as a positive reinforcing consequence when it is the result a person is currently trying to produce or is a result he or she values, and as a negative reinforcing consequence when it is not. Stated in more technical terms, a positive reinforcing consequence is one that helps reduce the discrepancy between current and preferred states, and a negative reinforcing consequence does not and may increase the discrepancy. Therefore the selection criteria lie within the BES guiding that episode. Those behavior patterns that a person evaluates as contributing to achieving the goal(s) in that context (i.e., as a successful "try") will become a part of the guiding BES and those not so evaluated will not. Thus the regulatory processes play a key role in learning or incremental development.

Because new development must start from existing patterns, developmental possibilities at any time are constrained and facilitated by current capabilities and characteristics, called the *principle of developmental flexibility and sequencing.* The greater the diversity of a person's behavioral repertoire, the less habitual they are in their performances and the fewer the prohibitions against trying something new, the greater is their developmental flexibility, that is, the more diverse are the options available in their current repertoire, the more diverse are their potential developmental pathways. Moreover, because new development starts with existing patterns, it follows that some development must be sequential, that is, some capabilities must develop before others can do so. For example, learning to walk depends upon prior motor developments. Developmental stage theories emphasize this sequencing principle.

It is important to reemphasize that the evaluative/regulatory processes that perform the selection operations involve both affective and cognitive evaluations. (See Chapter 4; Chapters 12 and 13 in Ford, 1987, and M. Ford, in press.) Affective evaluations are the most primitive (in evolutionary terms) and are dominant in infancy. In simple terms, babies regulate their activity in terms of what hurts or feels good or what makes them happy, frightened, angry, contented, or sad. This powerful regulatory function is one of the reasons that emotions play such an important part in human life and are so heavily implicated in many forms of psychopathology and biobehavioral disorders.

Cognitive regulation plays an increasingly important role as cognitive capabilities develop, but rather than replacing affective regulation (e.g., the regulatory influence of pain and emotions), cognitive and affective regulation typically operate in coordinated fashion. When they do not, conflict results, and conflicting regulatory processes are one important focus of many psychotherapy theories (Ford & Urban, 1963).

Achieving a goal (i.e., producing a desired consequence or preferred state) does not necessarily occur in an all or none fashion. A provisional try may be only partially successful. Therefore using the same pattern repetitively in similar episodes (i.e., "practicing" it) contributes to further revision of the BES to improve the effectiveness of the behavior by eliminating unnecessary parts, improving the coherence of the pattern's organization, and improving its fluency in performance. The concept of standards refers to the level of performance proficiency and degree of desired outcome a person will consider adequate. The "reinforcing" consequence does not need to represent complete accomplishment of the goal, but it does need to be evaluated as representing progress toward the desired consequence, that is, it must be evaluated as producing some decrease in the discrepancy between the current and preferred states.

Here is where spatial-temporal contiguity of events may lead to learned components of BES that may be irrelevant to successful completion of the BE and may produce irrelevant or erroneous behavior in future BEs. Any events perceived in spatial-temporal contiguity to the occurrences of relevant consequences may be interpreted as related to those consequences and the behavior thought to have produced them. Technically this illustrates what Nesselroade (in preparation) calls a *selection effect*.

For example, in a classic learning study cats were given the task of learning to open a door to get out of a cage (Thorndike, 1904, 1906). One cat's first successful try resulted when it backed around the cage and then bumped the door with its rear end. Thereafter it backed around the cage before bumping the door. The backing-up behavior was irrelevant to the successful completion of the task, but because it was contiguous to the successful outcome, it was encompassed as part of the successful pattern. Such contiguity is the basic dynamic of classical conditioning. For example, when a neutral event (e.g., a toy clown) is paired with another event that frightens a child (e.g., sudden, loud thunder and lightening), the neutral event may become a fear elicitor.

Errors in *causal attribution* often represent erroneous evaluations of contiguous events (i.e., covariation) as representing causal influences. For example, it was discovered that a girl in a sustained depression felt very guilty because during a period of anger and resentment she had privately wished her brother dead and that day he was killed in an auto accident. She felt responsible. She incorrectly evaluated her private thoughts as having contributed to his death. Superstitious behaviors are often the result of faulty evaluations of the relationships among contiguous events.

Of course the BEs from which a BES is constructed (learned) are only similar; they are not identical. Therefore the behavior pattern that "works" or is "reinforced" in each BE may be somewhat different as a function of variations in the person's current bodily state and of variations in the environment from one BE to another. When that occurs different ways of producing the same desired consequence(s) will be learned as a set of *alternative subroutines* within the relevant BES.

It is useful to distinguish between two types of outcomes that can be called performance change and capability change. Different behavior patterns (BES) develop to serve different purposes in different kinds of behavior episodes. Once a behavioral component has been constructed in any BES, it is potentially available for use in some other kind of BE if it can be activated (potentiated) as a possibility in that new episode. Thus *performance change* involves beginning to use an existing component of one's behavioral repertoire in a different kind of BE or discontinuing the use of some component. One does not learn a new competence, he or she just uses an old one in a new way. It must be emphasized that performance change does not occur automatically. The set of BES potentiated by the episode conditions must make available potentially relevant alternate behavior components. Then to become a permanent part of the BES for that new kind of episode, the new components must be subject to selection by consequences, that is, cognitive/affective processes must evaluate them as "working."

Goldstein and Kanfer (1979), through a review of research on generalization or transfer of training, found and labeled three characteristics that appear to facilitate performance change as follows:

1. *Identical elements*—the likelihood of transfer increases with increased similarity between the current BE and the BES that contains the potentially relevant response;
2. *Response availability*—the more frequently a behavioral component is used, the greater is the likelihood it may be tried in different situations; and
3. *Stimulus variability*—the greater the diversity of situations in which the behavior component has been performed previously, the more likely it is to be potentiated as a possibility in a new situation.

For example, a behaviorally conservative man retired from his job as an accountant and, to the surprise of many, he then participated in a diversity of more adventuresome kinds of BEs, such as buying and driving a little race car. His retirement was similar to his youth in the freedom and opportunity to pursue personal interests that it provided (identical elements). He had participated in many adventuresome activities as a teenager and young adult (response availability) and in a diversity of situations at home, in the navy, and at college (stimulus variability). Retirement BEs potentiated components of old BES active during his adolescent and young adult years.

Knowledge of the nature of performance change can be useful to professional change agents such as teachers, counselors, and psychotherapists. Everyone constructs BES at one phase of life for BEs that no longer occur in other phases of life (e.g., student BES after formal schooling is finished; pilot BES after one is no longer in the air force; dating BES after one marries). Such BES may still represent potentials in the person's "library of behavioral programs," although they may remain "on the shelf" for many years. Thus performance change may occur through the creation of BEs in which some "dormant" BES is potentiated and used in new circumstances as illustrated above. Retirement counselors sometimes focus on such possibilities with their clients (e.g., "Are there any interests you used to have that your job has prevented you from continuing to pursue?").

Recognizing that a person's performance in a specific kind of BE is a function of the BES that particular BE activates can help avoid inaccurate conclusions about individuals' capabilities. The person may have the capability, but that particular BE did not activate it. For example, Piaget concluded (1950, 1970; Inhelder & Piaget, 1958) that children were unable to perform certain kinds of cognitive tasks until they reached a certain developmental stage. Other researchers demonstrated that conclusion was incorrect by altering the design of the task (i.e., the BE) so that it elicited a relevant BES already in the children's repertoire (Gelman, 1978).

Performance change does not elaborate a person's capabilities; it only elaborates the circumstances in which he or she uses existing capabilities. *Capability change* involves elaboration of the behavioral repertoire itself, either by creating new components or by combining, reorganizing, or transforming existing components into different patterns. An infant learning to walk is a good example. A new capability may initially be tried through observational, imitative, discovery, or creative processes; however, whether or not its performance on those occasions leads to its permanent inclusion in a BES will be a function of the selection/evaluation/reinforcing processes that have been described.

In summary, through incremental change processes a person's existing capabilities are differentiated, elaborated, and combined in the form of BES as a result of demonstrated effectiveness in producing desired consequences. With practice, such revised BES can become habitual and can come to function in an "automated" or "machine-like" or habitual fashion, called an open loop in systems terms. This means that the pattern runs off as a unit without careful monitoring and ongoing adjustments of the flow of the activity. In other words the operation of the feedback side of Figure 5.1 is minimized. When

BES become "automated," their continuation in that form is protected by stability-maintaining processes. As a result, BES that were originally constructed because of their utility may be continued even when no longer effective because the feedback-regulatory processes are not operating to identify and correct the discrepancies.

INCREMENTAL CHANGE THROUGH POSITIVE FEEDBACK PROCESSES

Positive Feedback

The change-related processes discussed so far all represent manifestations of the dynamics of negative or discrepancy-reducing feedback. Positive feedback processes (described in Chapter 4) function differently. They operate to increase rather than decrease deviations from a specified state, so it is sometimes called discrepancy-amplifying feedback (Maruyama, 1963; Milsum, 1968). *When a process and its consequences are continually amplified by the effects of their own activity, the essence of positive feedback is present.* Profound effects can later result from the amplification of small initial deviations.

Deviation-amplifying feedback processes have been largely ignored in attempts to apply systems models to understanding human development. That is unfortunate because they are one important source of system change. A few examples may help make this less familiar concept more meaningful.

In some kinds of chemical reactions, products of the reaction provide ingredients necessary to maintain or increase the rate of reaction, sometimes termed *autocatalytic processes.* A similar, more familiar example is an atomic reactor. In the simplest terms, one material (uranium) is brought into contact with other materials under conditions that begin to break down or "disorganize" the uranium, thereby releasing energy that can provide useful thermal-electric power. Products of that process feed back to facilitate its continuation. If the positive feedback dynamics are carefully controlled, the rate of breakdown can be regulated to produce a slow, steady release of energy (i.e., through processes of controlled fission). If, however, the positive feedback dynamics get out of control, they will rapidly amplify the rate at which the breakdown of material is occurring and produce a runaway atomic reaction that can lead to an atomic explosion like that which occurred at an atomic power plant in Russia in the mid-1980s.

By amplifying deviations from current states, positive feedback processes produce instabilities or a form of increasing disorganization that, if continued unconstrained, will eventually destroy the system. It can, however, become a source of incremental change and precipitate some changes that will create a different, more stable pattern of organization. This happens when the increasing degree of discrepancy triggers negative feedback regulatory efforts to counteract the positve feedback processes and to resolve the discrepancy.

For example, in a marriage a wife carries out her daily activities in a highly planned, scheduled, efficient manner. In contrast, her husband is less planful, often does not stick with schedules, and often procrastinates on tasks that are of little interest or are distasteful. His wife begins nagging him about his unpredictable and procrastinating behavior. That irritates him; he becomes less responsive to her and avoids further doing the things about which he is being nagged. She increases her nagging, and he increases his avoidance and procrastinating pattern. This positive feedback pattern is driving them further and further away from the loving relationship they once had and both still seem to want. Finally, during a phone call in which her nagging is quite severe, he says some critical, nasty things about her behavior. She explodes in anger, hangs up, becomes more and more angry as she thinks about his behavior, packs her bags, and goes to visit her parents. The marriage is severely disorganized.

This separation temporarily suspends the positive feedback dynamics because it terminates the communicative interactions that fed the process. He finds her, states he wants to restore their marriage, she agrees, they enter relationship enhancement therapy, and, as a result, they change their communication patterns. She becomes less compulsive, he better organized, and a good relationship is restored between them. In effect they have constructed ways of controlling the previously troublesome positive feedback processes, thereby producing a more stable and satisfactory married state. More dramatic consequences of positive feedback will be discussed later under transformational change processes.

Escalation of positive rather than negative outcomes can result from positive feedback dynamics, but still produce distressing disruptions of existing patterns leading to incremental changes. For example, a man began going to public auctions with his wife and became interested in antiques. At one auction he bought an item for

$100 that he later learned was worth $5,000. He began to read about antiques and to develop expertise in distinguishing valuable antiques from copies or fakes. He and his wife increased their attendance at auctions and began making considerable amounts of money buying and selling antiques. People learned of his expertise and began hiring him to appraise their antiques and to seek out and buy antiques for them. Thus the consequences of the activity stimulated further elaboration of the activity and produced a growing discrepancy between time, energy, effort, and interest devoted to his current career and that devoted to his new hobby.

INCREMENTAL CHANGE THROUGH INTERRELATED POSITIVE AND NEGATIVE FEEDBACK PROCESSES

Positive and negative feedback arrangements can be coupled so that negative feedback processes limit the deviation-amplifying effects of a positive feedback process, and there are probably many such arrangements in humans. For example, a person's growth in height does not go unchecked. Children have growth "spurts" in which the rate of growth accelerates for a time, followed by plateaus in which the growth rate is drastically reduced, until the child reaches his or her mature adult height; then growth ends and stability-maintaining processes dominate. The pattern of a woman's menstrual cycle may be regulated by interrelated biochemical positive and negative feedback loops.

Such arrangements also operate in interpersonal relationships. For example, a wife and husband both have very busy careers that result in increasingly individualized lives and decreasing amounts of shared activity and time together. As a device to periodically interrupt that deviation-amplifying process and to protect their marriage, they establish the (stability-maintaining) practice of reserving one night a week for a "date," and of taking periodic weekend pleasure trips together whenever they think their work has begun to disrupt their married life too much. Unchecked positive feedback processes are one source of transformational change, as will be described later.

Biological Maturation

There is a species-typical pattern of biological growth and development that occurs normatively when the individual develops within a prototypical environmental niche. The unfolding of this pattern results from the interaction of individuals' genetic endowment with relevant features of his or her environmental niche and is called biological maturation. Much is still to be learned about the mechanisms by which organs and tissues are constructed during development (e.g., Bard, 1990).

Except for a few major transformational periods, this maturational elaboration occurs incrementally. For example, there is a normative sequence in which different organs and different biological functions emerge during embryonic and fetal development. As a new organ begins to form, cell division and tissue organization incrementally elaborate the organ until it reaches its prototypical adult size (assuming appropriate health, nutrition, and care). Changes in each biological component disturb the organizational coherence of the whole, so as one component changes others must also change to maintain or restore the unity of the whole.

For example, as bones in the arms and legs grow longer and stronger, changes in muscles, nerves, and blood supply must also occur to assure organizational unity. Subcomponents are organized through interacting input and output activities so that the internal functioning of any component may use the outputs resulting from the activities of other components as inputs to organize, fuel, and regulate its own functioning. Such incremental maturational development probably occurs through a form of controlled positive feedback linked to boundary-defining negative feedback processes, ones based on biochemical interactions (von Bertalanffy, 1968). Prigogine and Stengers (1984) emphasize pervasiveness of such arrangements in living systems:

> In far-from equilibrium conditions various types of self-organization processes may occur.... We have seen that the basic condition for the appearance of such phenomena is the existence of catalytic effects. Although the effects of "nonlinear" reactions (the presence of the reaction product) have a feedback action on their "cause" and are comparatively rare in the inorganic world, molecular biology has discovered that they are virtually the rule as far as living systems are concerned. Autocatalysis (the presence of X accelerates its own synthesis), autoinhibition (the presence of X blocks a catalysis needed to synthesize it), and crosscatalysis (two products belonging to two different reaction chains activate each other's synthesis) provide the classical regulation mechanism guaranteeing the coherence of the metabolic function. (p. 153)

For example, various phases of *embryonic and fetal development* are probably organized and fueled, at least in part, by such interacting catalytic processes. Cell-division processes and the tissue, organ, and organ system elaborations they produce display the properties of positive feedback processes, that is, the process and its consequences are continually amplified by the effects of their own activity. Physical growth through cell division appears to feed upon itself until some (as yet unclear) stability-maintaining regulatory processes are activated that terminate elaboration and then maintain the new steady state (e.g., size and organization). By controlled positive feedback we mean that not only is the rate of cell division controlled, but also the resulting organization of cells is constrained within the basic physical structures composed of that cell type.

Cancer appears to be an out-of-control positive feedback process of cell division. Cancers differ in terms of the kinds of cells in which this "snowballing" process is occurring (e.g., white blood cells, liver cells, kidney cells, skin cells). Further, in advanced stages they are not organizationally constrained. That is, cells may migrate to other tissues and trigger uncontrolled elaboration there. Effective prevention and control of cancer probably will rest upon knowledge of what activates the positive feedback processes that result in cell proliferation and upon the creation of means for interrupting intracellular or intercellular dynamics to prevent or interrupt those positive feedback processes.

As discussed in Chapter 3, there are important individual differences in maturational outcomes both because of differences in individuals' genetic heritage and because of variations in the environmental niche. (See assumptions 3, 3a, and 3b in Table 3.1.) Deficiencies in the environmental niche can reduce or increase the boundaries for physical growth and development. The malnourished, growth-stunted child described at the beginning of this chapter is an example of a nonnormative steady state established to fit the resources available; however, such deviations from normal maturational patterns can be corrected if the environmental deficiencies are remedied sufficiently early in the person's developmental pathway. For example, with proper nutrition, health care and love, positive feedback processes can be reactivated and a growth stunted child will "catch up" in his or her growth and can end up with an adult size prototypical for a person with his or her genetic endowment.

After biological maturity is reached, some kinds of material/energy-based incremental change processes can still occur. For example, the construction of new cells can occur in some, but not all, tissues of the body when disruptions require it (e.g., the healing of a cut finger or recovery from surgery). Sometimes significant qualitative change occurs fairly rapidly. We will examine those processes next.

Transformational Change Processes

While incremental change occurs through processes of differentiation and elaboration of existing organization, transformational change occurs through processes of reorganization. *Transformational change processes are the source of discontinuities in development.* How such transformational changes could come about has been an issue about which scholars in evolutionary theory, developmental biology, and developmental psychology have puzzled since the beginning of those fields. Advances in physics, chemistry, and cosmology have begun to reveal processes by which transformational change may occur. (See Capra, 1977; Jantsch, 1980; and Zukav, 1979, for less technical discussions of these developments.) Nobel prize winner Prigogine (1976) and Prigogine and Stengers (1984) have been particularly influential in disseminating these new ideas (e.g., see *Order Out of Chaos*, Prigogine & Stengers, 1984). Therefore we will use their work to convey their essence.

FAR-FROM-EQUILIBRIUM STATES AND ORGANIZATIONAL INSTABILITY

Recall that equilibrium is a state characterized by a balance among opposing forces. Therefore matter near equilibrium behaves in a "repetitive," "habitual," or stable way. Disequilibrium occurs when opposing forces become unbalanced, so disequilibrium may vary from a little to a lot. When extensive disequilibrium occurs, the material or system so affected is said to be operating far from equilibrium. For example, a liquid or chemical compound may be in equilibrium (i.e., a stable steady state). Heat is a form of energy, so by heating a liquid or chemical compound, energy is transferred to it, thus producing disequilibrium (the more heat, the more disequilibrium).

Recall that open systems are continually subject to disruptions of their existing states. The variations produced by such disruptions may be called fluctuations. In systems close to equilibrium, disruptions produce only minor fluctuations because stability-maintaining processes contain them; however, systems far from equilibrium are much less stable. They become inordinately sensitive to external influences. Small disruptions can be magnified to produce major fluctuations that shatter the existing organization (the proverbial "straw that broke the camel's back"). As a result the entire system may reorganize itself into a different organization or state. Prigogine & Stengers (1984) refer to such revolutionary moments as "bifurcation points," at which new types of organization may originate spontaneously. They emphasize that the form the reorganized state may take is not fully predictable, but they will "reflect the interaction of a given system with its surroundings" (p. 12). It is a stochastic process in which any one of several possibilities may be equally probable.

For example, when the flow rate of a fluid is increased to a certain level, turbulence suddenly appears in the flow. Similarly, at a certain threshold, heat moving evenly through a liquid suddenly converts into a convection current that radically alters the liquid, and millions of molecules suddenly reorganize into a collection of hexagonal cells called the Benard instability.

Phenomena whose organization is far from equilibrium are not rare. Prigogine & Stengers (1984) assert that both the biosphere and its components exist in far from equilibrium conditions. Living itself involves such far from equilibrium organization that can be maintained through the exchange processes of open systems, and life "appears as the supreme expression of the self-organizing processes" that characterize the broader natural order (p. 175). They cite many examples in the natural sciences when "the amplification of a microscopic fluctuation occurring at the 'right moment' resulted in favoring one reaction path over a number of other equally possible paths" (p. 176). In human terms this means that at critical moments the role played by individual behavior can be decisive in cultivating one developmental pathway or another. There are both predictable and unpredictable aspects to this process. Prigogine and Stengers (1984) assert that "self-organizing processes in far-from-equilibrium conditions correspond to a delicate interplay between chance and necessity, between fluctuations and deterministic laws" (pp. 175-176).

Because organisms are complex material organizations and thermodynamic energy systems, Prigogine and Stengers (1984) speculate "that the basic mechanism of evolution is based on the play between bifurcations as mechanisms of exploration and the selection of chemical interactions stabilizing a particular trajectory" (p. 172). In other words the transformational changes resulting from a bifurcation point that evolutionary theorists call "punctuated equilibrium" is necessarily followed by the selection processes of the gradualism doctrine.

ORGANIZATION-DISORGANIZATION-REORGANIZATION

By moving from an energy-based equilibrium-disequilibrium framework to the analogous framework of organization-disorganization, we propose that the same ideas can apply to information-based psychological/behavioral transformations as well as material/energy-based biological ones. Biochemical positive feedback processes can drive biological organization toward increasingly unstable states until some reorganization or transformation occurs to create a new steady state. Analogously, information-based positive feedback processes can make behavioral organization increasingly unstable until it goes through a transformation to a new steady state. Finally sudden unexpected events can severely disrupt both biological and/or behavioral patterns requiring reorganization to reach new steady states. For example, some suicide attempts result from positive feedback escalation of some emotional states and related through patterns, for example, discouragement-depression-despair. Some neuroses and psychoses represent maladaptive personality reorganization that serve to interrupt such unintended but distressing positive feedback dynamics.

Because humans are an exceedingly complex, hierarchical organization of components, the age-old conflict between reductionism and holism can be avoided. As Developmental Systems Theory emphasizes, (see assumptions 1, 1a, 2, 2a, and 2c in Table 3.1), changes may occur at any level, and the levels are intertwined and mutually influential. Both parts and wholes are important; each part is also a whole in its own right, but wholes have special properties that result from the ways the parts are organized. Prigogine and Stengers (1984) state:

> Ever since Aristotle . . . the same conviction has been expressed; a
> concept of complex organization is required to connect the various

levels of description and account for the relationship between the whole and the behavior of the parts. In answer to the reductionists, for whom the sole 'cause' of organization can lie only in the part, Aristotle with his formal cause, Hegel with his emergence of Spirit in Nature, and Bergson with his simple, irrepressible, organization-creating act, assert that the whole is predominant. (p. 173)

Biological Transformation

Extensive evidence reveals an astonishing ability of the embryo and fetus to withstand perturbations from its environment and to develop into a normal, functional infant despite such perturbations. The dynamics of genetically regulated maturational processes provide for developmental homeostasis of the embryo and fetus within a broad range of environmental variations. Within that broad picture, however, there are periods of transformational change. "When we observe development on film, we 'see' jumps corresponding to radical reorganizations followed by periods of more 'pacific' quantitative growth" (Prigogine and Stengers, 1984, p. 171).

Because transformational change results from processes of disorganization and reorganization, and because the form the reorganization will take is influenced by the specific conditions present at the "bifurcation point" at which the transitional disorganization occurs, it follows that an organism's future developmental pathway is most vulnerable to alterations during the transitional phase of transformational change. The nature of the developmental pathway deviation that occurs will be a function of the developmental phase of the embryo or fetus at that point of transition and of the nature of the perturbation. For example, the baby born with no arms mentioned at the beginning of this chapter probably emerged with that developmental outcome as a product of the mother having a drug called Thalidomide in her system during a developmental transition period when arms would normally begin to develop. The same developmental deviation would not have occurred if Thalidomide were present in a later developmental phase.

Some maturational transitions also occur after birth. The most familiar are puberty and menopause. Both represent a transition from one hormonal steady state to another and, although the causes of those transitions are not yet fully understood, one potential explanation lies in some kind of deviation-amplifying positive feedback process.

Biological disorganization-reorganization processes can also occur after birth if a person suffers a physical trauma or his or her material/energy transactions produce a toxic result. For example, a child fell into a lake and was under water for a brief period of time. She was revived, but the oxygen deprivation she suffered produced permanent brain damage and drastically altered her neurological capabilities for certain cognitive and motoric development. A college student fell on a trampoline, damaged his spinal cord, and became a quadriplegic. A man in an auto accident suffered a head trauma and lost the ability to speak. In all such instances the biological capabilities must achieve a new steady state if the person survives; that will also precipitate disorganization-reorganization processes involving psychological/behavioral functions disrupted by the lost neural capabilities. We will now consider information-based transformational change.

Psychological/Behavioral Transformations

There are a number of concepts, such as intrapsychic conflict and cognitive dissonance, that represent psychological states of disorganization. One indicator of the existence of such states is subjective feelings of tension or distress. The more extensive the disorganization, the more intense are those feelings. In more technical terms, the greater the discrepancy between existing and preferred states, the more intense will be the resulting evaluations. Behavior patterns used to try to minimize, reduce, or overcome such disorganization have been called coping strategies and defense mechanisms.

If psychological/behavioral disorganization becomes extensive, analogous to a system far from equilibrium, and if stability-maintaining and incremental change processes are insufficiently effective, then the only way to restore coherent organization is to reorganize the entire pattern. For example, a person whose negative self-evaluations and emotions of guilt and depression escalate through positive feedback processes to the point where they are unbearable will often go through some transformational change to relieve themselves of the disorganized state and its noxious consequences. The disorganization-reorganization can occur in a diversity of ways. For example, the most drastic is to commit suicide; the ultimate reorganization. Another is to go through an emotional decompensation and end up in a psychotic state. A third is to sedate oneself with alcohol or drugs. A fourth is to forget the whole thing and develop an amnesia. A fifth is to experience a religious conversion and resolve the disorganization with a new faith in powers greater than oneself. Very intense behavior episodes may trigger significant disorganization and reorganization. The various kinds of psychological and behavioral disruptions and reorganizations displayed by soldiers as a result of traumatic battle experiences are dramatic examples. Drastic sudden changes in a person's habitual environment can also produce severe functional disorganization. The death of a beloved spouse, the imprisonment of a successful and well-to-do person, and retirement all illustrate life events that are severely disorganizing for some people. Prolonged periods of severe stress can lead to system breakdown (or disorganization) and reorganization, producing "diseases of adaptation" as described by Selye (1976).

FACTORS THAT INFLUENCE THE REORGANIZATION PROCESS

Not all disorganization-reorganization patterns carry such negative connotations. For example, one form of *creative thought* is to juxtapose conflicting or contradictory ideas, creating severe cognitive dissonance, and then to try to reorganize the ideas so that they fit together coherently.

Disorganization Flexibility

One characteristic of the transitional period between disorganization and reorganization is called *disorganization flexibility*. In such states greater diversity in functional patterns is more likely to occur than when life is flowing smoothly in habitual steady states, because old BES are no longer functional. For example, a person may try things he or she never considered before. As a result more developmental options may be open. This is illustrated with the basketball player example at the beginning of the chapter. The sudden death of her husband and child produced severe intraperson and person-context disruptions, including loss of her job. As she struggled to reorganize her life, she tried a diversity of possibilities, for example, she moved to live with her husband's parents, she tried three other jobs, and she tried to renew a relationship with an old boyfriend.

This increased variability is a key reason why crisis intervention methods are so valuable. If a therapist can work with a person when he or she is in this transition period it is much easier to help him or her construct an effective reorganization than it is after he or she has reorganized into a different steady state. That is, during transitional periods the person is more likely to consider and to try a diversity of possibilities. Once reorganization occurs, stability-maintaining processes protect the new steady state and make change more difficult. Under those circumstances it may be necessary to try to disrupt a faulty steady state to open up new developmental alternatives. This rationale is implicit in procedures such as removing a child from an abusing family, electric shock therapy for severely depressed persons, and imprisonment of criminal offenders to disrupt their criminal behavior and to create rehabilitation possibilities.

Stability-Instability Ratio

A second factor that influences the ease with which a reorganization can be accomplished is called the stability-instability ratio. The more aspects of a person's life that are disrupted, the more extensive and difficult is the reorganization task. For example, a man was devastated to discover his wife was cheating on him. He not only decided to divorce his wife but also was planning to quit his job (at which he was quite successful), move to a different part of the country, and change his career. In other words he was considering disrupting most major aspects of his life. His counselor convinced him that he should delay the other disrupting actions until he had completed his marital transition. It is helpful to keep some aspects of life stable when dealing with major disruptions of other aspects.

Transition Protection

A third factor that can influence the reorganization process is called *transition protection*. As illustrated earlier in regard to embryonic development, living systems are more vulnerable when they are in transitional disorganized states. When people are going through significant personal or life disruptions, they are usually less capable of coping with other life demands that ordinarily would not be a problem. Therefore the reorganization process is often facilitated if they can be buffered somewhat from typical life demands until some new steady state begins to be effective. Bed rest of the ill, temporary hospitalization, a temporary leave from a job, the help of caring family and friends, and social support or self-help groups illustrate various forms of such transition protection. In our basketball player example, her temporary hospitalization and living with her husband's parents thereafter illustrate transition protection arrangements. A more positive example is a scholar struggling to make sense out of diverse and conflicting evidence and ideas. Large blocks of uninterrupted time facilitate that cognitive reorganization process by protecting the efforts at mental reorganization from being interrupted by other kinds of BEs.

Developmental Pathways Through Life Emerge From the Operation of All Three Processes

Each incremental or transformational change alters the possibilities and probabilities for future kinds of change. This is because the organismic boundary conditions have changed and development always starts with what exists. In addition, environments also display incremental and transformational, predictable and unpredictable change, thereby altering the environmental boundary conditions for change. Therefore development is probabilistic, open ended, and somewhat unpredictable. (See assumptions 4 and 4c in Table 3.1.) Figures 5.2 and 5.3, presented as an analogy to a Scrabble game, can be used to illustrate this process. The basic rules of Scrabble are that (a) any new word formed must use at least one letter of an existing word, and (b) no letters can be juxtaposed that do not form a word. This is analogous to saying that all development must start with something that already exists, and that any change must preserve the organizational coherence of the whole.

Figure 5.2 and the example of the basketball player presented in the beginning of this chapter will be used to illustrate the open-ended and unpredictable nature of developmental pathways shaped by incremental and transformational change processes. This woman started life in an impoverished, illiterate, physically abusing family that involved many developmentally constraining conditions and few facilitating ones. Figure 5.2 represents early phases of her development. A newborn baby, she started with limited "built-in" capabilities as the starting point for further development (Phase I). As an infant and young child she had few possibilities for learning and doing new things. This is symbolized by a tightly organized combination of

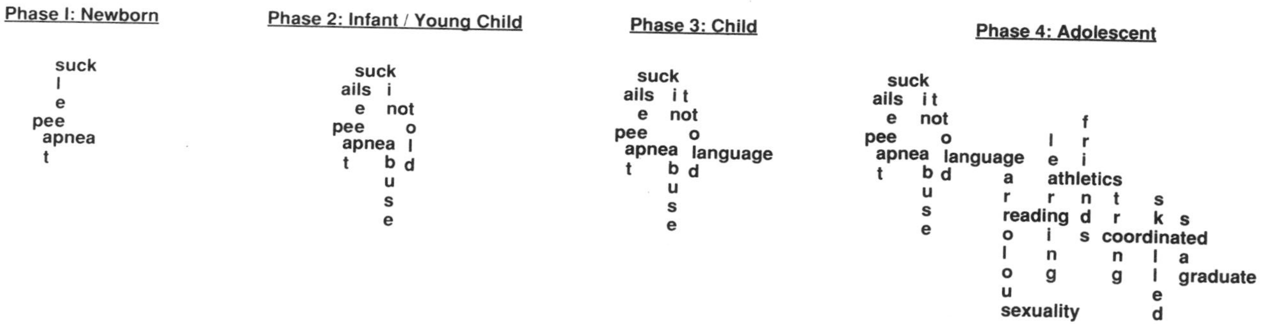

Figure 5.2. The ways in which changes in existing capabilities constrain or expand future development possibilities is illustrated using a Scrabble game as an analogy. The basic developmental rules are that new words (new capabilities) can only be created by adding letters to the existing set of words (elaborating existing capabilities to create new ones), and the developmental outcome must always be a coherent new word (a new capability that is compatible with existing ones). Therefore the greater the number of letters available to start new words, the greater the diversity of possible new words (the greater the diversity of existing capabilities, the more opportunities there are for elaborations into new capabilities). Each new word created thus opens new possibilities (each new capability constructed opens new behavioral possibilities).

words in Phase 2 of the Scrabble game; this organization provides only a few possibilities for constructing new words.

Then, when the girl started to school (Phase 3), a grade-school teacher concluded that she was a "diamond in the rough," and the teacher decided to use the girl's athletic ambitions and skills as motivation for cultivating her other capabilities. He tells her that she cannot be on the basketball team unless she learns to read. Note in Phase 3 of the Scrabble game that the word "language" provides most of the opportunities for constructing new words, just as it provides the basis for much new learning in real life. Building on her existing talking and listening language capability, and with special reading classes, she learns to read, enjoys it, and begins reading all kinds of material. Adding reading skill to her Scrabble game of life opens up many new possibilities for her as symbolized by all of the words linked to the word "reading" in Phase 4. The woman learns much more in her classes, starts earning superior grades, becomes a high school basketball star, has many good times with her school friends, and graduates from high school in the top 30% of her class and with the respect of her teachers.

Compare Phases 3 and 4 in Figure 5.2. Note three things. First, the life pattern symbolized in Phase 3 is now a minor part of the elaborated life pattern she has constructed as symbolized in Phase 4. Second, development progresses by elaborating from component letters rather than from entire words. The adding of new words symbolizes outcomes called elaborations, while the spelling of a word to represent an idea symbolizes differentiation processes. Third, not everything is connected to everything else. This is symbolized by letters that are only a part of their original word. The "undeveloped letters" (undeveloped potentials) symbolize components of a person's behavior repertoire or personality that are potential starting points for alternate developmental pathways.

Consider for a moment all the new possibilities in her life contained in Phase 4. She has excellent athletic skills, a high school diploma with good grades, well-developed intellectual skills, and a network of good friends and admiring adults. Where might she go from here?

One possibility is that she could have an accident that crippled her for life (an unpredictable change), eliminating the potential of her using her athletic competence and reputation as a basis for building her future life. Instead a different kind of pathway opened up for this hypothetical young woman as summarized in Phases

5-7, in Figure 5.3. Phase 5 represents her post-high school, young adulthood development. The father of a friend knew the basketball coach at a major university and told that coach about her (serendipity again). The coach offered her a basketball scholarship, so she went to the university, became an all-American player, completed a degree in business, and got a good job as a young business executive. She fell in love, married, had a child, and began saving for what appeared to be a bright future.

All of this probably would not have happened if a teacher and coach had not taken an interest in her, helped her learn to read, and cultivated her athletic skills in Phases 3 and 4 of Figure 5.2. These new competencies dramatically changed both the organismic and environmental facilitating and constraining conditions in her life, leading her step-by-step down a developmental pathway no one could have predicted from her humble, impoverished beginning.

But then the relatively smooth, progressive elaboration of a happy life was unexpectedly and drastically disorganized by the sudden tragic death of her husband and child in an auto accident. In the aftermath she lost her job. As a result, most major aspects of her life were severely disorganized, as symbolized by the scattered letters in Phase 6 of the Scrabble game. Her life hit bottom in a severe, prolonged depression, culminating in a suicidal attempt and hospitalization. As she began to recover from that episode she made sporadic attempts to start a new life, all without success (the transitional phase between disorganization and reorganization). Then fortuitously she attended an Easter service in a Catholic church, was deeply moved, and experienced a dramatic transformation in her feelings about herself and her life (transformational change through reorganization). As a result she committed herself to a new direction and through incremental change processes progressively elaborated a new and very different life for herself as symbolized in Phase 7 of Figure 5.3.

Summary and Implications

Life is full of a smooth flow of events as well as unpredictable, fortuitous occurrences. Some people see and seize the opportunities that come to them and some do not. Some suffer from many more constraints on their possibilities than do others. Some suffer major

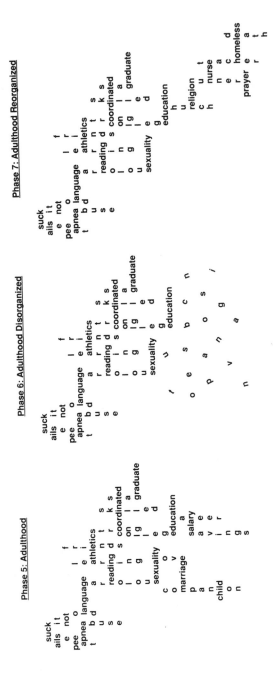

Figure 5.3. A continuation of the Scrabble game analogy presented in Figure 5.2. Illustrated by analogy is the transformation of a person's development pathway as a result of fortuitous events that precipitate disorganization-reorganization processes.

life disruptions and create a reorganized life that is fulfilling in new ways, whereas others go through transformations that restrict rather than elaborate their lives. But the basic process is the same for all of us. The initial conditions of life do not determine one's life course. One's life course is constructed phase by phase as events and one's own efforts successively and incrementally or transformationally change the constraints and possibilities through life.

Equifinality

One of the characteristics of open, living systems is that starting from different initial conditions and following different developmental pathways, similar developmental outcomes can result. Biologists have labeled this phenomenon *equifinality* (von Bertalanffy, 1968). In mechanical, deterministic systems the outcome is fully predictable from knowledge of initial conditions and the forces applied thereafter. This is not true for living systems because they are self-organizing and self-constructing rather than simply reactive in environments that are also self-organizing and self-constructing. For example, our young basketball player had a classmate from a well-to-do middle-class family (very different initial conditions). They both ended up graduating in business and both became successful young executives. Different initial conditions and different developmental pathways led to similar outcomes. The opposite may also occur. For example, imagine an equally talented twin sister of our basketball player. A friend introduced her to drugs, she got hooked, dropped out of school, became a prostitute, and eventually died of AIDS.

The principle of equifinality and the other principles of DST have very important social implications. DST emphasizes that one should not assume that certain developmental outcomes are predetermined by the organismic and environmental boundary conditions currently operative in a person's life. At any time of life the organismic and environmental boundary conditions for development that exist may be changeable. Even within the existing boundary conditions more than one developmental pathway is possible. Perhaps by starting with whatever current strengths or potentials a person has (e.g., undeveloped letters in their Scrabble game of life) and by creating a different environment and sequence of experiences, he or she can construct a developmental pathway that leads to quite different outcomes than those that appear probable in his or her initial circumstances.

For example, one should not assume that a person's heredity (e.g., their "bad blood") dooms him or her to certain developmental outcomes such as criminology, madness, or heart disease (Lerner, 1992). Alternatively, one should seek to create conditions and behavior episodes that create better developmental pathways. This is essentially the premise and rationale underlying activities as diverse as genetic engineering to prevent or cure various biologically based difficulties, developmental programming for mentally retarded and physically handicapped children, preschool Headstart educational programs, rehabilitative programs for physically damaged people, and retirement planning for older adults.

From the most humble initial conditions, great lives have been constructed, and from the most favorable initial conditions, lives of incompetence and degradation have been created. In Developmental Systems Theory, developmental pathways do not unfold along a predetermined course; they are constructed through processes of living that involve both continuities and discontinuities and that result both from smooth sailing and by transcending stormy seas.

Final Steps

The presentation has now been completed of the metamodel (Chapter 3) and the operational model (Chapters 4 and 5) of Developmental Systems Theory. Its purpose is to provide a more comprehensive approach to understanding the content of developmental pathways and outcomes as well as the change processes that generate different kinds of developmental patterns. We have not done this because it is an interesting intellectual exercise; rather, our purpose has been to create a useful tool for both developmental scientists and professionals. Therefore in the final chapter we will illustrate how DST might be useful in guiding develomental research and designing developmental interventions.

CHAPTER SIX

The Present as Prologue to the Future

IN CHAPTER ONE we considered how metamodels of development constructed in the past have influenced developmental theory and research during this century. Horowitz (1987) notes that the major influential theories of development were largely formulated prior to 1930. She asserts that they have remained relatively unmodified (except for Piaget's theory) by empirical evidence about development, most of which has accumulated since they were constructed. We proposed that developmental contextualism and the Living Systems Framework have emerged as products of a growing effort since 1970 to create alternative approaches that more adequately capture existing knowledge, especially about the complexity and diversity of development. We believe that their fusion into Developmental Systems Theory produces a new and more comprehensive theory of human development than any that presently exist.

Analogous to individual development as represented by the model presented in this book, theory development occurs through differentiation, elaboration, combination, and transformation of the fruits of past formulations. (See Piaget & Garcia, 1989, for a similar view of science.) DST is no exception. No single idea within it is new. Each component idea has a history, and therefore DST is deeply indebted to the creative efforts of many other scholars, as illustrated by the range of citations in this book. What we believe is new is the way the component ideas are organized to provide a more comprehensive representation of both the substance and dynamics of contextually fused human development across the life span. It represents (and hopefully encompasses) a family of proposals resting on similar assumptions, ranging from those of the Russians Basov and Bogdanov early in this century (Valsiner, 1988) to proposals presented during the 1980s such as those by Baltes (1987), Brim and Kagan (1980), Featherman (1983), Horowitz (1987), Oyama (1985), Samaroff (1983), and Piaget's (1983) most recent theorizing.

The purpose of this chapter is to focus on possible futures for developmental research and interventions based upon what is presently known and upon more recent theorizing, rather than upon the past. We, along with many others, have argued that different kinds of models and theories have practical consequences for both research and developmental interventions. In this chapter we will first illustrate the implications of DST for formulating research questions. Then we will consider implications for the kinds of research designs and methods used, followed by implications for professional and social applications.

Implications for Research Questions

DST proposes that both stability and change in all facets of humans result from mutual causal processes among multiple variables (i.e., from networks or organizations of variables), that somewhat different combinations of variables may lead to the same developmental outcome, and that development does not result solely from simple linear, additive processes but also from combinations of stability maintaining states altered or interrupted by periods of incremental and transformational change (cf. Featherman, 1983; Featherman & Lerner, 1985; Tobach, 1981). Moreover, different developmental possibilities and dynamics will emerge as successive developmental changes are manifest in both individuals and their contexts. Development is open ended; it has a direction but not fixed end points. The same variable may have one influence in one organization of variables at one developmental moment and a different influence in a different network of variables at a different developmental moment. Therefore questions of the form "To what extent do genes influence development?" or "To what extent does the environment influence development?" are considered inappropriate. Rather, questions take a more multivariate, multidimensional, dynamic form in which the relationships among variables represent mutual causal processes that are often nonlinear in character.

A diversity of examples of research questions suggested by DST will illustrate its heuristic implications. This is not meant to imply that no evidence exists with regard to many of the illustrative questions. In fact, one way to use DST (and any other theory) as a research tool is to use research questions derived from them to try to synthesize and interpret existing evidence about development and to identify shortcomings in existing research.

EARLY DEVELOPMENT: THE BIOBEHAVIORAL PERSON

From conception through early infancy the complexly and hierarchically organized person develops into a full human form that makes possible all the basic human functional capabilities, including those that make possible psychological and behavioral self-organization and self-construction (Tobach & Schneirla, 1968). If some marked deviation in the normative range of organism-context relations occurs during this phase of development, then the foundations for future development will be different and this variation could create lifelong constraints on future developmental possibilities. Organisms are particularly vulnerable during periods of transformational change. Therefore there are many important questions to be answered about that developmental phase as illustrated by the following.

What are the significant points of *transformational change* during embryonic and fetal development; what individual differences exist in their timing and nature, and what genetic/environment combinations might produce such differences? What specific genetic characteristics and biochemical and tissues states appear to combine to regulate each of these transformational changes? What characteristics of the embryonic/fetal biochemical environment are most likely to produce unwanted deviations in the species-typical developmental outcome(s) of each of those transformational periods (e.g., fetal alcohol syndrome)? What kinds of individual differences can be identified in the nature of developmental vulnerabilities during these transformational periods, and what might be the sources of such individual differences? What biochemical and/or genetic interventions might enhance the efficiency and effectiveness of, or overcome vulnerabilities that might exist in, each of those transformational periods? What kinds of individual differences in development can be identified in response to such interventions?

Because the nervous system provides the biological foundation for information-based self-organization and self-construction and for alteration of psychological/behavioral patterns, the nature of its early development is critical for later development. When, in what ways, and to what extent can different kinds and patterns of information transactions and motor activity optimize or retard neurological development during the embryonic, fetal, infancy, and adult periods of life? How may different kinds of material/energy exchanges (e.g., nutrition; inefficient kidney or lung function) affect neurological development during these periods. How do these material/energy-based processes interact with information-based transactions and motor activity to facilitate or constrain neurological development? What kinds of individual differences in neurological development can be identified in relationship to the capability for, timing of, and outcomes of such patterns of information transactions, motor activity, and material/energy exchanges (e.g., exposure to sounds in utero; constraint of movement or sensory exploration of the environment during the first few weeks of life)? Are there developmental differences related to cultural differences in the occurrence of and combinations of these kinds of variables?

EARLY DEVELOPMENT:
THE PSYCHOLOGICAL/BEHAVIORAL PERSON

What patterns of relationships exist between states of neurological development and functioning and information-based self-organizing and self-constructing capabilities and outcomes during infancy and early childhood (e.g., development of motor skills; cognitive processes and concept formation; comprehension and use of language)? In what ways, in what combinations, and at what times can different kinds of, and efficiency of, information-based functioning (e.g., sensoriperceptual, cognitive, communicative, and motoric) facilitate or constrain psychological and behavioral development and the development of the biological structures and processes that make those functions possible?

What kinds of psychological and behavioral developmental outcomes will be manifest in essentially similar ways in all normal humans who develop in a species-typical environmental niche (e.g., sensoriperceptual capabilities and basic motor patterns; modes of information processing; emotional arousal processes)? Is there a standard sequence in which any "universal" developmental outcomes appear in normal fetal/infant development, or may they emerge in multiple sequential patterns?

When and how in the course of development are differences in environmental factors likely to be most significant? What material/energy-based or information-based interventions might alter the developmental pathway from an unwanted direction to a desired direction, and when may this be done to, for example, prevent or overcome unwanted deviations in neurological, attentional, cognitive, or motoric capabilities?

DEVELOPMENT OF COMPONENT PSYCHOLOGICAL/BEHAVIORAL PROCESSES

Development is a multilevel process, so understanding development at component levels is one important objective (Schneirla, 1957; Tobach, 1981). What neurological and biochemical structures and processes undergird the development and functioning of prototypical human attentional, emotional arousal, sensoriperceptual, cognitive, action, and information-based self-organizing and self-constructing processes? How do these neurological and biochemical structures and processes change across the life course, and how do those changes affect psychological/behavioral development and functioning (e.g., puberty; menopause; decline in the efficiency of production of different kinds of neurochemicals)? What kinds of conditions of living (e.g., environmental characteristics interacting with patterns of behavior) will optimize the development, maintenance, and functioning of these neurological and biochemical bases of each kind of component capability?

Attentional Processes

DST proposes that attentional processes operate to selectively activate the nervous system to produce coherently organized and selectively effective intraperson and person-context patterns. Therefore their operation is critical for the development and functioning of complex behavior patterns.

What conditions may facilitate or constrain the optimal development and functioning of selective attentional processes related both to intraperson and person-context psychological/behavioral patterns at different phases of life? What are the consequences of developmental deviations in attentional capabilities for other kinds of psychological and behavioral development (e.g., of cognitive development or task persistence) at different phases of life? What kinds of interventions might alter unwanted deviations in attentional capabilities.

Emotional Arousal Patterns

DST proposes that emotional arousal patterns contribute to three critical system functions:

1. They alter biological functioning in support of actual or anticipated variations in activity patterns and environmental contingencies.
2. They interact with cognitive processes in evaluating and regulating the flow of behavior.
3. Affective displays influence person-context transactions. Therefore their operation has implications both for the construction of and effectiveness of complex behavior patterns and for healthy biological functioning of humans.

What basic kinds of emotional arousal patterns are prototypically present in infants, what are the characteristics of and individual differences in each kind of pattern (e.g., in regard to temperament), and what are the prototypical conditions under which they occur? When, under what conditions, and in what ways are emotional arousal patterns and their eliciting conditions elaborated or altered? How do different kinds of emotional arousal patterns facilitate and constrain functioning in different kinds of behavior episodes and influence the development of behavior episode schemata (e.g., memories, personal goals, values, coping strategies)? What developmental patterns exist concerning how different kinds of emotional arousal patterns influence the nature of individuals' reactions to, expectations of, and strategies for dealing with interpersonal relationships? What are the biological/health effects of persistent or chronic occurrence of each kind of emotional arousal pattern of which humans are capable (e.g., anger, fear, affection, pleasure) and how do these differ interindividually and in different developmental phases?

Sensoriperceptual Processes

DST proposes that sensoriperceptual processes operate to selectively collect information about the internal functioning of the person, about characteristics of his or her environment, and about the nature and dynamics of person-environment relationships. It is proposed that direct perceptions represent consistencies in the flow of stimulation across sensory receptors, and perceptual information serves the feedback processes on which the dynamics of system regulation depend. Perception also provides one starting point from which cognitive construction begins. Therefore the nature and accuracy of sensoriperceptual processes is critical for psychological/behavioral self-organization and self-construction.

To what extent and how can cognitive, attentional, or emotional-arousal processes selectively "tune" each kind of sensory structure to be more or less sensitive to different aspects of the information flow across it? In what ways and how do different sensoriperceptual modalities interact to produce coherent multimodal perceptions that integrate information of different kinds? If a particular sensoriperceptual modality malfunctions, to what extent can other modalities be trained to compensate for that malfunction, and does this differ at different phases of life? What biological, environmental, and behavioral conditions produce and maintain optimal development and functioning of the various sensoriperceptual processes? What life course developmental patterns exist in the various aspects of sensoriperceptual processes?

Cognitive Processes

DST proposes that cognitive processes operate to construct information-based representations that combine perceptual, abstract, and linguistic codes, and to use those representations to construct, organize, guide, and regulate individual's behavior patterns in relationship to their contexts. The elaborateness and flexibility of human cognitive capabilities enable humans not only to react to but also to anticipate and shape environments and events as well as their own capabilities (Kendall, Lerner, & Craighead, 1984; Lerner, Baker, & Lerner, 1985). Therefore understanding cognitive development is crucial for understanding humans.

What kinds of information processing and problem-solving strategies do people use to construct different kinds of cognitive representations (e.g., of quantitative and qualitative differences among objects; propositional knowledge representing both static and dynamic relationships among objects, events, and themselves)? When, under what conditions, and how do people use perceptual, abstract, and linguistic codes, singly and in combination, to construct, revise, elaborate, manipulate, and use cognitive representations? Are there points of transformational change in the nature of the strategies and codes used? If so, is there a fixed developmental sequence or may such transformational changes occur at different times depending upon the nature of the flow of the person's behavior-environment transactions? Do the information processing strategies and codes people use change as they progress through life? To what extent are different kinds of information processing and problem-solving strategies and codes learnable, and does this vary with different phases of life and across cultures?

When and how do infants/children begin to construct and use personal goals to selectively organize their behavior? What are the characteristics of behavior episodes (e.g., task definitions; nature of interpersonal interactions; emotional states) that facilitate or constrain the construction of such representations and their use by individuals in organizing and guiding their behavior? When, under what circumstances, and how do children and adults construct personal goal hierarchies and learn to organize and execute behavior episodes that simultaneously or sequentially serve several goals? What kinds of behavior episode (e.g., task) conditions facilitate or constrain people learning to persist in and to vary their activities in the pursuit of desired outcomes in the face of delays and obstacles to their accomplishment? What kinds of conditions disrupt or alter patterns of goal-directed activity (e.g., panic attacks)? How and under what conditions do personal goal construction, modification, and use change across the life course? Does this vary across cultures, and if so, why and how? (e.g. see Baltes & Baltes, 1986, for discussion of the importance of control beliefs and behaviors.)

When do infants/children begin to construct and use patterns of evaluative thoughts (e.g., values or personal agency beliefs) to regulate the flow of their behavior? What are the characteristics of behavior episodes that facilitate or constrain the development and use of different patterns of evaluative thought? Because emotional arousal patterns also perform regulatory functions, how do different kinds of emotional arousal patterns and interpersonal observations and experiences influence the kinds of evaluative thought patterns children construct and use? When, under what conditions, and how do people learn to resolve value conflicts (e.g., cognitive-affective and cognitive-cognitive conflicts)? Do patterns of cognitive and affective self-regulation change with different phases of life (e.g., adolescence, adult years, old age), and, if so, when and how? Are there cultural differences in these processes, and, if so, why?

When, under what conditions, and how do infants and children develop different skills for carrying out transactions with their contexts, for example, motor and communication skills? How do attentional, cognitive, affective, and environmental processes interact in influencing the development of such skills? What conditions facilitate and constrain the elaboration of such skills across the life course? If the biological structures that make such skills possible become damaged, to what extent, when and how can alternative structures be organized to provide alternate ways of carrying out the same kinds of transactions (e.g., communication; object manipulation)? Do the patterns of development of transactional skills vary in different cultures, and, if so, why?

THE DEVELOPMENT OF COMPLEX BEHAVIOR PATTERNS AND PERSONALITY

DST proposes that individuals always function as a unit in a context. Therefore component structures and processes cannot develop separately from one another. In both processes and outcomes they must maintain coherent intraperson and person-context organization. DST proposes that *behavior episodes (BE)* and *behavior episode schemata (BES)* are units of analysis that can be used for understanding the development and functioning of complex behavior patterns. It is also proposed that *personality development* may be represented by changes in individuals' repertoire of BES and their operation. Therefore understanding how BES are constructed, maintained, modified, and elaborated from BE experiences, and how BES operate to organize, guide, and regulate functioning within different kinds of BEs, is very important.

What BE conditions facilitate and constrain the construction and modification of efficient, effective BES in different life phases? When, under what conditions, and how do infants and small children begin to construct BES and to use them in organizing later episodes of behavior? In what ways do different characteristics of behavior episodes (e.g., task design) facilitate or constrain the construction of effective behavior episode schemata or the activation and use of previously constructed BES in new behavior episodes? Are some kinds of BES more easily constructed than others in certain periods of development? What characteristics of behavior episodes facilitate or constrain the revision, elaboration, or combining of previously constructed BES or their components (e.g., in skill development; in acquisition of knowledge)?

What characteristics of behavior episodes facilitate or constrain the activation and use in new situations of previously constructed BES (e.g., transfer of training)? What characteristics of BE experiences produce BES with greater or lesser degrees of resilience or generative flexibility and are there developmental differences in these capabilities? What kinds of behavior episode conditions can overcome stability-maintaining processes so that further change in habitual BES becomes possible and are there developmental differences in this regard? What kinds of BE or biological conditions within a person are likely to be sufficiently disruptive so as to precipitate some kind of psychological/behavioral transformational change? How might the development of such transformational change conditions be anticipated and prevented, facilitated, or channeled into preferred directions?

What characteristics of people's BES repertoire facilitate or constrain further psychological/behavioral change or development throughout their adult life? If there are changes in biological factors that constrain further development, in what ways might those be overcome or compensated for?

How do different kinds of social and cultural conditions (e.g., social-economic status [SES], customs, shared beliefs, laws, or religions) facilitate or constrain the kinds of BEs in which individuals are likely to participate at different phases of life and the kinds of elaborations of their BES repertoire that might be possible for them?

How do observational, instrumental, and thinking types of behavior episodes interact in individuals' construction, maintenance, modification, elaboration, and combining of BES, and are there particular combinations that are most effective in facilitating the construction of certain kinds of BES and related performances (e.g., doing chemistry vs. athletics)?

Implications for Research Methods

DST and its distinctions between variability, decremental and elaborative change, and development presents certain implications for the selection of research methodologies for the study of human development. As Nesselroade (1991) put it:

> Instead of conceptualizing the individual as a rather static package of more or less stable true scores that change only relatively slowly and gradually according to developmental (and learning) principles, the individual should be thought of as a dynamic, labile, fluctuating, changing entity, some of whose attributes are relatively stable over time but which change developmentally. (p. 19)

Individuals would also be different in different contexts, from the perspective of DST. One consequence of this view, Nesselroade (1991) asserts, "is that intraindividual changes in the parameters of intraindividual variability distributions become a focus of research on developmental pathways" (p. 20).

Development cannot be adequately studied with research designs that yield only information about single-occasion interindividual differences because the study of change and development requires the comparison of multiple states of the same person. (See Chapter 2.) Therefore the basic form of developmental research design must focus first on identifying patterns of intraindividual consistency, variability, and change in relevant states across multiple occasions. Then it becomes possible to examine patterns of interindividual consistencies and differences in patterns of intraindividual consistency and change. (See Baltes, Reese, & Nesselroade, 1977; Nesselroade, 1987, 1988, 1990a, 1990b, 1991; Nesselroade & Ford, 1985, 1987; Nesselroade & von Eye, 1985; Wohlwill, 1973.)

Also, because humans function and develop as complex, open systems in contexts, consistencies and changes in any single variable or pair of variables usually cannot be adequately identified and understood outside the network of variables in which they are embedded. Unlike the passengers on Noah's Ark, human development cannot be understood by examining variables two by two. Moreover, the multidimensional nature of development requires that research designs permit examination of multiple developmental pathways that may yield the same or different developmental outcomes. Therefore *sound developmental research should involve multivariate, multioccasion designs.*

Because it is not practical to simultaneously study every aspect of a complex system, however, subsets of variables must be selected for examination in any particular research project. It becomes important, then, to select those subsets of variables in such a way that they can be linked across sets of studies to represent the larger network of variables of which they are components, for example, through use of "marker variables." One possibility for simplifying the number of variables studied simultaneously is to construct coefficients that summarize relationships for many variables with one value (von Eye, 1985). Another is to have some kind of model of the larger system that can be used to guide such selection and integration of variables and empirical evidence. DST provides one such model. Another way is to use sampling designs that facilitate the integration of results across multiple studies.

Developmental research designs involve at least three basic kinds of sampling decisions:

1. Selection of the subset of variables to be examined and of methods for assessing those variables that will be sensitive to possible intraindividual changes and amenable to revealing the network of relationships among them;
2. Selection of the phase of life in which to examine the specific kinds of change/development of interest (e.g., infancy or middle age), of the population of persons to be studied within that phase of life (e.g., female infants), and some number of specific individuals to be studied who represent that population and phase of life; and
3. Selection of the kinds of behavior episodes or occasions in which the state of each variable and its interactions will be observed/measured (e.g., context for the observation; nature of the task conditions; procedures for obtaining the information); the "size" of the observational frame (e.g., temporal length) and number of episodes or occasions on which the relevant information will be determined and the time intervals between those occasions will be set.

These three kinds of sampling decisions must be interrelated because they must be appropriately linked if one is to capture accurate information about development. Traditionally, discussions of sampling and sample size have emphasized number 2 above, that is, the sampling of persons. This has led to guidelines for evaluating the adequacy of a study's sample that rest solely on the number of persons (or other units) studied. "The sample size is too small" typically means "You haven't studied enough people." In the study of development, however, the adequacy of the other samples is equally important. "The sample size is too small" can also mean "You haven't studied each person on sufficient relevant occasions to capture accurate information about development" or "Your sample of variables is inadequate."

A fourth issue, observational vantage points for obtaining information about relevant variables, could be considered a sampling issue. Information about a person could be obtained through self-observation and report, through observations and reports of significant others or some neutral observers, through direct measures of various functions or of task accomplishments. Phenomena may appear different from different observational vantage points so multimethod approaches permit identifying convergences among methods.

Within DST the following basic research design sampling strategy is suggested. First, specify the period of life to be studied. Second, identify the sample of variables (both individual and contextual) that needs to be included in the study to provide the desired information for understanding one person in that phase of life. Third, decide on the sample of occasions (type, length and number of BEs; time between occasions) that will be necessary to provide the needed information about patterns of consistency, variability, and change for one person. This combination of sampling decisions will lead to the necessary information concerning intraindividual patterns. Then decide with how many persons it is desirable to replicate that information to provide a reasonable basis for identifying patterns of *interindividual* consistency and differences. That approach is sometimes called a *replicated, multivariate, single-subject design*. Generalizability is a function of the combination of several kinds of sampling decisions, not just the number of people studied! (See Siegler & Crowley, 1991, for a discussion of the use of "microgenetic methods" in studying cognitive development.)

There are tradeoffs. For example, which combination of samples is likely to be most valuable in the study of development: (a) to collect a small amount of information about a lot of people on one or two occasions or (b) to collect a larger amount of information about a smaller number of people on a larger number of occasions? Empirical study of which combinations of samples will be most powerful for different kinds of research questions is sorely needed. We suspect that such empirical investigations will reveal that a sounder generalizability base for understanding development can be produced from studying a much smaller number of persons than is often recommended *if* a more adequate number of variables and occasions is sampled for each person. Moreover, it is often more practical and feasible to study fewer people more intensively. The utility of studying fewer subjects more intensively is impressively demonstrated by the lifetime research programs of Freud, Piaget and Skinner; however, if the objective is to understand or predict group functioning on a specific occasion, then other sampling combinations may be more useful. For example, samples of many people on few occasions produce relatively accurate predictions of election returns. (See Nesselroade, 1991, for an extended examination of these and related issues and for proposals about how to proceed.)

There are also implications for data analysis methods. The selection of a data analysis model for any study should be closely integrated with decisions about the assumptions concerning the phenomena to be studied, the research questions being addressed, and the research design being used. Data analysis models are tools for trying to reveal the patterns of organization in the samples of variables, occasions, and persons included in the study. Unfortunately, research in the social and behavioral sciences tends to be dominated by one family of data analysis approaches sometimes called *the linear model*, a family not adequate for many developmental research questions. Nesselroade and Ford (1987) state:

> The prevailing methodological orientation in social and behavioral science research is to model relationships among variables using linear, additive representations that apply to relatively small selections of occasions of measurement. Various ANOVA models as well as the regression-based structural models fitted by programs such as LISREL exemplify these representations. When such mathematical and statistical models are used with multioccasion data to model process and change, they tend not to be dynamic in character (i.e., the parameters of the models do not change as a function of time). (p. 73)

DST and the kinds of research questions it generates require, according to Nesselroade and Ford (1987):

> the use of mathematical models that are capable of simultaneously attending to multiple individuals, multiple variables, and multiple occasions of measurement. This means that we must be able to deal

not only with patterns of both intraindividual change and stability but also with interindividual differences in those intraindividual change and stability patterns, all within a multivariate framework that is capable of capturing pertinent features of the organism and its context. (p. 74)

There are some data analytic approaches presently available to social and behavioral scientists that come closer to these requirements. For example, von Eye (1990) describes methods for identifying patterns of organization in sets of categorical variables. Structural P-technique (Nesselroade & McArdle, 1986) uses sophisticated mathematical and statistical procedures that combine time-series and factor-analysis modeling (McArdle, 1990; Molenaar, 1985). The increased popularity of qualitative methods reflects increasing disillusionment with traditional data analytic models, and the growing desire of many scholars to find ways of more adequately identifying and representing the complex and often nonlinear patterns of consistency and change that are characteristic of humans. The ultimate goal should be to find ways of merging the informational richness of qualitative methods with the precision of mathematically based data analytic models.

Developmental research needs some new data analysis tools that can more adequately model dynamic, complex systems such as humans. We hope that some of the mathematically sophisticated developmentalists will devote their attention to the creation of such tools. There are other mathematical forms that hold promise for application to developmental research. For example, chaos theory (see Gleick, 1987, for a simplified presentation) and other methods that rest upon the use of sets of differential equations appear to hold considerable potential. Similarly the possibilities of mathematical group theory might be explored. As has been true in other fields of science, we think some methodological breakthroughs in developmental science could have a significant impact in producing advances in the field, and the field would be wise to encourage, promote, and support such efforts.

Implications for Professional Interventions

There are also implications for professional applications in fields such as parenting, education, health care, and mental health services. A few such implications will be described.

If DST is correct in representing individuals as self-organizing, self-constructing open systems fused with their environments, then it follows that it is not possible to change persons simply by doing something "to them." Rather, what interventions can do is to facilitate or constrain individuals' own self-organizing and self-constructing processes. This is true for the biobehavioral person as well as for the psychological and social or action persons. It is impossible to over-emphasize that, in the final analysis, each of us must do it for our-selves! It is also critical to understand that what we can do and construct, however, is significantly constrained and facilitated by contextual conditions and current personal characteristics. Several examples of material/energy-based biological interventions will illustrate this point.

Healthy infant biological growth and development is a function of the materials they ingest. Infant caretakers can create conditions to facilitate healthy biological development by providing a nutritionally sound diet; however, if the infant will not eat, cannot adequately digest the materials ingested, cannot adequately absorb into the bloodstream the essential nutrients, cannot adequately circulate them to all parts of the body, cannot carry out essential biological processes, or cannot excrete waste products that accrue during the process, then healthy development will be constrained regardless of caretaker ef-forts. For example, an infant was fed a nutritionally sound formula but nearly died from an allergic reaction to one of its ingredients. Analogously, sound development is not possible when available nu-trition is seriously deficient.

When people contract an infection, their immune systems (which provide biological stability-maintaining processes) mount a battle to overcome the infection and to restore a healthy steady state. A physi-cian may prescribe an antibiotic drug to help fight the infection; however, such drugs can only supplement and assist the immune system in the destruction of the infection; the drugs are not, by themselves, a cure.

Recognizing that humans are open systems leads to the design of interventions to shape environmental contingencies to reduce the possibility that environmental transactions will produce infections or other disruptions of healthy steady states. This is the primary focus of public health programs. For example, at the turn of the century in Philadelphia, Pennsylvania, 8,000 to 10,000 cases of typhoid fever occurred each year. By 1925 this had been reduced to approximately

200 cases a year. This change resulted from water purification as a result of the introduction of filtration in 1906 and chlorination in 1913. These environmental manipulations focused on preventing rather than combating invasions by infectious agents.

A person may develop a biological dysfunction that requires surgery either to repair some damaged tissue, to remove some malfunctioning tissue or organ, or to replace some damaged organ with a substitute. Surgery by itself, however, will not solve the person's biological problem. All the surgery does is to create conditions that facilitate the body's functioning to restore a healthy steady state. Only the patients' self-constructing processes can heal the wounds caused by the surgery, can construct tissue to integrate the implanted substitute into the larger system, and can provide the blood circulation to support continued functioning. Only the patient can perform the exercises necessary to restore strength and healthy functioning. Medical specialists cannot cure anyone; they can only function as assistants to the body's own self-constructing, self-organizing capabilities. That statement is not meant to minimize the importance of the facilitating conditions medical specialists provide patients, because they are often critical to patients' survival. They are often necessary but not sufficient for the maintenance or restoration of health. This is an ancient idea, appearing, for example, in the formulations of Hippocrates and ancient classical Chinese medicine (Capra, 1982).

Similar examples can be given for information-based psychological and behavioral development. DST's emphasis on relative plasticity and on development as multidimensional and open-ended (see Chapter 3) leads to a stance with regard to intervention that differs appreciably from those associated with either a mechanistic metamodel or a predetermined epigenetic-organismic metamodel. (See Chapter 1 for the differences.)

For example, the concepts of genetic inheritance and instinct as propounded by Konrad Lorenz (1940, 1965, 1966), it may be argued (Eisenberg, 1972, Lehrman, 1953; Schneirla, 1956;), rely on a presupposition of unalterable limits. Lorenz (1940, 1965) argued that genetic inheritance represents a "blueprint" for development and behavior, a set of directives unalterable by environment, experience, learning, socialization, and so on (cf. Lehrman, 1953, 1970). Genetic inheritance, according to Lorenz, circumscribes behavior by leading directly to the formation of an "instinct," a preformed, innate, and unmodifiable pattern of species-specific behavior. To emphasize how such theoretical views can influence not just scientific activity but also practical human affairs as well—consider the following written by Lorenz (as translated by Eisenberg, 1972) in Nazi Germany in 1940:

The only resistance which mankind of healthy stock can offer . . . against being penetrated by symptoms of degeneracy is based on the existence of certain innate schemata . . . . Our species-specific sensitivity to the beauty and ugliness of members of our species is intimately connected with the symptoms of degeneration, caused by domestication, which threatens our race . . . . Usually, a man of high value is disgusted with special intensity by slight symptoms of degeneracy in men of the other race . . . . In certain instances, however, we find not only a lack of this selectivity . . . but even a reversal to being attracted by symptoms of degeneracy. . . . Decadent art provides many examples of such a change of signs. . . . The immensely high reproduction rate in the moral imbecile has long been established. . . . This phenomenon leads everywhere . . . to the fact that socially inferior human material is enabled . . . to penetrate and finally to annihilate the healthy nation. *The selection for toughness, heroism, social utility . . . must be accomplished by some human institution if mankind, in default of selective factors, is not to be ruined by domestication-induced degeneracy. The racial idea as the basis of our state has already accomplished much in this respect.* The most effective race-preserving measure is . . . the greatest support of the natural defenses. . . . We must—and should—rely on the healthy feelings of our Best and charge them with the selection which will determine the prosperity or the decay of our people. [Italics added] (pp. 56-75)

This view persisted in his later work on aggression (Lorenz, 1966) in which he argued that aggression is instinctual in humans, that social conflict is an innate component of the human behavioral repertoire, and that there is an instinctual "militant enthusiasm" among youth. Lorenz recommended that civilization find methods for ritualizing aggressive instincts as a means of containing them—that is, that we make the best of an inevitably negative situation (Schneirla, 1966), because humans are universally and unalterably destructively aggressive.

In contrast to such views of fixed qualities of human nature and development, DST emphasizes relative plasticity and describes developmental processes that can produce multidimensional, open-ended developmental pathways (Lerner, 1982; Tobach, Gianutsos, Topoff, & Gross, 1974). This implies that means may be found to prevent, ameliorate, or enhance undesired, nonvalued, or desired developments or behaviors. Moreover, given the multiple integrated levels of person context organization, it is clear that a search for such means should be multilevel and multidisciplinary in scope (Baltes & Danish, 1980; Lerner, 1984).

Interventions that include only one source of influence (i.e., univariate/unilevel interventions) are more likely to provide only short-lived benefits and to produce relatively little change due to a lack of attention to altering concurrently relevant variables from other levels of analysis. For example, Goldstein and Keller (1983) describe the importance of multitargeted, multichannel, multiprocess, multidisciplinary approaches to aggression prevention and control. In addition the idea of developmental embeddedness suggests that one may take a historical approach to intervention and, for instance, devise long-term preventative strategies (Lerner & Ryff, 1978). Individual ontogeny, however, is not the only aspect of history that may be considered here. One should appreciate also features of intergenerational transmission (e.g., see Bengtson & Troll, 1978).

Because the potential for plasticity is not equipotential in all phases of life, and relative plasticity may differ in different human components at different phases of life (Baltes, 1987; Baltes & Baltes, 1980; Clarke & Clarke, 1976; Greenough & Green, 1981), it follows that some interventions may be more appropriate in some phases of life than others. Some kinds of changes may only be possible at certain times of life (e.g., organ development in certain embryonic/fetal phases). On the other hand it may be that some kinds of changes do not become impossible later in development, but, rather, only more difficult to achieve.

For example, although means may be found across life to decrease or even eliminate habits of cigarette smoking, alcohol consumption, or drug use, interventions later in life—after a longer history of those habits have produced BES more resistant to change—may require a greater expenditure of time and a more intricate involvement of the person's social context.

Also, DST suggests that *changes triggered by interventions may be thought of as changes in developmental pathways. They function to change not only current functioning but also the facilitating and constraining conditions for future developmental possibilities.* We should not expect that a single intervention, even early in life, will typically have an enduring influence on the person (there are some exceptions, for example, surgery to remove an infected appendix). Because the person retains some degree of plasticity across life, events and self-constructing processes subsequent to an initial intervention can usually alter the developmental pathway (Sigman, 1982). Stability-maintaining processes may, over time, overcome a change and restore the previous steady state, or an alternate equally deleterious pattern may emerge. Therefore, for example, repeatedly applying preventive or remedial measures may be necessary to produce enduring, desired outcomes and stable developmental pathways (e.g., lifelong dietary and exercise regimens).

Because a person always functions as a unit in a context, it follows that interventions focused on any component may precipitate changes throughout the system. (See Figure 4.3 in Chapter 4.) For example, environmental contingencies and consequences of a person's behavior may be changed (e.g., through schedules of reinforcement). This may result in changes in the way he or she feels (e.g., reduction of fear), which may be accompanied by changes in the way he or she thinks about and act in such circumstances. Or by changing how a person thinks (e.g., by helping him or her clarify his or her goals or alter troublesome self-evaluative thoughts), the person's feelings may change (e.g., he or she may become less depressed), resulting in changes in how he or she acts and the environmental contingencies and consequences he or she produces or selects. Or drugs may be used to alter neurochemical processes, which leads to changes in the way the person feels, thinks, and interacts with his or her environments. Or the person may be helped to change the way he or she acts (e.g., through skill training), which may produce different environmental contingencies or consequences, which facilitate changes in how he or she feels and thinks.

Because a person always functions as a unit in a context, interventionists who focus only on one aspect of a person without considering its impact on other aspects of the system may produce other unintended and potentially undesirable "side effects" outcomes. For example, a teacher may focus on teaching a student some subject matter, but use methods that lead the student to fear or hate the teacher and the subject; a parent may discipline a child with physical abuse and fear-inducing strategies without realizing that the child may model those strategies and use them against his or her friends, or later his or her own children. Different interventions may lead to similar outcomes (the concept of equifinality), so alternative interventions should be considered. DST would predict that combinations of interventions would be most effective.

One final example will illustrate the utility of a theoretical model for designing interventions. DST proposes that it is BES that organize, guide, and regulate the way a person functions in different kinds of BEs. It follows that permanent changes in psychological/behavioral functioning must be accomplished through changes in relevant BES; but BES cannot be changed unless they are activated and functioning (behavior and behavior change always occurs in the here and now). BES are activated by current behavior episode conditions that are similar to those from which the BES was constructed. Therefore interventions require designing behavior episodes that will activate the BES one wants to change, and then altering the behavior episode conditions in ways that will facilitate the desired change.

Three illustrations will demonstrate such interventions. First, the dominant approach to altering a phobia is to arrange for the person to experience a BE that activates the phobic BES, but to design it in such a way that the fear component does not occur or is reduced. So, for example, a person afraid of snakes make view a snake on the other side of a window, then later go into the room with the snake, and then finally hold the snake. The objective is to eliminate or reduce to manageable levels the fear component of the phobic BES. Second, in psychoanalytic treatments much is made of "transference." Transference occurs when a patient behaves toward the analyst in ways similar to the ways they behave(d) toward some other person significant to them, for example, their father. In other words, a "father BES" is activated by a current episode. Once activated, the analyst can then try to help the person recognize the nature of his or her BES and help him or her modify it. Third, practice or rehearsal of any skill involves activating the relevant BES in a current BE and then trying to change the BES so that performances are improved. For example, this is what happens in piano lessons and in practices by athletes.

Because BES contain context as well as person components, however, the modified BES may be activated only in the kinds of contexts in which it was constructed (e.g., the therapists office, the classroom, the practice setting). The problem of getting a modified BES to guide a person's behavior in other types of behavior episodes is often referred to as *transfer of training* or *generalization*. DST proposes that the solution to this problem is to build into the modified BES context components as much as possible like those of potential future behavior episodes in which one wants the revised BES to operate.

For example, teachers do this by having students practice using principles and problem-solving strategies they are being taught on a diversity of problems (i.e., each problem-solving task may be considered a specific BE). Football coaches do this by having their team practice against a group of players who simulate the upcoming opponents playing style (the "foreign team"). Drama coaches do it with dress rehearsals. Psychotherapists do it with procedures such as role-playing. (See Goldstein & Kanfer, 1979, for a review of relevant literature about, and multiple examples of, training for transfer of behavior change.)

Transformational change occurs as a result of processes of disorganization and reorganization, as discussed in Chapter 5. One characteristic of the phase of disorganization is that more options for future developmental pathways are open and likely to be tried than when the BES are in stable steady states. Therefore under some circumstances it may be necessary to design interventions for the purpose of disorganizing the relevant BES to open up possibilities for desired changes. Such periods of disorganization, however, are not only times of opportunity but also times of danger because individuals are most vulnerable during such periods. Therefore disorganizing interventions should be accompanied by interventions that (a) provide transition protection and (b) that facilitate the person's reorganization into a new, more desirable steady state (e.g., drug withdrawal as a means of altering drug addictions).

Implications for Social Policy

As emphasized in Chapter 3, biology and context in dynamic interaction are seen as liberators of human potential, not as an irrevocable constraint. Because of the relative plasticity, stability-maintaining, and self-constructing properties of human development, we simply cannot be absolutely sure what will result from altering person-context dynamic interactions. Therefore an "experimental" orientation to social policy is needed: Society should commit itself to testing and evaluating the range of possible outcomes that may arise when people are allowed to develop within altered social arenas and institutional settings.

From a DST perspective, existing social policies, institutions and arrangements may be viewed as one set of "planned attempts" (i.e., interventions) to influence human life and development. For example, Birkel, Lerner, and Smyer (1989) state:

> Key elements of a national economic policy, for instance, the availability of financial credit, current interest rates, and the securability of desirable retirement packages, have important effects on the lifecourse decisions and plans made by large numbers of individuals. Deciding whether and when to go to college, to marry, to have children, to buy a home, to change jobs, and to retire are all influenced by economic policies consciously designed by lawmakers with intercohort and developmental impacts in mind. (p. 430)

Social policy considerations would be strengthened by explicit recognition of the value of multilevel, multimethod interventions. For instance, Birkel et al. (1987) speak to this issue with regard to formulating policies associated with interventions to optimize intellectual functioning in the later years of life:

> The range of options available to promote intellectual activity and prevent cognitive decline among retirees would include: counseling individuals about nutritional requirements; helping retired couples to cultivate joint interests; educating children and grandchildren in ways they can contribute to a rich cognitive experience for their elders; assisting communities in developing meaningful volunteer experiences for older adults; extending elder hostel programming; fostering positive social attitudes toward employing retired individuals; encouraging corporations to target older adults in the development and marketing of new technologies; and lobbying for reductions in the tax rate for retired persons who choose to work. (p. 431)

DST also emphasizes that individuals are not only entities but are simultaneously components in multiple social groups. (See Figure 3.3 in Chapter 3.) Therefore a policy aimed at some individuals (e.g., one generation) may affect others as well (e.g., other generations). For example, early education programs, such as Head Start, have as their primary focus the facilitation of current developmental pathways that are expected to enhance the later-life academic functioning of the children. Such efforts, however, may also alter parents' perceptions about their children's intellectual abilities and, indeed, the entire family's commitment to education as a means to increase people's life chances.

In fact these possibilities are confirmed by the results of a follow-up study of several samples of children from low-income families who had been enrolled in infant and preschool early childhood education programs (Lazar, Darlington, Murray, Royce, & Snipper, 1982). At the time of the follow-up, when the children were between 9 and 19 years of age, they were: (a) more likely to meet their schools' basic requirements, less likely to be assigned to special education classes, and less likely to be retained a grade than were children in comparison (control) groups and (b) more likely than children in the control groups to give achievement-related reasons for being proud of themselves. In addition, children in these programs did better than control group children on standardized mental ability tests, and children who participated in the program had better nutritional practices and generally better health. Furthermore, and indicative of the intergenerational influence of this intervention, program participation altered children's familial context. Participation in the program influenced mothers' attitudes concerning school performance and, as well, enhanced the mothers' vocational aspirations for their children.

The existence of numerous potentially successful developmental pathways and routes to a successful intervention gives great flexibility to social planners. DST not only emphasizes that there is not just "one right way" for human development to proceed, but also indicates that there is great adaptive and social value in the human diversity that exists. This points to the conclusion that social policy leaders and interventionists of all sorts should both recognize and value pluralism in society and should be conscious of the diversity of healthy and desirable developmental pathways that may exist in an open society.

In Conclusion

We began this book by asserting that the assumptions we hold about the nature of humans and our relationships with the world in which we live, and that we use to guide our lives, have powerful influences upon what we do, how we live, how we deal with and try to influence one another, the social policies, attitudes, and institutions we construct, and, therefore, upon the evolution of the future we will construct for ourselves and in which we will have to live. One way of assessing any theory of human development is to consider its potential implications for our lives and work. We have tried to do that in this chapter with some examples with regard to implications for both research and applications.

We do not view DST as a complete or perfect representation of human development; there are undoubtedly many deficiencies in these proposals. Rather, we see it as only one more step in a scientific and social developmental pathway being pursued by many people directed toward trying to understand ourselves and human life better. We are deeply indebted to the efforts of others during the past 100 years; we build upon the work of those who have preceded us. *The past is prologue to the present.*

We hope that this present effort will stimulate others, particularly young scholars and professionals in training, to explore the heuristic utility of DST in their own work, to modify and elaborate it to improve upon it, or to try to formulate alternate and better frameworks to serve these same purposes.

Of this we are convinced: Without the construction of more integrative and comprehensive frameworks than those that presently exist, we are likely to be increasingly overwhelmed with mountains of data and empirical generalizations. They continue to accumulate as a pile of "bricks" of knowledge, each of which can contribute toward the construction of a cathedral of knowledge we have not yet built. The role of integrative theorizing is to help decide how to combine those "bricks" in a way that represents a more accurate and less passive mechanistic view of ourselves and that will help us learn how to construct more humane societies. *The present is prologue to the future.*

References

Abravanel, E. (1968). The development of intersensory patterning with regard to selected spatial dimensions. *Monographs of the Society for Research in Child Development, 33(2)*, Serial No. 18.

Alexander, C. N., & Langer, E. J. (Eds.). (1990). *Higher stages of human development: Perspectives on adult growth.* New York: Oxford University Press.

Altman, I., & Wohlwill, J. F. (1978). *Children and the environment.* New York: Plenum.

Anastasi, A. (1958). Heredity, environment, and the question "how?" *Psychological Review, 65,* 197-208.

Anderson, P. W. (1978). Local moments and localized states. *Science, 201,* 307-316.

Angell, J. R. (1907). The province of functional psychology. *Psychological Review, 14,* 61-69.

Antonovsky, A. (1979). *Health, stress, and coping.* San Francisco: Jossey-Bass.

Arbib, M. A. (1989). *The metaphorical brain 2: Neural networks and beyond.* New York: John Wiley.

Arbib, M. A., & Hesse, M. B. (1986). *The construction of reality.* Cambridge: Cambridge University Press.

Ashby, W. R. (1962). Principles of the self-organizing system. In H. VonFoerster & G. W. Zopf (Eds.), *Principles of self-organization* (pp. 108-118). New York: Pergamon.

Bain, A. (1855). *The senses and the intellect.* London: Parker.

Baldwin, J. M. (1894). *The development of the child and the race.* New York: Macmillan.

Baltes, M. M., & Baltes, P. B. (1986). *The psychology of control and aging.* Hillsdale, NJ: Lawrence Erlbaum.

Baltes, P. B. (1979, Summer). On the potential and limits of child development: Life-span developmental perspectives. *Newsletter of the Society for Research in Child Development,* 1-4.

Baltes, P. B. (1987). Theoretical propositions of life-span developmental psychology: On the dynamics between growth and decline. *Developmental Psychology, 23,* 611-626.

Baltes, P. B., & Baltes, M. M. (1980). Plasticity and variability in psychological aging: Methodological and theoretical issues. In G. E. Gurski (Ed.), *Determining the effects of aging on the central nervous system* (pp. 41-60). Berlin: Schering AG, (Oraniendruck).

Baltes, P. B., Cornelius, S. W., & Nesselroade, J. R. (1977). Cohort effects in behavioral development: Theoretical and methodological perspectives. In W. A. Collins (Ed.), *Minnesota symposia on child psychology* (Vol. 2, pp. 1-63). New York: Thomas Y. Crowell.

Baltes, P. B., & Danish, S. (1980). Intervention in life-span development and aging: Issues and concepts. In R. R. Turner & H. W. Reese (Eds.), *Life-span developmental psychology: Interventions* (p. 346). New York: Academic Press.

Baltes, P. B., Dittman-Kohli, F., & Dixon, R. A. (1984). New perspectives on the development of intelligence in adulthood: Toward a dual-process conception and a model of selective optimization with compensation. In P. B. Baltes & O. G. Brim, Jr. (Eds.), *Life-span development and behavior* (Vol. 6). New York: Academic Press.

Baltes, P. B., & Nesselroade, J. R. (1973). The developmental analysis of individual differences on multiple measures. In J. R. Nesselroade & H. W. Reese (Eds.), *Life-span developmental psychology: Introduction to research methodological issues* (pp. 219-251). New York: Academic Press.

Baltes, P. B., Reese, H. W., & Lipsitt, L. P. (1980). Life-span developmental psychology. *Annual Review of Psychology, 31,* 65-110.

Baltes, P. B., Reese, H. W., & Nesselroade, J. R. (1977). *Life-span developmental psychology: Introduction to research methods.* Monterey, CA: Brooks/Cole.

Baltes, P. B., & Willis, S. L. (1977). Towards psychological theories of aging and development. In J. E. Birren & K. W. Schaie (Eds.), *Handbook of the psychology of aging* (pp. 128-154). New York: Van Nostrand Reinhold.

Bandura, A. (1965). Influence of models' reinforcement contingencies on the acquisition of imitative responses. *Journal of Personality and Social Psychology, 1,* 589-595.

Bandura, A. (1978). The self system in reciprocal determinism. *American Psychologist, 33,* 344-358.

Bandura, A. (1986). *Social foundations of thought and action: A social cognitive theory.* Englewood Cliffs, NJ: Prentice-Hall.

Bandura, A., & Walters, R. H. (1959). *Adolescent aggression.* New York: Ronald Press.

Bard, J. (1990). *Morphogenesis: The cellular and molecular processes of developmental anatomy.* New York: Cambridge University Press.

Barker, R. G. (1968). *Ecological psychology: Concepts and methods for studying the environment of human behavior.* Stanford, CA: Stanford University Press.

Bartlett, F. C. (1932). *Remembering: An experimental and social study.* Cambridge, UK: Cambridge University Press.

Bengston, V. L., & Troll, L. (1978). Youth and their parents: Feedback and intergenerational influence in socialization. In R. M. Lerner & G. B. Stanier (Eds.), *Child influences on marital and family interaction: A life-span perspective* (pp. 215-240). New York: Academic Press.

Bentler, P. M. (1980). Multivariate analysis with latent variables: Causal modeling. *Annual Review of Psychology, 31,* 419-456.

Bernstein, N. A. (1967). *The coordination and regulation of movements.* London: Pergamon.

Bijou, S. W. (1976). *Child development: The basic stage of early childhood.* Englewood Cliffs, NJ: Prentice-Hall.

Bijou, S. W., & Baer, D. M. (1961). *Child development: A systematic and empirical theory* (Vol. 1). New York: Appleton-Century-Crofts.

Bijou, S. W., & Baer, D. M. (1978). *Behavior analysis of child development.* Englewood Cliffs, NJ: Prentice-Hall.

Birch, H. G., & Lefford, A. (1963). Intersensory development in children. *Monographs of the Society for Research in Child Development, 28(5),* Serial No. 89.

Birkel, R., Lerner, R. M., & Smyer, M. A. (1989). Applied developmental psychology as an implementation of a life-span view of human development. *Journal of Applied Developmental Psychology, 10,* 425-445.

Block, J. (1971). *Lives through time.* Berkeley, CA: Bancroft.

Braine, M. D. S., & Rumain, B. (1983). Logical reasoning. In P. H. Mussen (Ed.), *Handbook of child psychology: Cognitive development* (Vol. 3, pp. 263-340). New York: John Wiley.

Brent, S. B. (1978). Motivation, steady-state, and structural development: A general model of psychological homeostasis. *Motivation and Emotion, 2,* 299-332.

Brent, S. B. (1984). *Psychological and social structures: Their organization, activity, and development.* Hillsdale, NJ: Lawrence Erlbaum.

Brim, O. G., Jr., & Kagan, J. (Eds.). (1980). Constancy and change: A view of the issues. *Constancy and change in human development* (pp. 1-25). Cambridge, MA: Harvard University Press.

Bronfenbrenner, U. (1977). Toward an experimental ecology of human development. *American Psychologist, 32,* 513-531.

Bronfenbrenner, U. (1979). *The ecology of human development.* Cambridge, MA: Harvard University Press.

Brown, J. F. (1951). Topology and hodological space. In M. H. Marx (Ed.), *Psychological theory* (pp. 233-256). New York: Macmillan.

Bruner, J. S. (1982). The nature of adult-infant transaction. In M. Von Cranach & R. Harre (Eds.), *The analysis of action* (pp. 313-327). Cambridge: Cambridge University Press.

Buck, J., & Buck, E. (1968). Mechanism of rhythmic synchronous flashing of fireflies. *Science, 159,* 1319-1327.

Burke, J. F. (1989). *Contemporary approaches to psychotherapy and counseling: The self-regulation and maturity model.* Pacific Grove, CA: Brooks/Cole.

Buss, A. H. (1990). Personality as traits. *American Psychologist, 44,* 1378-1388.

Cannon, W. B. (1939). *The wisdom of the body* (rev. ed.). New York: Norton.

Capra, F. (1977). *The tao of physics.* New York: Bantam.

Capra, F. (1982). *The turning point: Science, society, and the rising culture.* New York: Bantam.

Case, R. (1985). *Intellectual development: Birth to adulthood.* Orlando, FL: Academic Press.

Chauchard, P. (1979). Cerebral Control and Attention. *Psychotherapy and Psychosomatics, 31,* 334-343.

Clarke, A. M., & Clarke, A. D. B. (Eds.). (1976). *Early experiences: Myth and evidence.* New York: Free Press.

Colombo, S. (1982). The critical period concept: Research, methodology and theoretical issues. *Psychological Bulletin, 91,* 260-275.

Comments. (1951). *American Psychologist, 45,* 70-72.

Corneal, C. C. (1989). *A stepchild's experience across two households: An investigation of emotional response patterns.* Unpublished master's thesis, The Pennsylvania State University, University Park.

Corneal, C. C. (1990). *Stepdaughters' experiences of the stepdaughter/stepfather relationship: An investigation of emotional response patterns.* Unpublished doctoral dissertation, The Pennsylvania State University, University Park.

Cornwall, K. (1990). *The power of long engagement: Important relationships and their effect upon role behavior in adult women.* Doctoral dissertation: The Pennsylvania State University.

Dannefer, D. (1984). Adult development and socialization theory: A paradigmatic reappraisal. *American Sociological Review, 49,* 100-116.

Darwin, C. (1872). *The expression of emotion in man and animals.* London: John Murray.

Darwin, C. (1964). *On the origin of the species by means of natural selection, or the preservation of forward races in the struggle for life.* Cambridge, MA: Harvard University Press (Original work published in 1859).

Davis, A. (1944). Socialization and the adolescent personality. In *Forty-third yearbook of the national society for the study of education* (Vol. 43, Part 1). Chicago: University of Chicago Press.

Deutsch, K. W. (1951). Mechanism, organism, and society. *Philosophy of Science, 18,* 230-252.

DeWan, E. M. (1976). Consciousness as an emergent causal agent in the context of control system theory. In G. G. Globes, G. Maxwell, & I. Savodnnik (Eds.), *Consciousness and the brain: A scientific and philosophical inquiry* (pp. 181-199). New York: Plenum.

Dixon, R. A., & Lerner, R. M. (1988). A history of systems in developmental psychology. In M. H. Bornstein & M. E. Lamb (Eds.), *Developmental psychology: An advanced textbook* (2nd ed., pp. 3-50). Hillsdale, NJ: Erlbaum.

Dixon, R. A., Lerner, R. M., & Hultsch, D. F. (1991). Maneuvering among models of developmental psychology. In P. van Geert & L. P. Mos (Eds.), *Annals of theoretical psychology* (Vol. 7). New York: Plenum.

Dollard, J., & Miller, N. E. (1950). *Personality and psychotherapy.* New York: McGraw-Hill.

Duffy, E. (1951). The concept of energy mobilization. *Psychological Review, 58,* 30-40.

Eichorn, D. H., Clausen, J. A., Haan, N., Honzik, M. P., & Mussen, P. H. (Eds.). (1981). *Present and past in middle life.* New York: Academic Press.

Eisenberg, L. (1972). The human nature of human nature. *Science, 176,* 123-128.

Elder, G. H., Jr. (1974). *Children of the great depression.* Chicago: University of Chicago Press.

Elder, G. H., Jr. (1975). Age differentiation and the life courses. In A. Inkeles, J. Coleman, & N. Smelser (Eds.), *Annual review of sociology* (Vol. 1, pp. 165-190). Palo Alto, CA: Annual Reviews.

Eldredge, N., & Gould, S. J. (1972). Punctuated equilibria: An alternative to phyletic gradualism. In T. J. M. Schoof (Ed.), *Models in paleoluogy* (pp. 82-115). San Francisco: Freeman Cooper.

Emmerich, W. (1968). Personality development and concepts of structure. *Child Development, 39,* 671-690.

Erikson, E. H. (1959). Identity and the life-cycle. *Psychological Issues, 1,* 18-164.

Erikson, E. H. (1968). *Identity, youth, and crisis.* New York: Norton.

Farber, M. L. (1968). *Theory of suicide.* New York: Funk & Wagnalls.

Featherman, D. L. (1983). Life-span perspectives in social science research. In P. B. Baltes & O. G. Brim, Jr. (Eds.), *Life-span development and behavior* (Vol. 5, pp. 1-57). New York: Academic Press.

Featherman, D. L., & Lerner, R. M. (1985). Ontogenesis and sociogenesis: Problematics for theory about development across the life span. *American Sociological Review, 50,* 659-676.

Ferster, C., & Skinner, B. F. (1958). *Schedules of reinforcements.* New York: Appleton-Century-Crofts.

Finkelstein, J. (1980). The endocrinology of adolescence. *Pediatric Clinics of North America, 27,* 53-69.

Ford, C. (1987). The role of emotions in an executive's workday. In M. E. Ford & D. H. Ford (Eds.), *Humans as self-constructing living systems: Putting the framework to work* (pp. 235-260). Hillsdale, NJ: Lawrence Erlbaum.

Ford, D. H. (1987). *Humans as self-constructing living systems: A developmental perspective on personality and behavior.* Hillsdale, NJ: Lawrence Erlbaum.

Ford, D. H., & Urban, H. B. (1963). *Systems and psychotherapy.* New York: John Wiley.

Ford, M. E. (in press). *Motivating humans: Goals, emotions, and personal agency beliefs.* Newbury Park, CA: Sage.

Ford, M. E., & Ford, D. H. (1987). *Humans as self-constructing living systems: Putting the framework to work.* Hillsdale, NJ: Lawrence Erlbaum.

Ford, M. E., & Nichols, C. W. (1987). A taxonomy of human goals and some possible applications. In M. E. Ford & D. H. Ford (Eds.), *Humans as self-constructing living systems: Putting the framework to work* (pp. 289-312). Hillsdale, NJ: Lawrence Erlbaum.

Forgas, J. (1979). Social episodes: The study of interaction routines. *European monographs in social psychology.* London: Academic Press.

Fowler, W. (1977). Sequence and styles in cognitive development. In I. C. Uzgiris & F. Weizmann (Eds.), *The structuring of experience* (pp. 265-296). New York: Plenum.

Frank, J. (1968). The role of hope in psychotherapy. *International Journal of Psychiatry, 15,* 383-395.

Frankl, V. E. (1963). *Man's search for meaning: An introduction to logotherapy.* New York: Washington Square Press.

Freud, S. (1905/1930). *Three contributions to the theory of sex.* Washington, DC: Nervous and Mental Disease Publishing Company.

Freud, S. (1949). *Outline of psychoanalysis.* New York: Norton.

Gallistel, C. R. (1980). *The organization of action: A new synthesis.* Hillsdale, NJ: Lawrence Erlbaum.

Gelman, R. (1978). Cognitive development. *Annual Review of Psychology, 29,* 297-332.

Gesell, A. L. (1946). The ontogenesis of infant behavior. In L. Carmichael (Ed.), *Manual of child psychology* (pp. 259-331). New York: John Wiley.

Gewirtz, J. L., & Stingle, K. G. (1968). Learning of generalized imitation as the basis for identification. *Psychological Review, 75,* 374-397.

Gibbs, J. C. (1979). The meaning of ecologically oriented inquiry in contemporary psychology. *American Psychologist, 34,* 127-140.

Gibson, J. J. (1979). *The ecological approach to visual perception.* Boston: Houghton Mifflin.

Glaser, R. (1990). The reemergence of learning theory within instructional research. *American Psychologist, 45,* 29-39.

Glaser, G., & Bassok, M. (1989). Learning theory and the study of instruction. *Annual Review of Psychology, 40,* 631-66.

Gleick, J. (1987). *Chaos: Making a new science.* New York: Viking Penguin.

Goldschmidt, R. (1940). *The material basis of evolution.* New Haven, CT: Yale University Press.

Goldstein, A. P., & Kanfer, F. H. (Eds.). (1979). *Maximizing treatment gains, transfer enhancement in psychotherapy.* New York: Academic Press.

Goldstein, A. P., & Keller, H. R. (1983). Aggression prevention and control: Multi-targeted, multichannel, multipress, multidisciplinary. In A. P. Goldstein & L. Krasner (Eds.), *Prevention and control of aggression* (pp. 338-350). New York: Pergamon.

Gollin, E. S. (1981). Development and plasticity. In E. S. Gollin (Ed.), *Developmental plasticity: Behavioral and biological aspects of variations in development* (pp. 231-331). New York: Academic Press.

Gottlieb, G. (1970). Concepts of prenatal behavior. In L. R. Aronson, E. Tobach, D. S. Lehrman, & J. S. Rosenblatt (Eds.), *Development and evolution of behavior: Essays in memory of T. C. Schneirla* (pp. 111-137). San Francisco: Freeman.

Gottlieb, G. (1976). The roles of experience in the development of behavior and the nervous system. In G. Gottlieb (Ed.), *Neural and behavioral specificity: Studies on the development of behavior and the nervous system* (Vol. 3, pp. 25-54). New York: Academic Press.

Gottlieb, G. (1983). The psychobiological approach to developmental issues. In M. M. Haith & J. J. Campos (Eds.), *Handbook of child psychology: Infancy and developmental psychobiology* (4th ed., pp. 1-26). New York: John Wiley.

Gottlieb, G. (1991). The experiential canalization of behavioral developmental theory. *Developmental Psychology, 27,* 4-13.

Gould, S. J., & Vrba, E. (1982). Exaptation: A missing term in the science of form. *Paleobiology, 8,* 4-15.

Greenough, W. T., & Green, E. J. (1981). Experience and the changing brain. In J. L. McGaugh, J. G. March, & S. B. Kiesler (Eds.), *Aging: Biology and behavior* (pp. 159-200). New York: Academic Press.

Grinker, R. R. (Ed.). (1956). *Toward a unified theory of human behavior.* New York: Basic Books.

Grinker, R. R., Korchin, S. J., Bosowitz, H., Hamburg, D. A., Sabshin, M., Persky, H., Chevalier, J. A., & Borad, F. A. (1956). A theoretical and experimental approach to problems of anxiety. *AMA Archives of Neurology and Psychiatry, 76,* 420-431.

Grouse, L. D., Schrier, B. K., & Nelson, P. G. (1979). Effect of visual experience on gene expression during the development of stimulus specificity in cat brain. *Experimental Neurology, 64,* 354-364.

Haan, N., & Day, D. (1974). A longitudinal study of change and sameness in personality development, adolescence to later adulthood. *Aging and Human Development, 5,* 11-39.

Hamburger, V. (1957). The concept of development in biology. In D. B. Harris (Ed.), *The concept of development* (pp. 49-58). Minneapolis: University of Minnesota Press.

Heidbreder, E. (1924). An experimental study of thinking. *Archives of Psychology* (No. 73).

Hetherington, E. M., Lerner, R. M., & Perlmutter, M. (Eds.). (1988). *Child development in life span perspective.* Hillsdale, NJ: Lawrence Erlbaum.

Hilgard, E. R. (1948). *Theories of learning.* New York: Appleton-Century-Crofts.

Hirsch, J. (1970). Behavior-genetic analysis and its biosocial consequences. *Seminars in Psychiatry, 2,* 89-105.

Homans, G. C. (1961). *Social behavior: Its elementary forms.* New York: Harcourt, Brace & World.

Homans, G. C. (1974). *Social behavior: Its elementary forms* (rev. ed.). New York: Harcourt Brace Jovanovich.

Horowitz, F. D. (1987). *Exploring developmental theories: Toward a structural behavioral model of development.* Hillsdale, NJ: Lawrence Erlbaum.

Hunt, N. (1967). *The world of Nigel Hunt: The diary of a Mongoloid youth.* New York: Garrett.

Inhelder, B., & Piaget, J. (1958). *The growth of logical thinking from childhood to adolescence.* New York: Basic Books.

Ittelson, W. H. (1978). Environmental perception and the urban experience. *Environment and Behavior, 10,* 193-213.

Jackson, J. B. C., & Cheetham, A. H. (1990). Evolutionary significance of morphospecies: A test with Cheilostonce Bryozoa. *Science, 248,* 579-582.

James, W. (1890). *Principles of psychology* (Vol. 1). New York: Henry Holt.

Janis, I. L., & Mann, L. (1977). *Decision making: A psychological analysis of conflict, choice, and commitment.* New York: Free Press.

Jantsch, E. (1980). *The self-organizing universe.* Oxford: Pergamon.

Jenkins, J. J. (1974). Remember that old theory of memory: Well forget it. *American Psychologist, 29,* 785-795.

Johanson, D. C., & Edey, M. A. (1981). *Lucy: The beginnings of humankind.* New York: Simon & Schuster.

Kagan, J. (1966). Psychological development of the father. Part I: Personality, behavior, and temperament. In F. Faulker (Ed.), *Human development* (pp. 326-366). Philadelphia: W. B. Saunders.

Kagan, J. (1980). Perspective on continuity. In O. G. Brim, Jr., & J. Kagan (Eds.), *Constancy and change in human development* (pp. 26-74). Cambridge: Harvard University Press.

Kagan, J. (1983). Developmental categories and the premise of connectivity. In R. M. Lerner (Ed.), *Developmental psychology: Historical and philosophical perspectives* (pp. 29-54). Hillsdale, NJ: Lawrence Erlbaum.

Kaplan, B. (1983). A trio of trails. In R. M. Lerner (Ed.), *Developmental psychology: Historical and philosophical perspectives* (pp. 185-239). Hillsdale, NJ: Lawrence Erlbaum.

Kendall, P. C., Lerner, R. M., & Craighead, W. E. (1984). Human development intervention in child psychopathology. *Child Development, 55,* 71-82.

Kendler, T. S. (1986). World views and the concept of development: A reply to Lerner and Kauffman. *Developmental Review, 6,* 80-95.

Kleigel, R., Smith, J., & Baltes, P. B. (1990). On the locus and process of magnification of age differences during mnemonic training. *Developmental Psychology, 26,* 894-904.

Kleinmuntz, B. (1966). *Problem, solving: Research method and theory.* New York: John Wiley.

Klinger, E. (1977). *Meaning and void: Inner experience and the incentives in people's lives.* Minneapolis: University of Minnesota Press.

Koestler, A. (1967). *The ghost in the machine.* New York: Macmillan.

Kohlberg, L. (1976). Moral stages and moralization. In T. Likora (Ed.), *Moral development: Current theory and research* (pp. 32-76). New York: Holt, Rinehart, & Winston.

Kohlberg, L. (1979). *The meaning and measurement of moral development. Heinz Werner Memorial Lecture.* Worcester, MA: Clark University Press.

Kreitler, H., & Kreitler, S. (1976). *Cognitive orientation and behavior.* New York: Springer.

Kuo, Z. Y. (1967). *The dynamics of behavior development.* New York: Random House.

Lashley, K. S. (1942). An examination of the "Continuity Theory" as applied to discriminate learning. *Journal of General Psychology, 26,* 241-265.

Lazar, I., Darlington, R., Murray, H., Royce, J., & Snipper, A. (1982). Lasting effects of early education: A report from the Consortium for Longitudinal Studies. *Monographs of the Society for Research in Child Development (47),* Serial No. 195, Nos. 2-3.

Lazarus, R. S. (1991). *Emotion and Adaptation.* New York: Oxford University Press.

Lehrman, D. S. (1953). A critique of Konrad Lorenz's theory of instinctive behavior. *Quarterly Review of Biology, 28,* 337-363.

Lehrman, D. S. (1970). Semantic and conceptual issues in the nature-nurture problem. In L. R. Aronson, E. Tobach, D. S. Lehrman, & J. S. Rosenblatt (Eds.), *Development and evolution of behavior: Essays in memory of T. C. Schneirla* (pp. 17-52). San Francisco: Freeman.

Lerner, J. V., Baker, N., & Lerner, R. M. (1985). A person-context goodness of fit model of adjustment. In P. C. Kendall (Ed.), *Advances in cognitive-behavioral research and therapy* (Vol. 4, pp. 111-136). New York: Academic Press.

Lerner, R. M. (1976). *Concepts and theories of human development.* Reading, MA: Addison-Wesley.

Lerner, R. M. (1978). Nature, nurture, and dynamic interactionism. *Human Development, 21,* 1-20.

Lerner, R. M. (1979). A dynamic interactional concept of individual and social relationship development. In R. Burgess & T. Huston (Eds.), *Social exchange in developing relationships* (pp. 271-305). New York: Academic Press.

Lerner, R. M. (1982). Children and adolescents as producers of their own development. *Developmental Review, 2,* 342-370.

Lerner, R. M. (1984). *On the nature of human plasticity.* New York: Cambridge University Press.

Lerner, R. M. (1986). *Concepts and theories of human development* (2nd ed.). New York: Random House.

Lerner, R. M. (1987). A life-span perspective for early adolescence. In R. M. Lerner & T. T. Foch (Eds.), *Biological-psychosocial interactions in early adolescence* (pp. 9-34). Hillsdale, NJ: Lawrence Erlbaum.

Lerner, R. M. (1988). Personality development: A life-span perspective. In E. M. Hetherington, R. M. Lerner, & M. Perlmutter (Eds.), *Child development in life-span perspective* (pp. 21-46). Hillsdale, NJ: Lawrence Erlbaum.

240 DEVELOPMENTAL SYSTEMS THEORY

Lerner, R. M. (1989). Developmental contextualism and the life-span view of person-context interaction. In M. Bornstein, & J. S. Bruner (Eds.), *Interaction in human development* (pp. 217-239). Hillsdale, NJ: Lawrence Erlbaum.

Lerner, R. M. (1990). Weaving development into the fabric of personality and social psychology—On the significance of Bandura's *Social foundations of thought and action. Psychological Inquiry, 1,* 92-95.

Lerner, R. M. (1992). *"Final Solutions": Biology, prejudice, and genocide.* University Park: Penn State Press.

Lerner, R. M., Hultsch, D. F., & Dixon, R. A. (1983). Contextualism and the character of developmental psychology in the 1970s. *Annals of the New York Academy of Sciences, 412,* 101-128.

Lerner, R. M., & Kauffman, M. B. (1985). The concept of development in contextualism. *Developmental Review, 5,* 309-333.

Lerner, R. M., & Lerner, J. V. (1983). Temperament-intelligence reciprocities in early childhood: A contextual model. In M. Lewis (Ed.), *Origins of intelligence: Infancy and early childhood* (2nd ed., pp. 399-421). New York: Plenum.

Lerner, R. M., & Lerner, J. V. (1987). Children in their contexts: A goodness of fit model. In J. B. Lancaster, J. Altmann, A. S. Rossi, & L. R. Sherrod (Eds.), *Parenting across the life span: Biosocial dimensions* (pp. 377-404). Chicago: Aldine.

Lerner, R. M., & Lerner, J. V. (1989). Organismic and social contextual bases of development: The sample case of adolescence. In W. Damon (Ed.), *Child development today and tomorrow* (pp. 69-85). San Francisco: Jossey-Bass.

Lerner, R. M., & Ryff, C. D. (1978). Implementation of the life-span view of human development. The sample case of attachment. In P. B. Baltes (Ed.), *Life-span development and behavior* (Vol. 1, pp. 2-44). New York: Academic Press.

Lerner, R. M., Skinner, E. A., & Sorell, G. T. (1980). Methodological implications of contextual/dialectic theories of development. *Human Development, 23,* 225-235.

Lerner, R. M., & Tubman, J. (1989). Conceptual issues in studying continuity and discontinuity in personality development across life. *Journal of Personality, 57,* 343-373.

Levin, D. A. (1970). Developmental instability and evolution in peripheral isolates. *American Naturalist, 104,* 343.

Levinson, D. J. (1978). *The seasons of a man's life.* New York: Knopf.

Lewin, K. (1939). Field theory and experiments in social psychology: Concepts and methods. *American Journal of Sociology, 44,* 688-696.

Lewontin, R. C. (1981). On constraints and adaptation. *Behavioral and Brain Sciences, 4,* 244-245.

Lewontin, R. C., & Levins, R., (1978). Evolution. *Encyclopedia* (Vol 5. Divino-Feine). Turino, Italy: Einaudi.

Little, B. (1983). Personal projects: A rationale and method for investigation. *Environment and Behavior, 15,* 273-309.

Looft, W. R. (1973). Socialization and personality throughout the life span: An examination of contemporary psychological approaches. In P. B. Baltes & K. W. Schaie (Eds.), *Life-span developmental psychology: Personality and socialization* (pp. 25-52). New York: Academic Press.

Lorenz, K. (1940). Durch Domestikation verursachte Storungen arteigenen Verhaltens. *Zeitschrift fur angewandte Psychologie und Charakterkunde, 59,* 2-81.

Lorenz, K. (1965). *Evolution and modification of behavior.* Chicago: University of Chicago Press.

Lorenz, K. (1966). *On aggression.* New York: Harcourt, Brace, & World.

MacCrimmon, K. R., & Taylor, R. N. (1983). Decision making and problem solving. In M. D. Dunnette, (Ed.), *Handbook of industrial and organizational psychology* (pp. 1397-1454). New York: John Wiley.

Magnusson, D. (Ed.). (1980). *Toward a psychology of situations: An interactional perspective.* Hillsdale, NJ: Lawrence Erlbaum.

Maruyama, M. (1963). The second cybernetics: Deviation-amplifying mutual causal processes. *American Scientist, 51,* 164-179.

Maturana, H. R. (1975). The organization of the living: A theory of the living organization. *International Journal of Man-Machine Studies, 7,* 313-332.

Mayr, E. (1963). *Animal species and evolution.* Cambridge, MA: Harvard University Press.

McArdle, J. J. (1990). Dynamic structural equation modeling of repeated measures. In J. R. Nesselroade & R. B. Cattell (Eds.), *Handbook of multivariate experimental psychology* (pp. 561-685). New York: Plenum.

McCandless, B. R. (1970). *Adolescents.* Hinsdale, IL: Dryden Press.

McClearn, G. E. (1981). Evolution and genetic variability. In E. S. Golin (Ed.), *Developmental plasticity: Behavioral and biological aspects of variations in development* (pp. 3-31). New York: Academic Press.

McGraw, M. (1935). *Growth: A study of Johnny and Jimmy.* New York: Appleton-Century-Crofts.

McGuire, T. R., & Hirsch, J. (1977). General intelligence and heritability. In I. C. Uzgiris & F. Weizmann (Eds.), *The structuring of experience* (pp. 25-72). New York: Plenum.

McMullen, E. (1983). Values in science. In P. D. Asquith & T. Mickles (Eds.), *Proceedings of the 1982 Philosophy of Science Association* (Vol. 2, pp. 3-23). East Lansing, MI: Philosophy of Science Association.

Meyer, J. W. (1988). The social construction of the psychology of childhood: Some contemporary processes. In E. M. Hetherington, R. M. Lerner, & M. Perlmutter (Eds.), *Child development in life-span perspective* (pp. 47-65). Hillsdale, NJ: Lawrence Erlbaum.

Miller, G. A., Galanter, E., & Pribram, K. H. (1960). *Plans and the structure of behavior.* New York: Holt, Rinehart & Winston.

Miller, J. G. (1978). *Living systems.* New York: McGraw-Hill.

Milsum, J. H. (1968). *Positive feedback.* Oxford: Pergamon.

Mischel, W. (1977). On the future of personality measurement. *American Psychologist, 32,* 246-254.

Molenaar, P. C. M. (1985). A dynamic factor model for the analysis of multivariate time series. *Psychometrika, 50,* 181-202.

Morris, E. K. (1988). Contextualism: The world view of behavioral analysis. *Journal of Experimental Child Psychology, 46,* 289-323.

Murphy, E. A. (1979). *Where are we going: Genetic analysis of common diseases: Applications to predictive factors in coronary disease.* New York: Alan Liss.

Murphy, G. (1949). *An historical introduction to modern psychology* (rev. ed.). New York: Harcourt-Brace.

Mussen, P. H. (1983). *Handbook of child psychology* (4th ed., Vols. 1-4). New York: John Wiley.

Nagel, E. (1957). Determinism in development. In D. B. Harris (Ed.), *The concept of development* (pp. 15-24). Minneapolis: University of Minnesota Press.

Neisser, V. (1976). *Cognition and reality: Principles and implications of cognitive psychology*. San Francisco: Freeman.

Nesselroade, J. R. (1987). Some implications of the trait-state distinction for the study of development over the life span: The case of personality. In P. B. Baltes, D. L. Featherman, & R. M. Lerner (Eds.), *Life-span development and behavior* (Vol. 8, pp. 163-189). Hillsdale, NJ: Lawrence Erlbaum.

Nesselroade, J. R. (1988). Sampling and generalizability: Adult development and the aging research issues examined within the general methodological framework of selection. In K. W. Schaie, R. T. Campbell, W. M. Meredith, & S. C. Rawlings (Eds.), *Methodological issues in aging research* (pp. 13-42). New York: Springer.

Nesselroade, J. R. (1990a). Adult personality development: Issues in assessing constancy and change. In A. I. Rabin, R. A. Zucker, R. A. Emmons, & S. Frank (Eds.), *Studying persons and lives* (pp. 41-85). New York: Springer.

Nesselroade, J. R. (1990b). Interindividual differences in intraindividual changes. In J. L. Horn & L. Collins (Eds.), *Best methods for studying change* (pp. 92-105). Washington, DC: American Psychological Association.

Nesselroade, J. R. (1991) The warp and the woof of the developmental fabric. In R. Downs, L. Liben, & D. S. Palermo (Eds.), *Visions of development, the environment, and aesthetics: The legacy of Joachim F. Wohlwill* (pp. 213-240). Hillsdale, NJ: Lawrence Erlbaum.

Nesselroade, J. R., & Baltes, P. B. (1974). Adolescent personality development and historical change: 1970-1972. *Monographs of the Society for Research in Child Development, 39.*

Nesselroade, J. R., & Ford, D. H. (1985). Multivariate, replicated, single-subject designs for research on older adults: P-technique comes of age. *Research on Aging, 7,* 46-80.

Nesselroade, J. R., & Ford, D. H. (1987). Methodological considerations in modeling living systems. In M. E. Ford & D. H. Ford (Eds.), *Humans as self-constructing living systems: Putting the framework to work* (pp. 47-80). Hillsdale, NJ: Lawrence Erlbaum.

Nesselroade, J. R., & McArdle, J. J. (1986). Multivariate causal modeling in alcohol research. *Social Biology, 32,* 272-296.

Nesselroade, J. R., & von Eye, A. (Eds.). (1985). *Individual development and social change: Explanatory analysis*. New York: Academic Press.

Neugarten, B. L., & Guttman, D. L. (1968). Age-sex roles and personality in middle ages. In B. B. Neurgarten (Ed.), *Middle age and aging* (pp. 58-71). Chicago: University of Chicago Press.

Overton, W. F., & Reese, H. W. (1973). Models of development: Methodological implications. In J. R. Nesselroade & H. W. Reese (Eds.), *Life-span developmental psychology: Methodological issues* (pp. 65-86). New York: Academic Press.

Overton, W. F., & Reese, H. W. (1981). Conceptual prerequisites for an understanding of stability-change and continuity-discontinuity. *International Journal of Behavioral Development, 4,* 99-123.

Oyama, S. (1985). *The ontogeny of information*. Cambridge, MA: Cambridge University Press.

Pascual-Leone, J. (1976). A view of cognition from a formalist's perspective. In K. F. Riegel & J. Meacham (Eds.), *The developing individual in a changing world* (pp. 89-100). The Hague, The Netherlands: Mouton.

Pepper, S. C. (1942). *World hypotheses.* Berkeley: University of California Press.

Petrinovich, L. (1979). Probabilistic functionalism: A conception of research method. *American Psychologist, 34,* 373-390.

Piaget, J. (1950). *The psychology of intelligence.* New York: Harcourt Brace.

Piaget, J. (1960). *The psychology of intelligence.* New York: Littlefield, Adams.

Piaget, J. (1970). Piaget's theory. In P. H. Mussen (Ed.), *Carmichael's manual of child psychology* (Vol. 1, pp. 703-732). New York: John Wiley.

Piaget, J. (1983). Piaget's theory. In P. H. Mussen (Ed.), *Handbook of child psychology* (Vol. 1, pp. 103-128). New York: John Wiley.

Piaget, J., & Garcia, R. (1989). *Psychogenesis and the history of science.* New York: Columbia University Press.

Plomin, R. (1986). *Developmental genetics and psychology.* Hillsdale, NJ: Lawrence Erlbaum.

Plutchik, R. (1980). *Emotion: A psychoevolutionary synthesis.* New York: Harper and Row.

Pribram, K. H. (1986). The cognitive resolution and mind/brain issues. *American Psychologist, 41,* 507-520.

Prigogine, I. (1976). Order through fluctuation: Self-organization and social system. In E. Jantsch & C. H. Waddington (Eds.), *Evolution and consciousness* (pp. 99-123). Reading, MA: Addison-Wesley.

Prigogine, I. (1978). Time, structure, and fluctuations. *Science, 201,* 777-785.

Prigogine, I., & Stengers, I. (1984). *Order out of chaos.* New York: Bantam.

Rapoport, A. (1968). A philosophical view. In J. H. Milsum (Ed.), *Positive feedback* (pp. 1-8). Oxford: Pergamon.

Reese, H. W., & Overton, W. F. (1970). Models of development and theories of development. In L. R. Goulet & P. B. Baltes (Eds.), *Life-span developmental psychology: Research and theory* (pp. 115-145). New York: Academic Press.

Revlin, R. & Mager, R. E. (Eds.). (1978). *Human reasoning.* Washington, DC: Winston.

Riegel, K. F. (1975). Toward a dialectical theory of development. *Human Development, 18,* 50-64.

Riegel, K. F. (1976a). The dialectics of human development. *American Psychologist, 31,* 689-700.

Riegel, K. F. (1976b). From traits and equilibrium toward developmental dialectics. In W. J. Arnold & J. K. Cole (Eds.), *Nebraska symposium on motivation, 1975* (pp. 349-408). Lincoln: University of Nebraska Press.

Riegel, K. F. (1978). *Psychology mon amour: A countertext.* Boston: Houghton Mifflin.

Riley, M. W. (Ed.). (1979). *Aging from birth to death.* Washington, DC: American Association for the Advancement of Science.

Rogosa, D., Brandt, D., & Zimowski, M. (1982). A growth curve approach to the measurement of change. *Psychological Bulletin, 92,* 726-748.

Rosnow, R., & Georgoudi, M. (Eds.). (1986). *Contextualism and understanding in behavioral research.* New York: Praeger.

Royce, J. E. (1961). *Man and his nature.* New York: McGraw-Hill.

Salisbury, H. E. (1969). *The 900 days: The siege of Leningrad.* New York: Harper & Row.

Sameroff, A. (1975). Transactional models in early social relations. *Human Development, 18,* 65-79.

Sameroff, A. J. (1983). Developmental systems: Contexts and evolution. In P. H. Mussen (Ed.), *Handbook of child psychology* (Vol. 1, pp. 237-294). New York: John Wiley.

Sarbin, T. R. (1977). Contextualism: A world view for modern psychology. In J. K. Cole & A. W. Lundfield (Eds.), *Nebraska symposium on motivation, 1976* (pp. 1-41). Lincoln: University of Nebraska Press.

Schaie, K. W. (1979). The primary mental abilities in adulthood: An exploration in the development of psychometric intelligence. In P. B. Baltes & O. G. Brim, Jr. (Eds.), *Life-span development and behavior* (Vol. 2, pp. 67-115). New York: Academic Press.

Schaie, K. W. (1984). Historical time and cohort effects. In K. A. McClusky & H. W. Reese (Eds.), *Life-span developmental psychology: Historical age generational effects* (pp. 1-15). New York: Academic Press.

Schaie, K. W., & Geiwitz, J. (1982). *Adult development and aging.* Boston: Little, Brown.

Schneirla, T. C. (1956). Interrelationships of the innate and the acquired in instinctive behavior. In P. P. Grasse (Ed.), *L'instinct dans le comportement des animaux et de l'homme* (pp. 387-452). Paris: Mason et Cie.

Schneirla, T. C. (1957). The concept of development in comparative psychology. In D. B. Harris (Ed.), *The concept of development* (pp. 78-108). Minneapolis: University of Minnesota Press.

Schneirla, T. C. (1966). Instinct and aggression. *Natural History, 75,* 16ff.

Schonfield, A. E. D. (1980). Learning, memory, and aging. In J. E. Birren & R. B. Sloane (Eds.), *Handbook of mental health and aging* (pp. 214-244). Englewood Cliffs, NJ: Prentice-Hall.

Sears, R. R. (1957). Identification as a form of behavioral development. In D. B. Harris (Ed.), *The concept of development* (pp. 149-161). Minneapolis: University of Minnesota Press.

Selye, H. (1976). *The stress of life* (rev. ed.). New York: McGraw-Hill.

Shaffer, L. H. (1980). Analyzing piano performance: A study of concert pianists. In G. E. Stelmach & J. Requin (Eds.), *Tutorials in motor behavior* (pp. 453-455). Amsterdam: North-Holland.

Siegler, R. S., & Crowley, K. (1991). The microgenetic method: A direct means for studying cognitive development. *American Psychologist, 46,* 606-620.

Sigman, M. (1982). Plasticity in development: Implications for intervention. In L. A. Bond & J. M. Joffe (Eds.), *Facilitating infant and early childhood development* (pp.98-116). Hanover, NH: University Press of New England.

Simon, H. A. (1969). *The sciences of the artificial.* Cambridge, MA: MIT Press.

Simon, H. A. (1978). Information-processing theory of human problem solving. In W. K. Estes (Ed.), *Handbook of learning and cognitive processes* (Vol. 5, pp. 271-286). Hillsdale, NJ: Lawrence Erlbaum.

Singer, R. N. (1975). *Motor learning and human performance.* New York: Macmillan.

Skinner, B. F. (1938). *The behavior of organisms: An experimental analysis.* New York: Appleton-Century-Crofts.

Skinner, B. F. (1957). *Verbal behavior.* New York: Appleton-Century-Crofts.

Skinner, B. F. (1981). Selection by consequences. *Science, 213,* 501-504.

Smotherman, W. P., & Robinson, S. R. (1990). The prenatal origins of behavioral organization. *Psychological Science, 1,* 97-106.

Sorensen, B., Weinert, E., & Sherrod, L. R. (Eds.). (1986). *Human development and the life course: Multidisciplinary perspectives.* Hillsdale, NJ: Erlbaum.

Sperry, R. W. (1988). Psychology's mentalist paradigm and the religion/science tension. *American Psychologist, 43,* 607-613.

Stanley, S. M. (1979). *Macroevolution: Pattern and process.* San Francisco: Freeman.

Stelmach, G. E., & J. Requin (Eds.). (1980). *Tutorials in motor behavior.* Amsterdam: North-Holland.

Sternberg, R. J. (Ed.). (1982). *Handbook of human intelligence.* Cambridge: Cambridge University Press.

Studer, R. G. (1980). Environmental design and management as evolutionary experimentation. *Design Studies, 1,* 365-371.

Thomas, A., & Chess, S. (1977). *Temperament and development.* New York: Brunner/Mazel.

Thorndike, E. L. (1904). The newest psychology. *Educational Review, 28* 217-227.

Thorndike, E. L. (1906). *Principles of teaching.* New York: Sieber.

Tobach, E. (1971). Some evolutionary aspects of human gender. *Journal of Orthopsychiatry, 41,* 710-715.

Tobach, E. (1972). The meaning of cryptanthroparian. In L. Ehrman, G. Omenn, & E. Caspari (Eds.), *Genetics, environment, and behavior* (pp. 219-390). New York: Academic Press.

Tobach, E. (1981). Evolutionary aspects of the activity of the organism and its development. In R. M. Lerner & N. A. Busch-Rossnagel (Eds.), *Individuals as producers of their development: A life-span perspective* (pp. 37-68). New York: Academic Press.

Tobach, E., Gianutsos, J., Topoff, H. R., & Gross, C. G. (1974). *The four horses: Racism, sexism, militarism, and social Darwinism.* New York: Behavioral Publications.

Tobach, E., & Greenberg, G. (1984). The significance of T. C. Schneirla's contribution to the concept of integration. In G. Greenberg & E. Tobach (Eds.), *Behavioral evolution and integrative levels* (pp. 1-7). Hillsdale, NJ: Erlbaum.

Tobach, E., & Schneirla, T. C. (1968). The biopsychology of social behavior of animals. In R. E. Cooke & S. Levin (Eds.), *Biological basis of pediatric practice* (pp. 68-82). New York: McGraw-Hill.

Tolman, E. C. (1932). *Purposive behavior in animals and men.* New York: Appleton-Century-Crofts.

Toulmin, S., & Goodfield, J. (1962). *The architecture of matter.* New York: Harper & Row.

Turkewitz, G. (1987).Psychology and developmental psychology: The influence of T. C. Schneirla on human developmental psychology. *Developmental Psychology, 20,* 369-375.

Turvey, M. T. (1990). Coordination. *American Psychologist, 45,* 938-953.

Uphouse, L. L., & Bonner, J. (1975). Preliminary evidence for the effects of environmental complexity on hybridization of rat brain RNA to rat brain DNA. *Developmental Psychobiology, 8,* 171-178.

Valsiner, J. (1988). *Developmental psychology in the Soviet Union.* Bloomington: Indiana University Press.

von Bertalanffy, L. (1933). Modern theories of development. London: Oxford University Press.

von Bertalanffly (1968). *General system theory.* New York: George Braziller.

von Eye, A. (1985). Structure identification using nonparametric models. In J. R. Nesselroade & A. von Eye (Eds.), *Individual development and social change: Explanatory analyses* (pp. 125-154). New York: Academic Press.

von Eye, A. (1990). *Introduction to configural frequency analysis. The search for type and antitype in classification.* Cambridge, UK: Cambridge University Press.

Vygotsky, L. S. (1962). *Thought and language.* Cambridge, MA: MIT Press.

Waddington, C. H. (1976). Evolution in the subhuman world. In E. Jantch & C. H. Waddington (Eds.), *Evolution and consciousness: Human systems in transition* (pp. 11-15). New York: Addison-Wesley.

Washburn, S. L. (1978). Human behavior and the behavior of other animals. *American Psychologist, 33*, 405-417.

Weiss, P. A. (Ed.). (1971). *Hierarchically organized systems in theory and practice*. New York: Hafner.

Werner, H. (1948). *Comparative psychology of mental development*. New York: International Universities Press.

Werner, H. (1957). The concept of development from a comparative and organismic point of view. In D. B. Harris (Ed.), *The concept of development* (pp. 125-148). Minneapolis: University of Minnesota Press.

Werner, H., & Kaplan, B. (1963). *Symbol formation: An organismic-developmental approach to language an the expression of thought*. New York: John Wiley.

White, P. A. (1990). Ideas about causation in philosophy and psychology. *Psychological Bulletin, 108*, 3-18.

Whitehead, A. N. (1925). *Science and the modern world*. New York: Macmillan.

Wicker, A. W. (1979). Ecological psychology: Some research and prospective developments. *American Psychologist, 34*, 755-765.

Wiener, N. (1961). *Cybernetics*. Cambridge, MA: MIT Press.

Williamson, P. G. (1981). Morphological stasis and developmental constraint: Real problems for neo-darwinism. *Nature, 294*, 214-215.

Willis, S. L. (1990). Cognitive training in later adulthood. *Developmental Psychology, 26*, 875-878.

Willis, S. L., & Nesselroade, C. S. (1990). Long-term effects of fluid ability training in old age. *Developmental Psychology, 26*, 905-910.

Winegrad, S. (1965). Energy exchange in striated muscle cells. In W. S. Yamamoto & J. R. Brobeck (Eds.), *Physiological controls and regulations* (pp. 239-252). Philadelphia: W. B. Saunders.

Winell, M. W. (1987). Personal goals: The key to self direction in adulthood. In M. E. Ford & D. H. Ford (Eds.), *Humans as self-constructing living systems: Putting the framework to work* (pp. 261-288). Hillsdale, NJ: Lawrence Erlbaum.

Wohlwill, J. F. (1973). *The study of behavioral development*. New York: Academic Press.

Wohlwill, J. F. (1991). The concept of development and the developmental research methodology. In P. van Geert & L. P. Mos (Eds.), *Annals of theoretical psychology* (Vol. 7, pp. 91-138). New York: Plenum.

Woodruff, D. S. (1985). Arousal, sleep, and aging. In J. E. Birren & K. Warner Schaie (Eds.), *Handbook of the psychology of aging* (pp. 261-295). New York: Van Nostrand Reinhold.

Yates, F. E., & Iberall, A. S. (1973). Temporal and hierarchical organization in biosystems. In J. Urquhart & F. E. Yates (Eds.), *Temporal aspects of therapeutics* (pp. 17-34). New York: Plenum.

Zeleny, M. (Ed.), (1981). *Autopoiesis: A theory of living organization*. New York: Elsevier North-Holland.

Zeman (1926.) (See Miller, 1978).

Zukav, G. (1979). *The dancing wuli masters*. New York: Bantam.

Name Index

Subject Index

About the Authors

Donald H. Ford received his Ph.D. in clinical psychology from The Pennsylvania State University in 1955. He has trained graduate students in clinical psychology, created and served as Director of Penn State's Division of Counseling, and served as the first Dean of Penn State's College of Health and Human Development. He is presently Professor of Human Development and Biobehavioral Health at The Pennsylvania State University. He is also a Fellow of the American Association for the Advancement of Science, the American Psychological Association and the American Psychological Society. His current scholarly work focuses on applying living systems theory to understanding personality development, systems of psychotherapy, and issues in biobehavioral health across the life span.

Richard M. Lerner, professor of family and child ecology, psychology, and pediatrics and human development directs the Institute for Children, Youth, and Families at Michigan State University. A developmental pyschologist, Lerner received his Ph.D. in 1971 from the City University of New York. He has taught at Hunter College, Eastern Michigan University, and The Pennsylvania State University. He has also been a Fellow at the Center for Advanced Study in the

Behavioral Sciences and is a Fellow of the American Association for the Advancement of Science, the American Psychological Association, the American Psychological Society, and the American Association of Applied and Preventive Psychology. At present, he serves as Membership Secretary of the International Society for the Study of Behavioral Development and is the founding editor of the *Journal of Research on Adolescence*. Lerner, the author or editor of more than 25 books and 150 scholarly articles and chapters, is an internationally recognized authority on contextual models of and methods for research on human development across the life span.